PROVEN TACTICS FOR GROWTH, INNOVATION, AND MARKET DOMINATION

100 BUSINESS STRATEGIES

BY DAN WAITE

REFERRAL PROGRAM STRATEGY	CUSTOMER-CENTRIC STRATEGY	BOOTSTRAPPING STRATEGY
VENTURE CAPITAL STRATEGY	CROWDFUNDING STRATEGY	PRIVATE EQUITY STRATEGY
DEFENSIVE STRATEGY	HYPERLOCAL STRATEGY	DROPSHIPPING STRATEGY
AUTOMATION STRATEGY	SURPRISE & DELIGHT STRATEGY	HYPERAUTOMATION STRATEGY
REVERSE LOGISTICS STRATEGY	SIX SIGMA STRATEGY	GAMIFICATION STRATEGY
HYPER-PERSONALIZATION STRATEGY	ECOSYSTEM STRATEGY	JUST-IN-TIME (JIT) STRATEGY

100 BUSINESS STRATEGIES

BLUE OCEAN EXPANSION	BLOCKCHAIN STRATEGY	UPSELLING STRATEGY
WEB3 STRATEGY	METAVERSE STRATEGY	SEO STRATEGY
BLUE OCEAN STRATEGY	GLOBAL EXPANSION STRATEGY	CONGLOMERATE STRATEGY
HORIZONTAL INTEGRATION	VERTICAL INTEGRATION	FIRST-MOVER ADVANTAGE
FAST-FOLLOWER STRATEGY	PLATFORM STRATEGY	COST LEADERSHIP STRATEGY
DIFFERENTIATION STRATEGY	ORGANIC GROWTH STRATEGY	GROWTH HACKING STRATEGY
OMNICHANNEL STRATEGY	LOYALTY PROGRAM STRATEGY	VIRAL MARKETING STRATEGY
STORYTELLING STRATEGY	NOSTALGIA MARKETING STRATEGY	AND MANY, MANY MORE

100 BUSINESS STRATEGIES PROVEN TACTICS FOR GROWTH, INNOVATION, AND MARKET DOMINATION

BY DAN WAITE

Published by LOCO TEMPUS LIMITED 2025

Copyright Dan Waite 2025

Cover design by Dan Waite

All rights reserved. Apart from brief extracts for the purpose of review, no part of this publication may be reproduced, stored in a retrieval system, or transmitted in any form or by any means, electronic, mechanical, photocopying, recording or otherwise without permission of the publisher.

Dan Waite has asserted his right under the Copyright, Designs and Patents Act 1988 to be identified as author of this work.

British Library Cataloguing in Publication Data

A catalogue record for this book is available from the British Library

ISBN: 978-1-917784-03-0

Dan Waite here, CEO of Better Noise Music.

Having worked at Virgin Records, Universal Records, MTV, AEG, BBC, NME and Better Noise Music and more, I have witnessed some of the business strategies of a variety of companies of different scale.

This book will explore the core principles of strategic thinking, providing insights into the frameworks and methodologies that drive business success. By understanding the importance of business strategy and how to apply it effectively, leaders, entrepreneurs, and professionals alike can position themselves for growth, innovation, and long-term sustainability.

Business strategies are not static; they evolve. The most successful companies continually assess and refine their strategies to adapt to market trends, economic shifts, and technological disruptions. Whether it's through cost leadership, differentiation, or market expansion, the right strategy allows businesses to anticipate challenges and seize opportunities before competitors do.

A well-crafted business strategy is more than just a plan; it is the foundation upon which successful enterprises are built. It provides clarity on objectives, identifies competitive advantages, and aligns resources to achieve long-term goals.

I hope that during the course of reading this book you will recognise the Business Strategy that your business needs, that may inspire you to adapt and transform your career.

Best of Luck applying these Business Strategies, Dan

This is dedicated to my wife Irena, my family & friends and work colleagues, present and past.

With thanks to Ade Adeluwoye, Nicolas Bate, Sir Richard Branson. Allen Kovac for your trust and guidance as a boss and mentor and Napolean Hill for the advice in spotting opportunity in hard work.

Thank you to inspirational contacts who as a result of their books and classes have me thinking differently, including Rory Sutherland and Will Page.

In memory of my father David Waite.

100 Business Strategies Proven Tactics for Growth, Innovation, and Market Domination

Corporate-Level Strategies

These focus on overall company direction and long-term vision:

1. Diversification Strategy – Expanding into new markets or industries.
2. Vertical Integration – Controlling more of the supply chain (forward or backward).
3. Horizontal Integration – Acquiring competitors to consolidate the market.
4. Conglomerate Strategy – Expanding into unrelated industries for risk reduction.
5. Global Expansion Strategy – Entering international markets for growth.
6. Blue Ocean Strategy – Creating untapped market space instead of competing in red oceans.
7. Franchising Strategy – Expanding via franchise partners rather than company-owned stores.
8. Joint Venture Strategy – Collaborating with another company to enter a market.
9. Strategic Alliance Strategy – Forming partnerships for mutual benefit.
10. Holding Company Strategy – Managing multiple independent businesses under one entity.

Competitive Strategies

These focus on gaining an edge over competitors:

11. Cost Leadership Strategy (Porter's Generic Strategy) – Becoming the lowest-cost producer.

12. Differentiation Strategy (Porter's Generic Strategy) – Standing out through unique offerings.

13. Focus Strategy (Porter's Generic Strategy) – Targeting a niche market.

14. First-Mover Advantage – Being the first in a market to gain dominance.

15. Fast-Follower Strategy – Learning from pioneers and improving on their innovations.

16. Customer Intimacy Strategy – Building deep relationships with customers.

17. Product Leadership Strategy – Constant innovation to be a market leader.

18. Platform Strategy – Creating a network effect (e.g., Airbnb, Uber).

19. Open Innovation Strategy – Leveraging external partnerships for R&D.

20. Defensive Strategy – Protecting market share from competitors.

Growth Strategies

Strategies aimed at scaling the business:

21. **Organic Growth Strategy** – Growing through internal resources rather than acquisitions.

22. **Mergers & Acquisitions Strategy (M&A)** – Buying other companies to grow.

23. **Market Penetration Strategy** – Increasing market share in

existing markets.
24. **Market Development Strategy** – Expanding existing products into new markets.
25. **Product Development Strategy** – Creating new products for existing customers.
26. **Blue Ocean Expansion** – Entering completely new and uncontested markets.
27. **Growth Hacking Strategy** – Using unconventional and rapid growth techniques.
28. **Freemium Strategy** – Offering free basic services with paid upgrades.
29. **Cross-Selling & Upselling Strategy** – Selling additional products to existing customers.
30. **Localization Strategy** – Adapting products for different cultural markets.

Marketing & Branding Strategies

How companies position themselves and attract customers:
31. **Content Marketing Strategy** – Using valuable content to attract customers.
32. **Influencer Marketing Strategy** – Leveraging influencers to build brand trust.
33. **SEO Strategy** – Optimizing online content for search engines.
34. **Viral Marketing Strategy** – Creating campaigns designed to be widely shared.
35. **Brand Differentiation Strategy** – Establishing a unique brand identity.
36. **Loyalty Program Strategy** – Encouraging repeat customers through rewards.
37. **Personalization Strategy** – Tailoring experiences for individual customers.

38. **Nostalgia Marketing Strategy** – Using past cultural references to connect emotionally.
39. **Storytelling Strategy** – Building a brand narrative that resonates.
40. **Omnichannel Strategy** – Providing seamless customer experiences across multiple channels.

Pricing Strategies

Approaches to setting the right price for profitability and competitiveness:
41. **Penetration Pricing Strategy** – Setting low prices to enter a market.
42. **Premium Pricing Strategy** – Charging higher prices to signal quality.
43. **Dynamic Pricing Strategy** – Adjusting prices in real-time (e.g., Uber surge pricing).
44. **Loss Leader Strategy** – Selling a product at a loss to attract future purchases.
45. **Bundling Strategy** – Selling multiple products together at a discount.
46. **Pay-What-You-Want Strategy** – Allowing customers to choose their price.
47. **Subscription Model Strategy** – Charging recurring fees for ongoing access.
48. **Skimming Pricing Strategy** – Setting high prices initially, then lowering them.
49. **Psychological Pricing Strategy** – Pricing to influence perception (e.g., $9.99 instead of $10).
50. **Geographical Pricing Strategy** – Adjusting prices by location or region.

Operational & Supply Chain Strategies

Enhancing efficiency, productivity, and logistics:
51. **Lean Manufacturing Strategy** – Eliminating waste for efficiency.
52. **Just-in-Time (JIT) Strategy** – Reducing inventory by producing only when needed.
53. **Six Sigma Strategy** – Improving processes to minimize defects.
54. **Outsourcing Strategy** – Using third-party providers to reduce costs.
55. **Vertical Supply Chain Control Strategy** – Owning the entire supply chain.
56. **Automation Strategy** – Using AI and robotics to streamline operations.
57. **Reshoring Strategy** – Bringing production back to domestic locations.
58. **Green Supply Chain Strategy** – Reducing environmental impact.
59. **Agile Manufacturing Strategy** – Quickly adapting to changing market demands.
60. **Vendor-Managed Inventory (VMI) Strategy** – Suppliers manage stock levels.

Financial & Investment Strategies

Managing money to maximize growth and profitability:
61. **Bootstrapping Strategy** – Growing without external funding.
62. **Venture Capital Strategy** – Seeking investment from VCs for rapid growth.
63. **Private Equity Strategy** – Leveraging buyouts to restructure companies.
64. **Crowdfunding Strategy** – Raising capital from the public.

65. **Leveraging Strategy** – Using debt to finance expansion.
66. **Dividend Strategy** – Paying dividends to attract investors.
67. **Stock Buyback Strategy** – Reinvesting profits by repurchasing shares.
68. **IPO Strategy** – Going public to raise capital.
69. **Tax Optimization Strategy** – Structuring finances to minimize taxes.
70. **Cash Flow Management Strategy** – Ensuring liquidity for sustainability.

Customer Experience & Retention Strategies

Building long-term customer relationships:
71. **Customer-Centric Strategy** – Designing business around customer needs.
72. **Customer Feedback Loop Strategy** – Using feedback to improve offerings.
73. **Hyper-Personalization Strategy** – Leveraging AI for highly customized experiences.
74. **Surprise & Delight Strategy** – Exceeding customer expectations unexpectedly.
75. **Social Proof Strategy** – Using reviews and testimonials to build trust.
76. **Community Building Strategy** – Creating loyal fan bases around brands.
77. **Gamification Strategy** – Using game mechanics to engage users.
78. **Self-Service Strategy** – Allowing customers to help themselves efficiently.
79. **Referral Program Strategy** – Encouraging word-of-mouth growth.
80. **Subscription Retention Strategy** – Reducing churn through engagement tactics.

Disruption & Future-Focused Strategies

Innovating for long-term dominance:
81. **AI & Data-Driven Strategy** – Leveraging AI for business decisions.
82. **Blockchain Strategy** – Using blockchain for transparency and efficiency.
83. **Metaverse Strategy** – Positioning brands in virtual spaces.
84. **Web3 Strategy** – Decentralizing business models.
85. **Sustainability-Driven Strategy** – Aligning business with environmental values.
86. **Crisis Management Strategy** – Preparing for unexpected events.
87. **Business Model Innovation Strategy** – Reinventing revenue streams.
88. **Hyperlocal Strategy** – Focusing on ultra-specific geographic markets.
89. **Reverse Innovation Strategy** – Adapting innovations from emerging markets.
90. **Subscription-Based Business Model** – Creating recurring revenue streams.

Industry-Specific Business Strategies

91. Direct-to-Consumer (DTC) Strategy – Selling directly to consumers without intermediaries (e.g., Warby Parker, Dollar Shave Club).
92. Dropshipping Strategy – Selling products without holding inventory; suppliers handle fulfilment.
93. On-Demand Economy Strategy – Providing services instantly via digital platforms (e.g., Uber, DoorDash).
94. Frugal Innovation Strategy – Developing cost-effective solutions for emerging markets (e.g., Tata Nano).

95. Hyperautomation Strategy – Automating every possible process using AI and machine learning.

96. Decentralized Business Strategy – Running businesses without a central authority (e.g., DAOs in Web3).

97. Co-Branding Strategy – Partnering with another brand to create mutual value (e.g., Nike & Apple Watch).

98. Ecosystem Strategy – Creating interconnected products/services to build customer loyalty (e.g., Apple's ecosystem).

99. User-Generated Content (UGC) Strategy – Encouraging customers to create content that promotes the brand.

100. Reverse Logistics Strategy – Managing product returns, recycling, and reusability efficiently.

Corporate-Level Strategies

1. Diversification Strategy

Theory Behind Diversification Strategy

Diversification strategy is a business approach where a company expands its operations by adding new products, services, markets, or business lines that differ from its existing offerings. It is a form of growth strategy aimed at reducing risk and increasing revenue by not relying on a single market or product line. Diversification can be classified into two main types:

1. **Related Diversification** – When a business expands into areas that are similar or complementary to its existing operations. For example, a car manufacturer launching an electric vehicle (EV) division.

2. **Unrelated Diversification** – When a business enters entirely different industries with no direct connection to its core business. For instance, a technology company acquiring a food processing business.

Harvard professor Igor Ansoff introduced the **Ansoff Matrix**, which highlights diversification as one of four key growth strategies, emphasizing its potential for high rewards alongside high risk.

Example of Diversification Strategy

A well-known example of successful diversification is **Apple Inc.** Initially a computer company, Apple expanded into consumer electronics by launching the iPod, iPhone, iPad, and Apple Watch, entering markets such as music, mobile phones, and wearables. This move allowed Apple to reduce dependency on its Mac computer sales and build a vast ecosystem of interconnected products and services.

Why Diversification Works

Diversification works because it spreads business risk across multiple products, services, and markets. If one sector underperforms, revenue from other areas can offset the losses. This approach ensures resilience against industry downturns, economic shifts, and changing consumer trends. Additionally, it enables companies to leverage existing resources, brand reputation, and expertise to tap into new opportunities.

For example, **Amazon's expansion from an online bookstore into cloud computing (AWS), streaming (Prime Video), and smart devices (Alexa) ensures financial stability by not relying solely on e-commerce revenue.**

How Diversification Works

Diversification is implemented through four main methods:

1. **Internal Development** – Expanding by creating new products or services within the company.

2. **Mergers & Acquisitions** – Buying existing businesses to enter new industries quickly.

3. **Joint Ventures & Partnerships** – Collaborating with other companies to share risks and resources.

4. **Investment in R&D** – Innovating to create new offerings that differentiate from competitors.

The success of diversification depends on **market research, financial capacity, operational capability, and strategic execution** to ensure the new venture complements the company's existing strengths.

Application of Diversification Strategy

Businesses use diversification for various reasons, such as:

- **Reducing market dependency** – A retail brand expanding into online services to mitigate the risk of declining physical store sales.

- **Capitalizing on emerging trends** – A car company investing in electric and autonomous vehicles.

- **Leveraging brand equity** – A fashion brand launching a cosmetics line under the same branding.

- **Risk mitigation** – A food company entering the health supplements market to counter changing consumer habits.

Key Insights on Diversification Strategy

- **High risk, high reward** – Diversification can generate immense success but requires careful planning and investment.

- **Strategic fit is crucial** – Related diversification often yields better results as businesses can utilize existing expertise.

- **Not always necessary** – Companies should diversify only when market conditions and internal capabilities align.

- **Strong execution is key** – Success depends on market research, financial health, and seamless integration of new ventures.

By understanding and effectively applying diversification, businesses can create long-term sustainability, capitalize on new opportunities, and safeguard against economic fluctuations.

2. Vertical Integration

Vertical Integration Strategy: A Comprehensive Breakdown

Theory Behind Vertical Integration

Vertical integration is a business strategy in which a company expands its control over multiple stages of its supply chain, from production to distribution. This strategy reduces dependency on external suppliers and improves efficiency, cost control, and quality. Vertical integration is classified into two main types:

1. **Forward Integration** – A company moves closer to the consumer by acquiring or developing distribution channels, retail outlets, or direct sales platforms. For example, a manufacturer opening its own retail stores instead of relying on third-party distributors.

2. **Backward Integration** – A company takes control of its supply sources, such as raw material suppliers or manufacturing facilities. For instance, a car company purchasing a steel factory to secure a steady supply of materials.

This strategy was famously discussed in Michael Porter's **Five Forces Model**, where controlling supply chain elements helps businesses reduce supplier power and create competitive advantages.

Example of Vertical Integration

A well-known example is **Tesla**. Unlike traditional automakers that rely on third-party suppliers for batteries and dealerships for sales, Tesla manufactures its own batteries (backward integration) and sells directly to consumers through its own stores and online platform (forward integration). This approach reduces costs, ensures quality control, and enhances customer experience.

Another example is **Amazon**, which has vertically integrated by owning its supply chain, warehouses, and delivery services (Amazon Logistics), reducing reliance on external shipping companies.

Why Vertical Integration Works

Vertical integration works because it provides:

- **Cost Reduction** – Eliminating intermediaries reduces expenses and increases profit margins.

- **Quality Control** – Companies maintain higher standards by overseeing production and distribution.

- **Supply Chain Stability** – Ensures access to raw materials and distribution channels, reducing reliance on third parties.

- **Market Control** – Increases pricing power by eliminating supplier or distributor markups.

For example, **Apple manufactures its own chips (M1, M2 processors), reducing dependency on external suppliers like Intel, improving product performance, and lowering costs.**

How Vertical Integration Works

A company can achieve vertical integration through:

1. **Acquisitions** – Buying suppliers, manufacturers, or distributors to control more of the supply chain.
2. **Internal Development** – Building capabilities to manufacture components or distribute products.
3. **Partnerships** – Forming exclusive agreements with suppliers or distributors for strategic advantages.

Successful vertical integration requires **significant capital investment, expertise in new business areas, and careful management** to avoid inefficiencies.

Application of Vertical Integration Strategy

Businesses implement vertical integration to:

- **Secure supply chains** – A restaurant chain acquiring farms to ensure consistent ingredient quality.
- **Improve customer experience** – A fashion brand opening its own stores instead of selling through third-party retailers.

- **Reduce dependency on suppliers** – A car company producing its own batteries rather than relying on external vendors.

- **Enhance profitability** – A tech company designing and manufacturing its own hardware components instead of outsourcing.

Key Insights on Vertical Integration

- **Not always cost-effective** – Large investments are required, and inefficiencies can arise if managed poorly.

- **Reduces flexibility** – Companies may struggle to adapt if market conditions change.

- **Best suited for stable industries** – Works well when supply chain control provides a long-term competitive advantage.

- **Can create monopolistic advantages** – Reducing supplier dependency can lead to industry dominance, as seen with companies like Amazon and Tesla.

When executed correctly, vertical integration enhances efficiency, strengthens market control, and improves profitability, making it a powerful strategy for companies seeking long-term sustainability.

3. Horizontal Integration

Horizontal Integration Strategy: A Comprehensive Breakdown

Theory Behind Horizontal Integration

Horizontal integration is a business strategy where a company expands by acquiring or merging with competitors in the same industry. Instead of diversifying into new markets or supply chains, horizontal integration focuses on consolidating market position, increasing market share, and achieving economies of scale.

This strategy is a key element of **Michael Porter's Competitive Strategy Framework**, where companies use horizontal integration to strengthen their industry position, reduce competition, and create synergies.

There are two main ways businesses achieve horizontal integration:

1. **Mergers** – When two companies in the same industry combine to form a single entity.

2. **Acquisitions** – When one company purchases another to expand its market presence.

This strategy is commonly used in industries with intense competition, such as technology, retail, healthcare, and manufacturing.

Example of Horizontal Integration

A classic example is **Disney's acquisition of Pixar, Marvel, Lucasfilm, and 21st Century Fox**. By acquiring these companies, Disney expanded its entertainment empire, gaining access to valuable intellectual property, reducing competition, and increasing its market dominance in movies, streaming, and theme parks.

Another example is **Facebook (now Meta) acquiring Instagram and WhatsApp**, allowing the company to control a larger share of the social media market, expand its user base, and integrate advertising revenue streams across platforms.

Why Horizontal Integration Works

Horizontal integration works because it provides several strategic advantages, including:

- **Market Power** – By acquiring competitors, companies reduce competition and increase their influence over pricing and market trends.
- **Cost Efficiency** – Merging businesses can eliminate duplicate operations, streamline supply chains, and increase efficiency.
- **Brand Expansion** – Acquiring well-known brands helps companies leverage existing customer loyalty.

- **Synergy & Innovation** – Sharing technology, research, and expertise across acquired companies leads to innovation and competitive advantages.

For example, **Google acquiring YouTube allowed it to dominate online video content, leveraging YouTube's existing user base and advertising model to enhance Google's overall revenue stream.**

How Horizontal Integration Works

Companies implement horizontal integration through:

1. **Acquiring direct competitors** – A beverage company purchasing a rival brand to control more market share.

2. **Merging with similar firms** – Two airlines merging to expand flight routes and reduce operational costs.

3. **Consolidating industry leaders** – A hotel chain buying competitors to dominate specific travel markets.

To succeed, companies must **navigate antitrust regulations, ensure strategic alignment, and integrate operations smoothly** to avoid inefficiencies.

Application of Horizontal Integration Strategy

Businesses use horizontal integration to:

- **Expand market dominance** – A telecom company acquiring regional providers to strengthen its national reach.

- **Eliminate competition** – A pharmaceutical firm buying rivals to control drug patents and market exclusivity.

- **Increase economies of scale** – A supermarket chain acquiring competitors to negotiate better deals with suppliers.

- **Enhance technological capabilities** – A software company merging with another to consolidate research and development efforts.

Key Insights on Horizontal Integration

- **Regulatory challenges** – Governments often scrutinize mergers and acquisitions to prevent monopolies.

- **Not always beneficial** – Poorly executed mergers can lead to integration challenges and cultural clashes.

- **Best for market consolidation** – Works well when gaining market share and eliminating competition provide a strategic advantage.

- **Requires strong leadership** – Effective management is needed to ensure operational integration and maximize synergy benefits.

When implemented successfully, horizontal integration helps companies strengthen their market position, reduce costs, and drive long-term growth, making it a powerful strategy for industry leaders.

4. Conglomerate Strategy

Conglomerate Strategy: A Comprehensive Breakdown

Theory Behind Conglomerate Strategy

A **conglomerate strategy** is a business approach where a company expands by entering completely unrelated industries. This diversification reduces dependence on a single market or product line, spreading risks and capitalizing on new growth opportunities.

Conglomerate strategy is a type of **unrelated diversification**, meaning the new businesses acquired or developed have no direct connection to the company's core industry. This strategy is commonly pursued by large corporations seeking to build a multi-industry presence.

Companies using a conglomerate strategy often grow through:

1. **Acquisitions** – Purchasing businesses in different sectors to diversify operations.
2. **Internal Development** – Creating new business units outside the company's core industry.

Economist **Richard Rumelt** categorized diversification into four types, with conglomerate diversification being the most complex due to the lack of synergy between business units. While risky, this approach can provide stability during economic downturns.

Example of Conglomerate Strategy

A well-known example is **General Electric (GE)**, which expanded into aviation, healthcare, finance, energy, and consumer electronics. Originally an electrical company, GE became a diversified conglomerate by acquiring businesses in unrelated industries, reducing reliance on any single market.

Another example is **Virgin Group**, which operates in sectors like music, airlines, telecommunications, space travel, and hospitality. Virgin's conglomerate approach allows it to leverage its brand across industries while reducing industry-specific risks.

Why Conglomerate Strategy Works

Conglomerate strategy works because it provides:

- **Risk Diversification** – By operating in multiple industries, a company reduces financial dependency on a single sector. If one industry declines, others may still be profitable.

- **Capital Allocation Flexibility** – Profits from successful business units can be reinvested into underperforming or new ventures.

- **Brand Leverage** – Established conglomerates can use their reputation to enter new industries with greater trust and customer recognition.

- **Access to New Revenue Streams** – Expanding into different industries opens up new markets and opportunities for sustained growth.

For example, **Berkshire Hathaway**, led by Warren Buffett, owns businesses in insurance (GEICO), energy (Berkshire Hathaway Energy), food (Dairy Queen), and retail (See's Candies). This diversification ensures consistent returns despite economic fluctuations.

How Conglomerate Strategy Works

A conglomerate strategy is executed through:

1. **Acquiring profitable businesses** – Purchasing well-established companies with strong financials in different industries.

2. **Building new ventures** – Developing independent business units under the parent company.

3. **Managing diverse portfolios** – Effectively allocating resources across industries to ensure profitability.

To succeed, conglomerates must **balance managerial focus, financial investment, and operational efficiency** across all business units.

Application of Conglomerate Strategy

Businesses use a conglomerate strategy to:

- **Minimize risk exposure** – If one industry underperforms, others can sustain overall profitability.

- **Expand global influence** – Entering multiple industries strengthens international presence.

- **Optimize investment opportunities** – Capital from high-performing sectors can fund new ventures.

- **Create financial stability** – Diversified revenue streams protect against market downturns.

For instance, **Samsung operates in electronics, construction, insurance, shipbuilding, and biotech, ensuring long-term sustainability despite changing industry trends.**

Key Insights on Conglomerate Strategy

- **Not always efficient** – Managing unrelated businesses can be complex and lead to inefficiencies.

- **Success depends on strong leadership** – Effective management is required to oversee diverse business units.

- **Can dilute brand identity** – Expanding into too many industries may weaken brand focus.

- **Best for financially strong companies** – Requires substantial capital to acquire and manage multiple businesses.

When executed well, a conglomerate strategy provides **financial stability, risk diversification, and long-term growth**, making it a powerful approach for companies looking to expand beyond their core industry.

5. Global Expansion Strategy

Global Expansion Strategy: A Comprehensive Breakdown

Theory Behind Global Expansion Strategy

A **global expansion strategy** is a business approach where a company expands its operations into international markets to increase revenue, market share, and competitive advantage. This strategy allows businesses to tap into new customer bases, access new resources, and benefit from global economies of scale.

Global expansion is often guided by **international business theories**, including:

1. **Uppsala Model** – Suggests companies gradually expand into foreign markets, starting with culturally and geographically close countries before entering more distant markets.

2. **Born Global Theory** – Some businesses, especially tech startups, expand internationally from the start without a gradual approach.

3. **Porter's Diamond Model** – Explains how a nation's competitive advantages influence a company's success in global markets.

Businesses can expand globally through various methods, including **exporting, franchising, joint ventures, mergers & acquisitions, and direct foreign investment**. The choice depends on factors like market conditions, regulatory environment, and company resources.

Example of Global Expansion Strategy

A prime example is **McDonald's**, which successfully expanded from the U.S. into over 100 countries. By adapting its menu to local tastes (such as the McAloo Tikki in India and Teriyaki Burgers in Japan) and using a franchising model, McDonald's became a dominant global fast-food brand.

Another example is **Netflix**, which expanded internationally by localizing its content, investing in regional productions, and adapting to different regulatory environments. This strategy allowed Netflix to grow its subscriber base beyond the U.S. and become a leader in global streaming services.

Why Global Expansion Strategy Works

Global expansion works because it provides:

- **Market Diversification** – Reduces dependence on a single domestic market and spreads risk across multiple regions.
- **Revenue Growth** – Access to larger customer bases increases potential sales and profitability.
- **Competitive Advantage** – Establishing an international presence strengthens brand recognition and industry positioning.

- **Economies of Scale** – Larger operations allow cost efficiencies in production, marketing, and logistics.
- **Access to Resources** – Companies can source raw materials, talent, and technology from different parts of the world at lower costs.

For example, **Apple manufactures its products in China, sources rare minerals from Africa, and sells devices globally, optimizing costs while maintaining global brand dominance.**

How Global Expansion Strategy Works

A business can expand internationally through:

1. **Exporting** – Selling products to foreign markets without establishing a local presence.
2. **Franchising & Licensing** – Allowing foreign partners to operate under the company's brand and business model.
3. **Joint Ventures & Partnerships** – Collaborating with local firms to share market risks and expertise.
4. **Direct Foreign Investment** – Establishing production facilities, offices, or stores in new countries.
5. **Mergers & Acquisitions** – Buying foreign businesses to enter a market quickly.

Success in global expansion requires **market research, regulatory compliance, cultural adaptation, and strong international logistics and supply chain management.**

Application of Global Expansion Strategy

Businesses use global expansion to:

- **Enter high-growth markets** – Companies like Starbucks expanding into China to tap into rising consumer demand.

- **Leverage brand strength** – Luxury brands like Gucci and Louis Vuitton expanding into emerging markets where demand for high-end goods is growing.

- **Access cost advantages** – Tech companies outsourcing manufacturing to regions with lower production costs.

- **Gain first-mover advantage** – Expanding early into new markets before competitors establish themselves.

For instance, **Amazon's global expansion strategy involves acquiring local e-commerce companies, adapting to regional logistics, and investing in cloud infrastructure to strengthen its international dominance.**

Key Insights on Global Expansion Strategy

- **Cultural adaptation is crucial** – Success depends on understanding and aligning with local consumer preferences.

- **Regulatory barriers exist** – Countries have different legal and economic environments that must be navigated.

- **Not always profitable in the short term** – Initial costs for market entry, localization, and logistics can be high.

- **Technology enables global reach** – Digital platforms, e-commerce, and streaming services have made international expansion easier.

When executed effectively, a **global expansion strategy unlocks new opportunities, enhances brand influence, and ensures long-term business sustainability** in an increasingly interconnected world.

6. Blue Ocean Strategy

Blue Ocean Strategy: A Comprehensive Breakdown

Theory Behind Blue Ocean Strategy

The **Blue Ocean Strategy** is a business approach that encourages companies to move away from highly competitive markets (red oceans) and instead create new, uncontested market spaces (blue oceans). It was introduced by **W. Chan Kim and Renée Mauborgne** in their book *Blue Ocean Strategy* (2005).

The strategy Is based on two key principles:

1. **Value Innovation** – Instead of competing on existing industry standards, companies create unique products or services that provide greater value at a lower cost.

2. **Reconstructing Market Boundaries** – Companies redefine industries by eliminating unnecessary features, reducing costs, and adding unique elements that appeal to untapped customers.

The **Red Ocean vs. Blue Ocean** analogy highlights:

- **Red Oceans** – Saturated, highly competitive markets where businesses fight over existing demand, leading to price wars and shrinking profit margins.

- **Blue Oceans** – New, unexplored markets where businesses generate fresh demand and create sustainable competitive advantages.

By shifting the focus from competition to innovation, companies following the **Blue Ocean Strategy** redefine their industries and capture new markets.

Example of Blue Ocean Strategy

A famous example is **Cirque du Soleil**. Instead of competing with traditional circuses, Cirque du Soleil created a new entertainment category by combining elements of theatre, acrobatics, and storytelling. By eliminating costly elements like animal acts and emphasizing artistic performances, Cirque du Soleil attracted a completely new audience and avoided competing with traditional circuses.

Another example is **Nintendo Wii**. Instead of competing with PlayStation and Xbox on hardware power, Nintendo targeted casual gamers and families with motion-based controls and simple, engaging games. This strategy created a new market beyond traditional gaming audiences.

Why Blue Ocean Strategy Works

The **Blue Ocean Strategy** works because it:

- **Eliminates Direct Competition** – By creating a unique value proposition, companies don't have to compete in saturated markets.
- **Generates New Demand** – Instead of stealing market share from competitors, businesses attract new

customers who were previously uninterested in the industry.

- **Increases Profitability** – By reducing unnecessary costs and offering differentiated value, companies achieve higher margins.

- **Builds Strong Brand Identity** – Unique offerings create strong customer loyalty and brand recognition.

For instance, **Tesla didn't just compete with traditional car manufacturers; it redefined the automobile industry by focusing on electric, sustainable, and high-tech vehicles, making EVs desirable and aspirational.**

How Blue Ocean Strategy Works

Companies apply the **Blue Ocean Strategy** through the **Four Actions Framework**:

1. **Eliminate** – Remove industry standards that are costly but add little value (e.g., Cirque du Soleil removing animals from its performances).

2. **Reduce** – Minimize factors that are overdesigned or unnecessary (e.g., Nintendo Wii focusing on simple gaming mechanics instead of high-end graphics).

3. **Raise** – Improve key elements that differentiate the product (e.g., Tesla enhancing battery technology and software capabilities).

4. **Create** – Introduce completely new elements that appeal to untapped customers (e.g., Airbnb creating a new lodging alternative by connecting travellers with homeowners).

Success requires **deep market research, customer insight, and a willingness to disrupt traditional business models.**

Application of Blue Ocean Strategy

Businesses use Blue Ocean Strategy to:

- **Escape market saturation** – Enter new spaces where competitors do not operate.

- **Expand customer reach** – Attract non-customers by offering something radically different.

- **Improve cost efficiency** – Eliminate unnecessary expenses while maximizing customer value.

- **Achieve sustainable growth** – Reduce reliance on competitive pricing and develop long-term brand loyalty.

For example, **Uber** transformed transportation by shifting from traditional taxi services to a ride-sharing model, creating a new market while bypassing regulatory challenges faced by traditional cab companies.

Key Insights on Blue Ocean Strategy

- **Innovation is key** – Businesses must challenge industry assumptions and find unique opportunities.

- **Not every new idea is a Blue Ocean** – Some attempts to create new markets fail if they lack customer demand.

- **Requires bold leadership** – Companies must be willing to take risks and break industry norms.

- **Timing matters** – Entering at the right moment ensures success before competitors adapt.

When executed effectively, the **Blue Ocean Strategy** helps companies **escape competition, maximize profits, and create lasting industry impact**, making it one of the most powerful business growth strategies.

7. Franchising Strategy

Franchising Strategy: A Comprehensive Breakdown

Theory Behind Franchising Strategy

A **franchising strategy** is a business growth model where a company (the franchisor) allows independent entrepreneurs (franchisees) to operate under its established brand, using its business model, trademarks, and operational processes in exchange for fees and royalties.

This strategy is widely used in industries like **food and beverage, retail, hospitality, and fitness**. The franchising model provides a way for businesses to scale quickly while minimizing the risks and capital investment associated with traditional expansion.

There are two main types of franchising:

1. **Product/Trade Name Franchising** – The franchisee sells the franchisor's branded products but operates independently (e.g., car dealerships).

2. **Business Format Franchising** – The franchisee adopts the entire business model, including branding, operations, and marketing (e.g., McDonald's, Subway).

3.

Franchising is based on the concept of **mutual benefit**:

- The **franchisor** expands its brand and revenue with lower capital risk.

- The **franchisee** gains access to a proven business model, reducing startup risk and increasing the likelihood of success.

Example of Franchising Strategy

A leading example is **McDonald's**, which operates in over 100 countries with more than 39,000 locations, most of which are franchised. McDonald's provides its franchisees with a complete operating system, including **branding, training, marketing, and supply chain support**, while franchisees pay an upfront fee and ongoing royalties.

Another example is **Subway**, which expanded aggressively through franchising, making it one of the largest restaurant chains globally. By offering a **low-cost, easy-to-operate model**, Subway attracted entrepreneurs worldwide.

Why Franchising Strategy Works

Franchising works because it:

- **Enables Rapid Expansion** – Companies can grow internationally without massive capital investments.
- **Shares Financial Risk** – Franchisees invest their own money, reducing the franchisor's financial burden.
- **Ensures Local Market Adaptation** – Franchisees, being local entrepreneurs, understand their market better, leading to more effective operations.

- **Maintains Brand Consistency** – Standardized processes ensure a uniform customer experience across locations.
- **Creates Passive Revenue Streams** – The franchisor earns royalties and fees without directly managing all outlets.

For example, **Starbucks initially focused on company-owned stores but later adopted a franchise-like licensing model to accelerate global growth while maintaining brand control.**

How Franchising Strategy Works

A franchising strategy is executed through the following steps:

1. **Developing a Scalable Business Model** – The franchisor must create an efficient, replicable system that can be easily adopted.
2. **Establishing a Franchise Agreement** – A legal contract defining terms, fees, training, support, and brand usage.
3. **Recruiting Franchisees** – Identifying motivated individuals who align with the brand's values and operational requirements.
4. **Providing Training & Support** – Ensuring franchisees follow company standards in operations, customer service, and marketing.
5. **Ongoing Management & Quality Control** – Monitoring franchisees to maintain brand consistency and high-quality service.

Successful franchises invest heavily in **training, marketing, and operational support** to ensure franchisees thrive while maintaining the brand's reputation.

Application of Franchising Strategy

Businesses use franchising to:

- **Expand internationally** – Brands like KFC and Domino's Pizza use franchising to grow globally while adapting to local tastes.

- **Scale quickly with minimal capital** – Fitness brands like Anytime Fitness have expanded rapidly without needing to build every location themselves.

- **Create passive revenue streams** – Hotel chains like Marriott license their brand while earning steady royalties from franchise operators.

- **Penetrate emerging markets** – Fast-food chains and retail brands use franchising to establish a foothold in new economies with minimal risk.

For example, **7-Eleven's franchising strategy allowed it to dominate the global convenience store market by leveraging local franchisee expertise.**

Key Insights on Franchising Strategy

- **Not every business is franchise-ready** – Companies must have a well-structured, scalable, and easily replicable model.

- **Brand consistency is critical** – Strong training and quality control prevent dilution of the brand's reputation.

- **Franchisee selection matters** – Choosing the right partners ensures operational success and brand alignment.

- **Regulations vary by country** – Franchisors must navigate legal requirements in different markets.

- **Ongoing innovation is key** – To stay competitive, franchises must adapt to changing consumer preferences and industry trends.

When executed effectively, **franchising is a powerful strategy that enables businesses to scale efficiently, expand globally, and generate long-term profitability while minimizing direct operational risks.**

8. Joint Venture Strategy

Joint Venture Strategy: A Comprehensive Breakdown

Theory Behind Joint Venture Strategy

A **joint venture (JV) strategy** is a business arrangement where two or more companies collaborate to achieve a shared goal while remaining independent entities. Joint ventures allow companies to pool resources, expertise, and market access without fully merging or acquiring one another.

Joint ventures are typically formed for **market expansion, technology sharing, risk reduction, and operational synergy.** This strategy is commonly used in industries such as **automotive, technology, pharmaceuticals, and energy** where high capital investment and specialized expertise are required.

There are two primary types of joint ventures:

1. **Equity Joint Venture** – Partners create a new, jointly owned entity with shared investments and profits (e.g., Sony Ericsson).

2. **Contractual Joint Venture** – Companies collaborate on a specific project without forming a new legal entity (e.g., construction projects, R&D collaborations).

The **Resource-Based View (RBV) Theory** supports joint ventures, emphasizing how firms can combine complementary assets to achieve a competitive advantage.

Example of Joint Venture Strategy

A well-known example is **Sony Ericsson**, a joint venture between Sony (Japan) and Ericsson (Sweden) in 2001. By combining Sony's expertise in consumer electronics and Ericsson's mobile technology, the venture created innovative mobile phones. Although the JV eventually dissolved, it allowed both companies to gain significant market experience and technology integration.

Another example is **BMW and Toyota's joint venture on hydrogen fuel cells**. Both companies combined their expertise to accelerate fuel cell development, reducing R&D costs while expanding their future vehicle portfolios.

Why Joint Venture Strategy Works

Joint ventures work because they:

- **Share Costs and Risks** – High-risk projects, such as research and development, become more manageable when costs are divided.

- **Enable Market Entry** – Foreign companies can enter new markets by partnering with local firms that understand regulations and consumer behaviour.

- **Enhance Competitive Advantage** – Partnering with a company that has complementary strengths can create a superior product or service.

- **Leverage Brand and Distribution** – Established companies can share branding and distribution networks, improving market reach.

For instance, **Starbucks partnered with Tata in India** to leverage Tata's deep knowledge of the Indian market, ensuring a smooth entry into a competitive coffee industry.

How Joint Venture Strategy Works

Companies create a successful joint venture through the following steps:

1. **Identifying Strategic Partners** – Selecting a company with complementary strengths, shared vision, and aligned goals.

2. **Structuring the Agreement** – Defining investment contributions, profit-sharing, management structure, and exit strategies.

3. **Legal and Regulatory Compliance** – Ensuring the JV complies with local business laws and industry regulations.

4. **Establishing Governance and Operations** – Implementing a framework for decision-making, conflict resolution, and day-to-day operations.

5. **Monitoring and Evaluation** – Regularly assessing performance, adjusting strategies, and determining long-term feasibility.

Clear communication and shared vision are crucial for avoiding conflicts and ensuring long-term success.

Application of Joint Venture Strategy

Businesses use joint ventures to:

- **Enter restricted foreign markets** – Many countries require foreign firms to partner with local entities (e.g., **McDonald's joint venture in China**).

- **Develop new technologies** – Companies collaborate to share R&D expenses and speed up innovation (e.g., **Ford and Volkswagen's JV on electric vehicles**).

- **Expand distribution networks** – Retail brands partner with regional firms to gain faster market access (e.g., **Nike's JV with local distributors**).

- **Improve operational efficiency** – Manufacturing companies form JVs to optimize supply chain efficiency and reduce costs.

For example, **Nestlé and General Mills created a joint venture for breakfast cereals** to leverage each other's market strengths globally.

Key Insights on Joint Venture Strategy

- **Not all JVs succeed** – Cultural differences, conflicting interests, and poor governance can lead to failure.

- **Legal and financial clarity is crucial** – Clearly defining roles, ownership, and responsibilities reduces future disputes.

- **JVs can be short-term or long-term** – Some last only for specific projects, while others become permanent business relationships.

- **Trust and transparency matter** – Open communication ensures smoother collaboration and goal alignment.

- **Exit strategy is important** – Companies must plan for dissolution if the JV no longer serves its purpose.

When executed correctly, a **joint venture strategy helps businesses expand efficiently, share risks, and achieve mutual growth**, making it a powerful tool for strategic partnerships and global expansion.

9. Strategic Alliance Strategy

Strategic Alliance Strategy: A Comprehensive Breakdown

Theory Behind Strategic Alliance Strategy

A **Strategic Alliance Strategy** is a business arrangement where two or more companies collaborate to achieve shared objectives while maintaining their independence. Unlike mergers or acquisitions, strategic alliances allow companies to leverage each other's strengths without full integration.

Strategic alliances are often used to **expand market reach, share expertise, develop new products, and improve operational efficiencies**. This strategy is particularly common in industries like **technology, pharmaceuticals, automotive, and retail**, where collaboration can accelerate innovation and market expansion.

There are three main types of strategic alliances:

1. **Joint Venture** – Two companies create a separate entity to pursue a specific goal (e.g., Sony Ericsson).

2. **Equity Strategic Alliance** – One company takes partial ownership in another to strengthen collaboration (e.g., Renault-Nissan alliance).

3. **Non-Equity Strategic Alliance** – Companies partner without ownership ties, focusing on contractual agreements (e.g., airline codeshare agreements).

The **Resource-Based View (RBV) Theory** supports strategic alliances by highlighting how companies gain a competitive edge by pooling resources and capabilities.

Example of Strategic Alliance Strategy

A well-known example is **Starbucks and PepsiCo**. Starbucks produces bottled coffee beverages, while PepsiCo handles distribution. This alliance allows Starbucks to enter the ready-to-drink coffee market without building its own distribution network, and PepsiCo benefits from Starbucks' brand strength.

Another example is **Apple and IBM**, which formed a strategic alliance to develop enterprise solutions for businesses. Apple leveraged IBM's corporate client relationships, while IBM utilized Apple's user-friendly hardware and software.

Why Strategic Alliance Strategy Works

Strategic alliances work because they:

- **Enhance Market Expansion** – Companies gain access to new markets by leveraging their partner's local expertise and distribution channels.

- **Reduce Costs and Risks** – Sharing resources lowers R&D costs, operational expenses, and market entry risks.

- **Accelerate Innovation** – Collaborations combine expertise and technology, leading to faster product development.

- **Improve Competitive Advantage** – Companies gain complementary skills and capabilities that strengthen their market position.

- **Increase Flexibility** – Unlike mergers, strategic alliances allow companies to collaborate without full integration, maintaining operational independence.

For example, **Boeing and General Electric's strategic alliance in aerospace enables both companies to develop advanced aircraft technologies while reducing individual R&D costs.**

How Strategic Alliance Strategy Works

A strategic alliance is formed through the following steps:

1. **Identifying the Right Partner** – Companies must ensure strategic alignment in goals, expertise, and market reach.

2. **Defining Objectives and Roles** – Clear agreements on responsibilities, contributions, and benefits prevent conflicts.

3. **Structuring the Alliance** – Establishing equity or non-equity partnerships based on the desired level of collaboration.

4. **Legal and Contractual Agreements** – Setting terms for intellectual property rights, revenue sharing, and dispute resolution.

5. **Ongoing Management and Evaluation** – Regularly assessing performance and making adjustments to optimize the partnership.

Strong governance and communication are critical for sustaining a successful alliance.

Application of Strategic Alliance Strategy

Businesses use strategic alliances to:

- **Enter foreign markets** – Companies collaborate with local firms to navigate regulations and cultural differences (e.g., **McDonald's alliances with regional suppliers**).

- **Develop new technologies** – Tech giants like **Google and Samsung collaborate to integrate software and hardware innovations**.

- **Strengthen supply chains** – Automotive brands form alliances with suppliers to improve efficiency (e.g., **Toyota partnering with battery manufacturers**).

- **Improve customer experience** – Airline alliances like **Star Alliance** provide seamless travel across multiple carriers.

For instance, **Nike and Apple partnered to develop fitness-tracking technology, combining Nike's expertise in sportswear with Apple's technological innovation**.

Key Insights on Strategic Alliance Strategy

- **Trust and transparency are crucial** – Misalignment in vision or expectations can lead to conflicts.

- **Not all alliances succeed** – Cultural differences, power imbalances, or poor execution can cause failure.

- **Legal agreements must be solid** – Intellectual property rights and financial terms should be clearly defined.

- **Continuous evaluation is necessary** – Adjustments may be required to adapt to market changes and evolving business needs.

- **Exit strategy planning is important** – Companies should plan for possible alliance termination to avoid disruption.

When executed effectively, a **strategic alliance strategy enables companies to scale efficiently, access new capabilities, and gain a competitive edge without the risks of full integration**, making it a powerful tool for long-term growth.

10. Holding Company Strategy

Holding Company Strategy: A Comprehensive Breakdown

Theory Behind Holding Company Strategy

A **holding company strategy** is a business model where a parent company (the holding company) owns and controls multiple subsidiary businesses without directly managing their day-to-day operations. The holding company primarily serves as a financial and strategic overseer, benefiting from the performance of its subsidiaries while maintaining legal and financial separation between them.

This strategy is commonly used in **finance, real estate, manufacturing, retail, and technology**, allowing companies to diversify investments, minimize risk, and optimize tax benefits.

There are two main types of holding companies:

1. **Pure Holding Company** – Exists solely to own shares in other businesses without engaging in operations.
2. **Mixed Holding Company** – Owns subsidiaries but also engages in its own business activities.

The **portfolio theory** supports the holding company strategy by emphasizing diversification as a means of risk reduction and value creation.

Example of Holding Company Strategy

A famous example is **Berkshire Hathaway**, led by Warren Buffett. It owns a diverse portfolio of businesses, including **Geico (insurance), Dairy Queen (food), Duracell (batteries), and BNSF Railway (transportation)**. Each subsidiary operates independently, while Berkshire Hathaway provides financial oversight and strategic direction.

Another example is **Alphabet Inc.**, the parent company of Google, YouTube, Waymo, and other subsidiaries. By structuring itself as a holding company, Alphabet enables its different business units to innovate independently while benefiting from shared resources and capital.

Why Holding Company Strategy Works

The holding company strategy is effective because it:

- **Reduces Risk** – Financial and legal separation of subsidiaries protects the parent company from liabilities.

- **Enhances Financial Efficiency** – Centralized capital allocation allows profitable subsidiaries to fund new ventures.

- **Encourages Business Autonomy** – Subsidiaries operate independently, fostering innovation and agility.

- **Optimizes Tax Benefits** – Holding companies can strategically manage taxes through subsidiaries in different jurisdictions.

- **Facilitates Expansion and Diversification** – Enables entry into multiple industries while reducing operational complexity.

For instance, **Johnson & Johnson operates as a holding company, overseeing multiple pharmaceutical, medical device, and consumer health businesses**, ensuring each segment remains focused on its niche.

How Holding Company Strategy Works

A holding company strategy is implemented through:

1. **Acquiring Majority Shares** – The parent company gains control over subsidiaries through majority ownership.

2. **Establishing Financial Oversight** – Managing investments, capital allocation, and financial reporting across businesses.

3. **Providing Strategic Guidance** – Setting long-term goals while allowing subsidiaries to operate independently.

4. **Mitigating Risk** – Ensuring financial and legal separation between the parent company and subsidiaries.

5. **Facilitating Growth** – Acquiring new businesses or spinning off subsidiaries based on market trends.

Effective governance and leadership are essential to maintaining balance between oversight and subsidiary autonomy.

Application of Holding Company Strategy

Businesses use a holding company strategy to:

- **Diversify investments** – Conglomerates like **Tata Group** operate in industries such as steel, technology, and automobiles.

- **Manage risk in regulated industries** – Banks and financial institutions create holding companies to separate banking from investment operations.

- **Optimize tax structures** – Companies use holding structures in tax-friendly jurisdictions to reduce tax burdens.

- **Spin off non-core businesses** – Large firms create holding companies to separate high-growth startups from legacy businesses.

For example, **Procter & Gamble owns multiple consumer brands like Gillette, Pampers, and Tide under a holding company structure**, allowing each brand to operate independently while benefiting from shared corporate resources.

Key Insights on Holding Company Strategy

- **Legal and financial expertise is critical** – Holding companies must navigate complex corporate governance structures.

- **Subsidiary autonomy drives innovation** – Allowing businesses to operate independently prevents bureaucracy and fosters growth.

- **Holding companies must create value** – Simply acquiring businesses is not enough; strategic oversight is required.

- **Exit strategies are necessary** – Selling or spinning off underperforming subsidiaries ensures long-term profitability.

- **Regulatory compliance varies** – Different countries impose specific regulations on holding company structures.

When executed effectively, a **holding company strategy provides financial stability, diversified growth, and long-term value creation**, making it a preferred approach for multinational corporations and investment firms.

Competitive Strategies; These focus on gaining an edge over competitors:

11. Cost Leadership Strategy

Cost Leadership Strategy: A Comprehensive Breakdown

Theory Behind Cost Leadership Strategy

A **Cost Leadership Strategy** is a business approach where a company aims to become the lowest-cost producer in its industry while maintaining acceptable quality. This strategy is one of **Michael Porter's Three Generic Strategies**, which include **Cost Leadership, Differentiation, and Focus**.

Cost leadership is achieved through:

1. **Economies of Scale** – Producing in large volumes to lower per-unit costs.
2. **Efficient Operations** – Streamlining supply chains, reducing waste, and optimizing production.
3. **Low-Cost Raw Materials** – Sourcing cheaper inputs without compromising quality.
4. **Technological Advancements** – Using automation and advanced systems to reduce labour and operational costs.

This strategy is common in **retail, manufacturing, airlines, and fast-moving consumer goods (FMCG)** industries, where price competition is intense.

Example of Cost Leadership Strategy

A well-known example is **Walmart**, which dominates the retail industry by offering the lowest prices through:

- **Bulk purchasing** – Buying large quantities from suppliers at discounted rates.
- **Operational efficiency** – Investing in technology and logistics to minimize costs.
- **Supplier negotiations** – Pressuring suppliers to lower prices in exchange for high sales volume.

Another example is **Ryanair**, a European low-cost airline that keeps fares low by:

- **Operating a single aircraft type (Boeing 737)** to reduce maintenance and training costs.
- **Using secondary airports** to lower landing fees.
- **Charging for additional services** to keep base ticket prices minimal.

Why Cost Leadership Strategy Works

Cost leadership works because it:

- **Attracts Price-Sensitive Customers** – Low-cost products appeal to budget-conscious consumers.

- **Creates a Competitive Advantage** – Competitors struggle to match lower prices without sacrificing profit margins.

- **Builds Market Share** – Lower prices encourage higher sales volume, leading to industry dominance.

- **Increases Profitability** – Even with thin margins, high sales volumes generate strong overall profits.

For example, **Amazon leverages cost leadership through its vast distribution network, warehouse automation, and bulk shipping discounts, allowing it to offer lower prices than traditional retailers.**

How Cost Leadership Strategy Works

A company implements cost leadership through:

1. **Investing in Cost-Efficient Production** – Automating processes and optimizing manufacturing.

2. **Standardizing Products** – Offering basic, no-frills versions to reduce production complexity.

3. **Streamlining Supply Chains** – Reducing transportation and warehousing costs.

4. **Negotiating with Suppliers** – Securing bulk discounts and favourable terms.

5. **Minimizing Overhead Costs** – Keeping administrative expenses and marketing budgets low.

To succeed, businesses must continuously find ways to cut costs without compromising essential product quality.

Application of Cost Leadership Strategy

Businesses use cost leadership to:

- **Dominate price-sensitive markets** – Discount retailers like **Dollar General** thrive by offering low-cost alternatives.
- **Expand globally** – Companies like **IKEA** use cost-efficient designs and self-assembly models to reduce costs in international markets.
- **Survive economic downturns** – Low-cost providers remain resilient when consumers cut spending.
- **Compete with private labels** – Grocery chains use cost leadership to compete against store-brand alternatives.

For instance, **McDonald's offers value meals and standardized processes to maintain affordability while ensuring profitability.**

Key Insights on Cost Leadership Strategy

- **Cost-cutting must not sacrifice quality** – If quality drops too low, customers may leave.
- **Economies of scale are crucial** – Larger production volumes drive cost reductions.

- **Competition is fierce** – Competitors may enter price wars, further squeezing margins.

- **Innovation matters** – Continuous process improvements keep costs low over time.

- **Brand perception can be affected** – Low prices may lead to an image of lower quality unless balanced with strong branding.

When executed effectively, a **cost leadership strategy enables companies to maximize profitability, dominate price-sensitive markets, and build a sustainable competitive advantage**, making it one of the most powerful business strategies in competitive industries.

12. Differentiation Strategy

Differentiation Strategy: A Comprehensive Breakdown

Theory Behind Differentiation Strategy

A **Differentiation Strategy** is a business approach where a company aims to offer unique products or services that distinguish it from competitors. Instead of competing on price, businesses focus on innovation, brand value, customer experience, or product quality to attract a loyal customer base.

This strategy is one of **Michael Porter's Three Generic Strategies**—the others being **Cost Leadership** and **Focus Strategy**. Differentiation allows companies to charge premium prices by providing value that customers perceive as superior.

Key elements of differentiation include:

1. **Unique Product Features** – Innovations, design, or performance enhancements.

2. **Strong Branding** – Creating an emotional connection and brand loyalty.

3. **Superior Customer Experience** – Personalized service, user-friendly design, or exceptional support.

4. **Technology and Innovation** – Using cutting-edge technology to stand out.

5. **Quality and Reliability** – Offering higher durability, better materials, or improved performance.

Differentiation is commonly used in industries like **luxury goods, electronics, automotive, hospitality, and technology**, where uniqueness justifies higher pricing.

Example of Differentiation Strategy

A prime example is **Apple**, which differentiates itself through:

- **Innovative Design** – Sleek, minimalist aesthetics that stand out.

- **Ecosystem Integration** – Seamless connectivity between iPhones, MacBooks, iPads, and Apple Watch.

- **Brand Prestige** – Apple's marketing creates an aspirational image.

- **Customer Experience** – High-quality support and user-friendly software.

Another example is **Nike**, which differentiates through:

- **Product Innovation** – Cutting-edge shoe technology (e.g., Air Zoom, Flyknit).

- **Emotional Branding** – Inspiring marketing campaigns featuring top athletes.

- **Customization** – Nike By You (personalized sneaker designs).

Why Differentiation Strategy Works

Differentiation works because it:

- **Reduces Price Competition** – Unique products reduce reliance on price wars.

- **Increases Brand Loyalty** – Customers are willing to pay more for brands they trust.

- **Enhances Profit Margins** – Higher perceived value justifies premium pricing.

- **Creates a Competitive Advantage** – Difficult for competitors to replicate unique offerings.

- **Encourages Customer Retention** – Strong emotional connections increase long-term loyalty.

For instance, **Tesla differentiates itself with cutting-edge electric vehicle technology, autopilot features, and a strong brand identity**, allowing it to dominate the premium EV market.

How Differentiation Strategy Works

A company implements differentiation by:

1. **Investing in R&D** – Developing new products that stand out from competitors.

2. **Building a Strong Brand Identity** – Crafting compelling marketing messages and storytelling.

3. **Enhancing Customer Service** – Offering superior support and personalized experiences.

4. **Leveraging Innovation** – Creating features that competitors don't offer.

5. **Focusing on Quality** – Using premium materials and meticulous craftsmanship.

Successful differentiation requires continuous **innovation, market research, and customer engagement**.

Application of Differentiation Strategy

Businesses use differentiation to:

- **Compete in saturated markets** – Luxury brands like **Rolex** thrive by focusing on exclusivity and craftsmanship.

- **Expand into new markets** – Electric vehicle makers like **Lucid Motors** differentiate through extended battery range and premium interiors.

- **Avoid price-based competition** – Premium hotels like **Ritz-Carlton** charge higher rates for superior service.

- **Increase brand value** – Tech firms like **Samsung** invest in innovation to distinguish themselves from rivals.

For example, **Netflix differentiates itself by investing in exclusive, high-quality content that competitors cannot replicate**.

Key Insights on Differentiation Strategy

- **Requires continuous innovation** – Stagnation can lead to loss of competitive edge.

- **Customer perception is crucial** – Marketing and branding must reinforce uniqueness.

- **High costs may be involved** – R&D, design, and branding require significant investment.

- **Not every customer values differentiation** – Some markets remain price-sensitive.

- **Competitors will try to copy success** – Companies must constantly evolve to maintain uniqueness.

When executed effectively, a **differentiation strategy enables businesses to command higher prices, build strong brand loyalty, and create long-term competitive advantages**, making it one of the most effective strategies for sustainable growth.

13. Focus Strategy

Focus Strategy: A Comprehensive Breakdown

Theory Behind Focus Strategy

A **Focus Strategy** is a business approach where a company targets a specific market segment, catering to a niche audience rather than competing across a broad industry. This strategy is one of **Michael Porter's Three Generic Strategies**, alongside **Cost Leadership** and **Differentiation**.

A company using a focus strategy can choose between:

1. **Cost Focus** – Offering the lowest prices within a niche market.

2. **Differentiation Focus** – Providing unique, high-value products tailored to a specific segment.

By narrowing its market scope, a business can **build expertise, enhance customer loyalty, and reduce direct competition** from larger, mass-market companies. This strategy is common in industries like **luxury goods, high-performance technology, boutique services, and specialized healthcare**.

Example of Focus Strategy

A strong example is **Rolls-Royce**, which follows a **differentiation focus strategy** by targeting high-net-worth individuals with **customized, ultra-luxury automobiles**. Unlike mass-market car brands, Rolls-Royce focuses on craftsmanship, exclusivity, and personalization, allowing it to charge premium prices.

Another example is **Dollar Tree**, which uses a **cost focus strategy** by offering budget-friendly products to price-sensitive consumers. By maintaining a strict $1.25 pricing model and targeting low-income shoppers, Dollar Tree differentiates itself from general retailers like Walmart.

Why Focus Strategy Works

A **Focus Strategy** works because it:

- **Builds Customer Loyalty** – Specialized products and services foster strong brand relationships.

- **Reduces Competition** – Operating in a niche segment limits direct competition from broad-market companies.

- **Enhances Brand Authority** – Businesses gain expertise and credibility by specializing in a particular field.

- **Allows for Higher Profit Margins** – Niche customers are often willing to pay more for tailored offerings.

- **Improves Operational Efficiency** – Serving a smaller, well-defined market reduces complexity in production and marketing.

For example, **Lululemon** has built a loyal following by focusing exclusively on premium athletic wear for yoga and fitness enthusiasts, allowing it to charge higher prices than mainstream sports brands.

How Focus Strategy Works

A business implements a focus strategy through:

1. **Identifying a Profitable Niche** – Conducting market research to find underserved customer segments.

2. **Developing Specialized Products or Services** – Tailoring offerings to meet the specific needs of the target audience.

3. **Optimizing Marketing Strategies** – Using niche-targeted advertising and brand positioning to attract the right customers.

4. **Maintaining Strong Customer Relationships** – Providing personalized experiences, superior service, and community engagement.

5. **Managing Costs Effectively** – For a **cost focus strategy**, streamlining operations to maintain low prices is crucial.

Success depends on **deep market understanding and consistent alignment with the target segment's needs.**

Application of Focus Strategy

Businesses use focus strategies to:

- **Dominate niche markets** – Tesla initially focused on the luxury EV segment before expanding.

- **Maximize brand loyalty** – Harley-Davidson appeals to a dedicated motorcycle enthusiast community.
- **Compete against larger firms** – Etsy thrives by catering to independent artisans and handmade product buyers.
- **Improve profit margins** – Boutique hotels like **The Ritz-Carlton** focus on high-end travellers, charging premium rates for personalized luxury experiences.

For example, **GoPro successfully used a focus strategy by targeting action sports enthusiasts and adventure travellers with high-performance cameras.**

Key Insights on Focus Strategy

- **Niche markets must be large enough** – The target segment should have sufficient demand for sustainable profits.
- **Brand loyalty is crucial** – A strong emotional connection with customers enhances long-term success.
- **Risk of market saturation** – If the niche becomes overcrowded, differentiation may be harder to maintain.
- **Scaling can be challenging** – Expanding beyond the niche may dilute brand identity.
- **Competitors may enter the niche** – If the segment proves highly profitable, larger firms might attempt to compete.

When executed well, a **focus strategy enables businesses to build strong customer loyalty, achieve high-profit margins, and establish a competitive edge in specialized markets**, making it a powerful strategy for sustainable success.

14. First-Mover Advantage

First-Mover Advantage: A Comprehensive Breakdown

Theory Behind First-Mover Advantage

The **First-Mover Advantage (FMA)** is a business strategy where a company gains a competitive edge by being the first to enter a market or introduce an innovative product. This early entry allows the company to establish brand recognition, build customer loyalty, and create barriers for future competitors.

The theory behind first-mover advantage is rooted in **game theory, market dynamics, and brand positioning**, where being first can lead to long-term dominance. However, this advantage is not guaranteed—companies must execute well and maintain their lead.

First-mover advantages typically arise from:

1. **Brand Recognition & Customer Loyalty** – Early adopters associate the brand with innovation.

2. **Economies of Scale** – Being first allows firms to refine operations and lower costs before competitors arrive.

3. **Switching Costs & Network Effects** – Customers may be reluctant to switch once they invest in a first-mover's product or ecosystem.

4. **Technological Leadership** – Owning patents or proprietary technology can block competitors from copying innovations.

5. **Control Over Distribution & Supply Chains** – Early entrants can secure exclusive supplier and retail agreements.

Despite these benefits, **first-mover disadvantages** exist, such as high research costs, market uncertainty, and the risk of competitors learning from early mistakes.

Example of First-Mover Advantage

A prime example is **Amazon**, which entered the e-commerce space in the 1990s before online shopping became mainstream. By being first, Amazon:

- Established strong brand recognition and customer trust.
- Developed a robust supply chain and fulfilment network.
- Created **Amazon Prime**, strengthening customer retention.
- Built technological leadership in logistics and cloud computing (AWS).

Another example is **Coca-Cola**, which pioneered the soft drink industry and remains the dominant brand globally due to **early market entry, strong branding, and exclusive distribution deals**.

Why First-Mover Advantage Works

First-mover advantage works because:

- **Early entrants set industry standards** – Google became the default search engine, making it hard for competitors to displace.

- **Market share is easier to secure** – Customers associate the first brand with innovation and reliability.

- **Competitive barriers increase** – Owning patents, partnerships, or proprietary technology makes it difficult for later entrants to compete.

- **Consumer habits are established** – Once customers adopt a first-mover's product, switching becomes costly or inconvenient.

For instance, **Netflix pioneered online streaming, securing content licensing deals before competitors like Disney+ entered the space.**

How First-Mover Advantage Works

Companies achieve first-mover status by:

1. **Investing in Research & Development (R&D)** – Innovation is critical to leading an industry.

2. **Capturing Market Share Quickly** – Aggressive marketing and partnerships solidify brand presence.

3. **Developing Customer Loyalty Programs** – Locking in early customers prevents them from switching later.

4. **Patenting Innovations** – Protecting technology and intellectual property prevents imitation.

5. **Building Strong Distribution Networks** – Securing suppliers and retailers makes entry harder for competitors.

However, **execution is key**—companies must capitalize on their lead before competitors catch up.

Application of First-Mover Advantage

Businesses use FMA to:

- **Dominate emerging industries** – Tesla leveraged FMA to lead the electric vehicle (EV) market before competitors reacted.

- **Secure exclusive partnerships** – Apple's early deals with music labels helped iTunes dominate digital music.

- **Develop industry standards** – Microsoft Windows became the default OS for personal computers by entering early.

- **Monopolize key resources** – Starbucks expanded aggressively to secure prime real estate locations before competitors.

For example, **Uber's early expansion into ride-sharing created strong brand dominance, making it difficult for new entrants to scale.**

Key Insights on First-Mover Advantage

- **Timing is critical** – Entering too early may mean high costs with little market readiness.

- **Fast followers can catch up** – Facebook wasn't the first social network but surpassed MySpace by executing better.

- **Innovation must continue** – Early success means nothing if competitors innovate faster.

- **Customer experience matters** – A weak first-mover with a poor product can be overtaken by a better-executing rival.

- **Not always an advantage** – Second-movers can **learn from first-mover mistakes, avoid high R&D costs, and execute more efficiently**.

When executed well, a **first-mover advantage can lead to market dominance, customer loyalty, and sustained profitability**, making it a powerful strategy in emerging and high-growth industries.

15. Fast-Follower Strategy

Fast-Follower Strategy: A Comprehensive Breakdown

Theory Behind Fast-Follower Strategy

The **Fast-Follower Strategy** is a business approach where a company quickly enters a market after a first-mover has introduced a new product or service. Instead of pioneering innovation, fast followers **observe early entrants, learn from their mistakes, and execute better**. This strategy allows companies to **reduce risk, optimize efficiency, and outperform first movers** in execution.

Fast followers take advantage of **the first-mover's challenges**, such as:

1. **High R&D Costs** – First movers invest heavily in research, while fast followers refine and improve existing innovations.

2. **Market Uncertainty** – Fast followers enter after demand has been established, avoiding costly miscalculations.

3. **Customer Feedback Loops** – They study early adopters' reactions and optimize their offerings accordingly.

4. **Technological Advancements** – Waiting allows them to leverage newer, more efficient technology.

5. **Brand Differentiation Opportunities** – They refine branding, pricing, and positioning based on first-mover shortcomings.

This strategy is often used in **technology, consumer electronics, pharmaceuticals, and automotive industries**, where product development cycles are rapid.

Example of Fast-Follower Strategy

A prime example is **Facebook**, which was not the first social network (MySpace, Friendster, and others came earlier). However, Facebook refined the social networking model by:

- Focusing on **clean design and real identities** (unlike MySpace's cluttered, anonymous model).

- Expanding globally with a **scalable infrastructure**.

- Introducing **new features** like the News Feed and targeted advertising, outpacing competitors.

Another example is **Samsung in smartphones**. While Apple pioneered the modern smartphone with the iPhone in 2007, Samsung:

- **Analysed Apple's success and weaknesses**, improving screen sizes and battery life.

- **Leveraged Android**, giving consumers an alternative to Apple's closed ecosystem.

- **Iterated faster**, launching multiple models per year to outpace Apple's one-year cycle.

Today, Samsung is one of the largest smartphone manufacturers, proving that **fast-followers can overtake first-movers with superior execution.**

Why Fast-Follower Strategy Works

The **Fast-Follower Strategy** works because:

- **Reduces Risk** – First movers absorb high R&D and market education costs, while followers capitalize on proven demand.

- **Allows for Iterative Improvements** – Companies refine product features based on first-mover feedback.

- **Enables Better Market Timing** – Entering at the right moment avoids early adopter scepticism.

- **Leverages Advanced Technology** – Later entrants use more refined and cost-effective tech.

- **Optimizes Cost Structure** – Fast followers avoid wasteful spending by learning from pioneers' inefficiencies.

For instance, **Google entered the search engine market after Yahoo and AltaVista but became dominant by improving algorithms and offering a cleaner user experience.**

How Fast-Follower Strategy Works

Companies successfully implement this strategy through:

1. **Market Surveillance** – Observing first movers, identifying weaknesses, and learning from early mistakes.

2. **Strategic Timing** – Entering the market once consumer demand is validated.

3. **Product Differentiation** – Improving key features or pricing to offer a superior alternative.

4. **Operational Efficiency** – Using updated technology to lower production and marketing costs.

5. **Aggressive Scaling** – Once a refined product is introduced, scaling quickly to capture market share.

Success depends on **speed, execution, and innovation**—waiting too long allows first-movers to entrench themselves, while rushing in without differentiation leads to failure.

Application of Fast-Follower Strategy

Businesses use fast-following to:

- **Compete in tech-driven industries** – Microsoft followed Apple in personal computing and became dominant with Windows.

- **Outpace pioneers in execution** – Netflix overtook Blockbuster by refining the streaming model.

- **Avoid excessive risk** – Pharmaceutical firms often wait for early drug development success before launching alternatives.

- **Improve affordability** – Tesla introduced luxury EVs, but brands like BYD and Rivian are fast-followers offering competitive, lower-cost alternatives.

For example, **TikTok wasn't the first short-video platform (Vine existed earlier), but superior execution, AI-driven recommendations, and aggressive marketing helped it dominate.**

Key Insights on Fast-Follower Strategy

- **Execution matters more than being first** – Many first-movers fail due to poor strategy and operations.

- **Timing is critical** – Enter too early, and the market may not be ready; enter too late, and competitors may dominate.

- **Differentiation is necessary** – Simply copying a first-mover won't work; successful fast-followers **improve and innovate**.

- **Branding plays a role** – Second entrants must position themselves as superior, not just alternatives.

- **Agility and adaptability win** – Fast-followers must iterate quickly to stay ahead of first movers and later competitors.

When done correctly, a **Fast-Follower Strategy enables companies to dominate markets without the high costs and** risks of pioneering, making it one of the most effective strategies in competitive industries.

16. Customer Intimacy Strategy

Customer Intimacy Strategy: A Comprehensive Breakdown

Theory Behind Customer Intimacy Strategy

A **Customer Intimacy Strategy** is a business approach where companies focus on **deeply understanding and serving the unique needs of their customers**. Instead of competing on price (Cost Leadership) or innovation (Differentiation), businesses using this strategy **build strong relationships, deliver personalized experiences, and provide exceptional service**.

This strategy is part of the **Value Discipline Model**, introduced by Michael Treacy and Fred Wiersema, which outlines three competitive approaches:

1. **Operational Excellence** – Competing on efficiency and low cost.
2. **Product Leadership** – Competing on innovation and cutting-edge products.
3. **Customer Intimacy** – Competing on deep customer relationships and personalized solutions.

Companies that adopt a Customer Intimacy Strategy **prioritize long-term customer loyalty over short-term profits** by delivering customized solutions, exceptional service, and strong engagement.

Example of Customer Intimacy Strategy

A well-known example is **Ritz-Carlton**, which sets itself apart in the luxury hotel industry by:

- Training employees to remember guest preferences and personalize services.
- Empowering staff to go above and beyond to create memorable experiences.
- Maintaining a "Gold Standards" approach that ensures high levels of service consistency.

Another example is **Amazon**, which personalizes the shopping experience through:

- **AI-driven recommendations** based on past purchases and browsing history.
- **One-click ordering and Prime benefits** to simplify and enhance customer satisfaction.
- **Superior customer service**, including hassle-free returns and 24/7 support.

Both companies excel by **building customer trust, loyalty, and repeat business** through personalized engagement.

Why Customer Intimacy Strategy Works

This strategy is effective because it:

- **Builds Strong Customer Loyalty** – Personalized experiences make customers feel valued, leading to long-term retention.

- **Encourages Higher Spending** – Loyal customers are willing to pay more for personalized service.

- **Creates Competitive Differentiation** – Unique customer relationships are difficult for competitors to replicate.

- **Enhances Customer Lifetime Value (CLV)** – Satisfied customers return repeatedly, increasing profitability.

- **Generates Positive Word-of-Mouth** – Happy customers become brand advocates, driving organic growth.

For instance, **Nordstrom is known for its outstanding customer service, offering flexible returns and personalized shopping assistance, making it a preferred brand for premium retail buyers.**

How Customer Intimacy Strategy Works

Companies implement customer intimacy by:

1. **Collecting and Analyzing Customer Data** – Using CRM systems to track customer preferences, behaviours, and feedback.

2. **Personalizing Customer Interactions** – Offering tailored product recommendations, customized services, and proactive engagement.

3. **Training Employees for High-Touch Service** – Empowering staff to make decisions that enhance customer satisfaction.

4. **Offering Flexible Solutions** – Adapting products and services to meet specific customer needs.

5. **Building Long-Term Relationships** – Prioritizing customer satisfaction over transactional sales.

For example, **Salesforce uses customer data to provide businesses with highly customized CRM solutions, strengthening its market dominance**.

Application of Customer Intimacy Strategy

Businesses apply customer intimacy in:

- **Luxury brands** – Companies like **Louis Vuitton** offer exclusive, high-touch shopping experiences.
- **B2B services** – Consulting firms like **McKinsey & Company** tailor solutions to specific client challenges.
- **Retail & E-commerce** – Sephora's **Beauty Insider loyalty program** provides customized product recommendations.
- **Technology & SaaS** – Netflix's **AI-driven content curation** enhances user experience.

For instance, **Zappos built its reputation on customer intimacy by offering free shipping, easy returns, and a no-time-limit refund policy, making online shoe shopping hassle-free**.

Key Insights on Customer Intimacy Strategy

- **It requires deep customer insights** – Businesses must invest in data collection, AI, and CRM systems.

- **Long-term focus is necessary** – Prioritizing customer loyalty over short-term sales pays off in sustained revenue.

- **Scalability can be challenging** – As businesses grow, maintaining personalized relationships requires strategic automation.

- **Employee empowerment is key** – Frontline staff should have the autonomy to enhance customer experiences.

- **Differentiation must be maintained** – Competitors can mimic aspects of customer intimacy, so businesses must continuously evolve their approach.

When executed effectively, a **Customer Intimacy Strategy leads to strong brand loyalty, high customer retention, and long-term profitability, making it a powerful strategy for premium and service-driven industries.**

17. Product Leadership Strategy

Product Leadership Strategy: A Comprehensive Breakdown

Theory Behind Product Leadership Strategy

A **Product Leadership Strategy** is a business approach where companies compete by consistently delivering **innovative, cutting-edge, and high-quality products**. This strategy prioritizes **breakthrough ideas, superior design, and technological advancements** to differentiate from competitors.

This strategy is one of the **Three Value Disciplines**, introduced by **Michael Treacy and Fred Wiersema**, which include:

1. **Operational Excellence** – Competing on efficiency and cost.

2. **Customer Intimacy** – Competing on relationships and personalized service.

3. **Product Leadership** – Competing on superior products and innovation.

Product leaders focus on **constant improvement, risk-taking, and a culture of innovation** to stay ahead. Their goal is to **set industry standards** and create demand by offering superior solutions.

Key characteristics of a product leadership strategy include:

- **Innovation and R&D investment** – High budgets allocated to research and technological advancements.

- **Fast-paced product development** – Rapid iteration and new releases to maintain market leadership.

- **High-quality design and functionality** – Emphasis on aesthetics, performance, and user experience.

- **Strong brand identity** – Companies position themselves as market trendsetters.

Industries where product leadership is common include **technology, consumer electronics, pharmaceuticals, automotive, and fashion.**

Example of Product Leadership Strategy

A prime example is **Apple**, which dominates through:

- **Groundbreaking product design** – Sleek, user-friendly devices with premium aesthetics.

- **Ecosystem integration** – Seamless connectivity between iPhones, MacBooks, iPads, and Apple Watches.

- **Continuous innovation** – Introduction of new features like Face ID, M1 chips, and Vision Pro.

Another example is **Tesla**, which revolutionized the electric vehicle (EV) market by:

- **Developing industry-first innovations**, such as self-driving technology and over-the-air software updates.

- **Expanding battery efficiency and range**, making EVs more viable for mainstream users.

- **Setting trends in sustainable technology,** forcing traditional automakers to adapt.

Both companies **consistently redefine their industries** and command premium pricing due to their reputation for cutting-edge innovation.

Why Product Leadership Strategy Works

The **Product Leadership Strategy** is effective because it:

- **Creates Market Differentiation** – Unique, high-quality products stand out from competitors.

- **Justifies Premium Pricing** – Customers are willing to pay more for superior technology and design.

- **Builds Brand Loyalty** – Early adopters and enthusiasts create strong communities around product leaders.

- **Encourages Repeat Purchases** – Frequent innovations drive customers to upgrade regularly.

- **Forces Competitors to Play Catch-Up** – First-mover advantage in innovation keeps rivals reacting rather than leading.

For instance, **Dyson transformed the vacuum cleaner industry by introducing bagless cyclonic technology, making its products both premium and high-performing.**

How Product Leadership Strategy Works

To implement a product leadership strategy, companies must:

1. **Invest Heavily in R&D** – Prioritize breakthrough technologies and continuous product improvement.

2. **Foster a Culture of Innovation** – Encourage employees to think creatively and take risks.

3. **Speed Up Product Development** – Quickly bring innovations to market before competitors.

4. **Prioritize Design and Usability** – Ensure products are not only functional but also aesthetically appealing and user-friendly.

5. **Leverage Branding and Marketing** – Position the company as an industry innovator and thought leader.

For example, **Nike invests in cutting-edge materials and designs, such as Flyknit technology, to maintain its edge in sports apparel innovation.**

Application of Product Leadership Strategy

Businesses apply product leadership when they:

- **Compete in innovation-driven markets** – Tech companies like **Google** lead through AI and software advancements.

- **Disrupt traditional industries** – Fintech firms like **Square and Stripe** innovate payment processing.

- **Offer premium products** – Luxury brands like **Rolex** differentiate through craftsmanship and design.

- **Capitalize on first-mover advantage** – Pharmaceutical companies invest in **groundbreaking drug patents** before competitors.

For example, **Netflix revolutionized entertainment by transitioning from DVD rentals to streaming, continuously investing in AI-driven recommendations and exclusive content.**

Key Insights on Product Leadership Strategy

- **Innovation must be continuous** – Companies must consistently push boundaries to stay relevant.

- **R&D investment is critical** – Cutting-edge developments require significant financial commitment.

- **Execution speed matters** – Delayed product launches can lead to competitors catching up.

- **Customer perception defines success** – Marketing must reinforce the brand's leadership position.

- **Not all innovations succeed** – Some risks will fail, requiring agility and adaptability.

When executed correctly, a **Product Leadership Strategy ensures long-term dominance, premium pricing power, and industry influence**, making it one of the most powerful strategies for sustainable business growth.

18. Platform Strategy

Platform Strategy: A Comprehensive Breakdown

Theory Behind Platform Strategy

A **Platform Strategy** is a business approach where companies create an ecosystem that facilitates exchanges between different user groups—typically **producers and consumers**. Instead of just selling products or services, platform businesses act as intermediaries, **connecting users, enabling interactions, and capturing value from network effects**.

This strategy is grounded in **two-sided and multi-sided market theory**, where success depends on attracting and balancing supply and demand. It is commonly used in **technology, e-commerce, finance, and social media** industries.

Key characteristics of a platform strategy include:

1. **Network Effects** – More users increase the platform's value (e.g., Facebook becomes more useful as more people join).

2. **Scalability** – Platforms grow rapidly without significant marginal costs (e.g., Airbnb doesn't own hotels).

3. **Value Creation via Ecosystem** – Third-party developers, service providers, or contributors enhance the platform (e.g., Apple's App Store).

4. **Low Asset Ownership** – Many platform businesses do not own the primary goods or services they facilitate (e.g., Uber doesn't own cars).

The platform model disrupts **traditional linear business models**, where companies control production and distribution directly.

Example of Platform Strategy

A strong example is **Amazon**, which transitioned from a retailer to a **marketplace platform**. Instead of just selling products, Amazon allows third-party sellers to list and sell items, significantly expanding product selection and revenue without additional inventory costs.

Another example is **Uber**, which:

- Connects drivers with riders instead of operating a fleet.
- Uses a **two-sided network**, where more drivers attract more passengers and vice versa.
- Leverages data and algorithms to optimize pricing and availability.

Both companies **dominate their markets by leveraging network effects and scalable business models**.

Why Platform Strategy Works

A **Platform Strategy** is effective because:

- **Network Effects Drive Growth** – More users attract more contributors, enhancing value.
- **High Scalability** – Digital platforms expand quickly with minimal infrastructure costs.
- **Creates Marketplaces with Lower Costs** – Platforms act as intermediaries without the need for inventory.
- **Increases Switching Costs** – Once users and providers are embedded in a platform, they are less likely to switch.
- **Encourages Innovation** – Third-party developers and businesses expand platform capabilities (e.g., Google's Android ecosystem).

For instance, **Facebook became dominant by building a social network that encouraged user-generated content and third-party integrations, keeping users engaged.**

How Platform Strategy Works

Companies implement a platform strategy through:

1. **Building a Core Infrastructure** – Developing the technology to facilitate interactions (e.g., app, website, API).
2. **Attracting Initial Users** – Using incentives, promotions, or exclusivity to grow early adoption.
3. **Creating Value for All Sides** – Ensuring both producers (sellers, drivers, creators) and consumers benefit.

4. **Leveraging Data and Algorithms** – Using AI to enhance matchmaking, recommendations, and dynamic pricing.

5. **Expanding the Ecosystem** – Encouraging third-party involvement, partnerships, and integrations.

For example, **Google's Android OS is a platform that allows developers to create apps, handset manufacturers to build devices, and users to access a vast ecosystem.**

Application of Platform Strategy

Businesses use platform strategies to:

- **Disrupt traditional industries** – Airbnb challenges hotels by creating a home-sharing marketplace.

- **Build digital ecosystems** – Apple's App Store enables developers to create and sell apps.

- **Monetize network effects** – LinkedIn's value increases as more professionals join and engage.

- **Lower operational costs** – YouTube generates content through users rather than producing videos itself.

- **Enhance customer engagement** – Video game platforms like PlayStation create vibrant online communities.

For instance, **Spotify connects music artists and listeners, offering personalized recommendations while monetizing through subscriptions and ads.**

Key Insights on Platform Strategy

- **Critical Mass is Essential** – Platforms must grow their user base rapidly to become valuable.

- **Winner-Takes-All Dynamics** – Many platform markets (e.g., social media, e-commerce) are dominated by a few players.

- **Data is the Competitive Advantage** – Successful platforms use AI and analytics to optimize experiences.

- **Trust and Security Matter** – Platforms must manage fraud, quality control, and user safety.

- **Monetization Must Be Balanced** – Charging too early or too much can limit network growth.

When executed effectively, a **Platform Strategy enables businesses to scale rapidly, dominate markets, and create sustainable competitive advantages by leveraging network effects and digital ecosystems**.

19. Open Innovation Strategy

Open Innovation Strategy: A Comprehensive Breakdown

Theory Behind Open Innovation Strategy

An **Open Innovation Strategy** is a business approach where companies **collaborate with external partners, startups, universities, customers, and research institutions** to drive innovation. Unlike traditional **closed innovation**, where companies develop new ideas internally, open innovation leverages **outside expertise, technologies, and intellectual property (IP)** to accelerate development and reduce costs.

The concept was introduced by **Henry Chesbrough**, who defined open innovation as "a distributed innovation process based on **purposefully managed knowledge flows across organizational boundaries**."

Open innovation takes two primary forms:

1. **Inbound Open Innovation** – Companies acquire ideas, technologies, or intellectual property from external sources. (e.g., licensing, partnerships, crowdsourcing).

2. **Outbound Open Innovation** – Companies share their own innovations, licensing technologies or forming strategic alliances to expand their reach.

This strategy is common in **technology, pharmaceuticals, automotive, and consumer goods** industries, where breakthroughs require collaboration and diverse expertise.

Example of Open Innovation Strategy

A leading example is **LEGO**, which:

- Engages customers in co-creation through the **LEGO Ideas platform**, where fans submit new designs.
- Develops winning ideas into official LEGO sets, rewarding contributors with recognition and royalties.
- Benefits from community-driven innovation without heavy internal R&D costs.

Another example is **Tesla**, which **open-sourced its electric vehicle (EV) patents** to encourage industry-wide EV adoption. This move:

- Increased collaboration and standardization across the EV sector.
- Expanded Tesla's influence in the sustainable transport industry.
- Encouraged competitors to innovate using Tesla's advancements.

Both companies show how open innovation fosters creativity and **accelerates industry growth**.

Why Open Innovation Strategy Works

Open innovation is effective because it:

- **Reduces R&D Costs** – External collaboration lowers internal research expenses.

- **Speeds Up Innovation** – Accessing external knowledge accelerates product development.
- **Encourages Cross-Industry Synergies** – Combining expertise from different fields creates breakthrough innovations.
- **Builds a Competitive Advantage** – Companies can leverage **startups, universities, and external partners** to stay ahead.
- **Enhances Customer Engagement** – Involving users in product creation strengthens brand loyalty.

For instance, **Google's Android OS is an open-source platform**, allowing third-party developers to build apps, fostering a massive ecosystem of innovation.

How Open Innovation Strategy Works

Companies implement open innovation by:

1. **Identifying Innovation Needs** – Determining gaps in technology, market trends, or research areas.
2. **Forming External Partnerships** – Collaborating with startups, universities, suppliers, and customers.
3. **Utilizing Crowdsourcing and Hackathons** – Engaging the public to generate fresh ideas.
4. **Leveraging Open-Source Models** – Sharing selected innovations to drive adoption and ecosystem growth.

5. **Licensing or Acquiring External Technologies** – Purchasing patents, software, or scientific breakthroughs.

For example, **Procter & Gamble's "Connect + Develop" program** sources innovation ideas externally, reducing in-house R&D risks.

Application of Open Innovation Strategy

Businesses use open innovation to:

- **Enhance product development – NASA collaborates with private companies** to develop aerospace technologies.
- **Expand into new markets – Xiaomi integrates customer feedback into smartphone design.**
- **Reduce costs while improving quality – Pfizer and BioNTech collaborated to rapidly develop the COVID-19 vaccine.**
- **Leverage external research – IBM's Watson AI integrates third-party datasets and research.**

For instance, **Microsoft collaborates with open-source developers** to enhance cloud services, making its Azure platform more adaptable and widely used.

Key Insights on Open Innovation Strategy

- **Collaboration is essential** – Success depends on strong partnerships and shared incentives.

- **IP protection must be managed** – Balancing openness with competitive advantage is crucial.

- **Customer involvement strengthens brands** – Co-creation builds deeper consumer relationships.

- **Innovation is democratized** – Companies no longer need to rely solely on internal R&D teams.

- **Execution matters** – Simply gathering ideas isn't enough; companies must **integrate external insights into actionable innovations**.

When executed effectively, an **Open Innovation Strategy accelerates growth, reduces costs, and fosters industry-wide collaboration**, making it a powerful tool for companies looking to stay ahead in fast-evolving markets.

20. Defensive Strategy

Defensive Strategy: A Comprehensive Breakdown

Theory Behind Defensive Strategy

A **Defensive Strategy** is a business approach where companies take proactive measures to protect their market position, brand reputation, and profitability from competitors. Instead of focusing on aggressive expansion, this strategy prioritizes **maintaining market share, fending off new entrants, and ensuring long-term stability**.

Defensive strategies are essential in industries with **high competition, market saturation, or disruptive innovations**. They align with **Michael Porter's Competitive Strategy Framework**, which emphasizes maintaining a competitive edge through:

1. **Barriers to Entry** – Making it difficult for new competitors to enter the market.

2. **Customer Retention** – Strengthening brand loyalty and reducing churn.

3. **Cost Leadership or Differentiation** – Ensuring competitive pricing or unique offerings to discourage switching.

4. **Legal and Regulatory Measures** – Patents, trademarks, and compliance to protect intellectual property.

Companies adopt **defensive strategies** when facing threats from **new market entrants, technological shifts, or changing consumer preferences**.

Example of Defensive Strategy

A classic example is **Coca-Cola**, which protects its market dominance by:

- **Heavy branding and advertising** to reinforce customer loyalty.
- **Global distribution dominance**, ensuring easy availability of products.
- **Product diversification**, such as launching Diet Coke and Coca-Cola Zero to counter shifting health trends.

Another example is **Microsoft**, which used defensive strategies to maintain dominance in the software industry by:

- **Bundling Microsoft Office with Windows**, making it harder for competitors to gain traction.
- **Acquiring potential threats**, such as buying LinkedIn and GitHub.
- **Adapting to cloud computing** through Azure to defend against Amazon AWS.

Both companies **use a mix of market control, innovation, and strategic acquisitions to prevent losing their competitive edge.**

Why Defensive Strategy Works

A **Defensive Strategy** is effective because:

- **Prevents Competitor Growth** – Strong market presence discourages new entrants.

- **Enhances Brand Loyalty** – Loyal customers are less likely to switch to competitors.

- **Reduces Price Wars** – Cost leadership makes it difficult for others to undercut prices.

- **Ensures Long-Term Stability** – Strategic positioning protects against sudden industry changes.

- **Maximizes Market Control** – Companies with strong defensive strategies dictate industry standards.

For example, **Apple defends its ecosystem by making iOS exclusive, ensuring customers stay within its product line (iPhones, iPads, Macs, and services like iCloud and Apple Music).**

How Defensive Strategy Works

Companies implement defensive strategies through:

1. **Brand Reinforcement** – Investing in marketing to keep the brand top-of-mind.

2. **Product Innovation** – Continuously improving products to stay ahead of competitors.

3. **Competitive Pricing** – Offering discounts, loyalty programs, or bundles to retain customers.

4. **Legal Protections** – Filing patents and enforcing intellectual property rights.

5. **Strategic Partnerships & Acquisitions** – Buying or collaborating with emerging competitors to neutralize threats.

For example, **Google ensures dominance in search engines by continuously refining its algorithms, acquiring competitors (YouTube, Android), and integrating AI features like Google Assistant.**

Application of Defensive Strategy

Businesses use defensive strategies to:

- **Maintain Market Leadership** – Amazon defends its position by investing heavily in logistics, cloud computing, and exclusive deals.

- **Counter Emerging Competitors** – Netflix invests in original content to prevent competition from Disney+ and HBO Max.

- **Adapt to Market Shifts** – McDonald's expanded its healthy menu options to counter trends favouring organic food.

- **Control Pricing Power** – Walmart's cost leadership strategy prevents competitors from undercutting prices.

For instance, **Samsung strategically counters Apple by launching premium smartphones with advanced features before iPhone releases.**

Key Insights on Defensive Strategy

- **Proactive defence is stronger than reactive moves** – Companies must anticipate threats rather than just responding to them.

- **Customer loyalty is crucial** – A strong brand following makes it harder for competitors to take market share.

- **Innovation remains important** – Defensive strategies should not lead to stagnation; continuous improvement is necessary.

- **Legal and regulatory measures can create barriers** – Companies should leverage patents and compliance to protect their market.

- **Cost efficiency matters** – Maintaining competitive pricing ensures affordability without sacrificing profitability.

When executed effectively, a **Defensive Strategy helps businesses sustain their leadership, protect profitability, and navigate competitive pressures without losing market relevance.**

Growth Strategies; Strategies aimed at scaling the business:

21. Organic Growth Strategy

Organic Growth Strategy: A Comprehensive Breakdown

Theory Behind Organic Growth Strategy

An **Organic Growth Strategy** is a business approach where a company expands through **internal development rather than mergers, acquisitions, or partnerships.** This means growth is driven by **increasing sales, improving efficiency, launching new products, expanding operations, and enhancing customer engagement.**

Unlike **inorganic growth** (which relies on acquisitions or external investments), organic growth is **sustainable, cost-effective, and focuses on long-term success.**

Organic growth is built on:

1. **Expanding Product or Service Offerings** – Innovating and launching new products that cater to market demand.

2. **Increasing Market Penetration** – Selling more of existing products to current customers or attracting new customers.

3. **Geographical Expansion** – Entering new markets through local distribution or direct presence.

4. **Enhancing Customer Experience** – Building brand loyalty and repeat business through quality and service.

This strategy is common in **retail, technology, consumer goods, and hospitality** industries, where customer satisfaction and innovation drive long-term success.

Example of Organic Growth Strategy

A great example is **Starbucks**, which has grown organically by:

- **Expanding its product lineup** – Introducing seasonal drinks, alternative milk options, and new food items.

- **Enhancing customer engagement** – Using the Starbucks Rewards program to increase customer loyalty.

- **Entering new markets** – Expanding internationally without relying on major acquisitions.

Another example is **Amazon**, which initially grew organically by:

- **Expanding its product categories** – From books to electronics, clothing, and cloud computing (AWS).

- **Focusing on customer experience** – Fast delivery, Prime membership, and personalized recommendations.

- **Developing its own technology** – Alexa, Kindle, and Echo devices were built in-house to enhance its ecosystem.

Both companies **prioritized sustainable internal growth over aggressive acquisitions**, leading to long-term success.

Why Organic Growth Strategy Works

An **Organic Growth Strategy** is effective because:

- **Sustainable and Low-Risk** – Growth is gradual and based on proven demand.

- **Strengthens Brand Identity** – Customers recognize and trust organically grown brands more.

- **Improves Profitability Over Time** – Since there's no acquisition debt, companies maintain financial health.

- **Encourages Innovation** – Companies focus on continuous product and service improvements.

- **Enhances Employee and Cultural Stability** – Internal growth maintains corporate culture, avoiding disruption from mergers.

For instance, **Nike continues to grow organically by innovating in sportswear technology and directly engaging customers through digital experiences**.

How Organic Growth Strategy Works

Companies achieve organic growth by:

1. **Investing in Product Development** – Creating better products based on customer needs and trends.

2. **Expanding Marketing and Sales Efforts** – Increasing brand visibility and customer outreach.

3. **Enhancing Customer Retention Strategies** – Using loyalty programs, personalization, and engagement.

4. **Improving Operational Efficiency** – Optimizing production, supply chain, and digital transformation.

5. **Expanding into New Markets Gradually** – Testing new locations and demographics before scaling.

For example, **Apple's organic growth comes from constant product innovation (iPhone, Mac, iPad), ecosystem expansion, and direct customer engagement through Apple Stores and online services.**

Application of Organic Growth Strategy

Businesses use organic growth strategies to:

- **Expand sustainably** – Tesla grows by continuously improving its battery technology and manufacturing capacity.

- **Enhance customer lifetime value** – Subscription models like Netflix increase user retention without acquiring new companies.

- **Build a competitive edge** – Google dominates search and cloud computing through internal R&D and AI investments.

- **Develop strong brand loyalty** – Disney grows organically by expanding its original content and theme parks.

For instance, **IKEA expands by opening new stores, refining logistics, and adapting to local market preferences instead of acquiring competitors.**

Key Insights on Organic Growth Strategy

- **Takes time and patience** – Unlike acquisitions, organic growth requires consistent effort and long-term planning.

- **Requires continuous innovation** – Companies must invest in R&D and market research to stay relevant.

- **Customer experience is key** – Loyalty, personalization, and engagement drive repeat business.

- **Scaling must be managed carefully** – Expanding too fast can strain resources and operations.

- **Financially stable growth** – Without acquisition costs, companies maintain stronger cash flow and profit margins.

When executed effectively, an **Organic Growth Strategy leads to strong brand loyalty, sustainable expansion, and long-term profitability**, making it a powerful approach for businesses focused on innovation and customer-centric growth.

22. Mergers & Acquisitions Strategy (M&A)

Mergers & Acquisitions (M&A) Strategy: A Comprehensive Breakdown

Theory Behind Mergers & Acquisitions Strategy

A **Mergers & Acquisitions (M&A) Strategy** is a business approach where companies expand by **combining with or acquiring other businesses**. This strategy is used to gain market share, diversify product offerings, enter new markets, or achieve cost efficiencies.

Mergers and acquisitions differ in structure:

1. **Merger** – Two companies combine to form a single entity (e.g., Exxon and Mobil merging to create ExxonMobil).
2. **Acquisition** – One company purchases another, which may continue operating under its own brand or be integrated (e.g., Facebook acquiring Instagram).

M&A is guided by **synergy theory**, where the combined value of two firms exceeds their separate values. Synergies may arise from:

- **Cost Savings** – Reduced operational redundancies and economies of scale.
- **Revenue Growth** – Expanding customer base or product lines.

- **Market Expansion** – Entering new geographical or industry markets.
- **Technology & Talent Acquisition** – Gaining intellectual property and skilled employees.

M&A is common in **finance, technology, pharmaceuticals, and consumer goods**, where consolidation creates competitive advantages.

Example of Mergers & Acquisitions Strategy

A well-known example is **Disney's acquisition of Marvel, Lucasfilm, and 21st Century Fox**, which:

- Expanded Disney's intellectual property portfolio.
- Strengthened its content library for streaming services like Disney+.
- Increased revenue through blockbuster franchises like Star Wars and the Marvel Cinematic Universe.

Another example is **Microsoft acquiring LinkedIn** to integrate professional networking with its cloud services, creating a strategic advantage in enterprise software.

Both examples showcase how M&A enables companies to **leverage existing assets and accelerate growth**.

Why Mergers & Acquisitions Strategy Works

An **M&A Strategy** is effective because:

- **Achieves Rapid Growth** – Expands market presence faster than organic growth.

- **Enhances Competitive Position** – Strengthens industry dominance by eliminating competition.

- **Diversifies Revenue Streams** – Reduces reliance on a single product or market.

- **Drives Innovation** – Acquiring technology firms accelerates R&D capabilities.

- **Maximizes Operational Efficiencies** – Shared resources reduce costs and improve margins.

For instance, **Google's acquisition of YouTube allowed it to dominate the online video market while leveraging its advertising expertise**.

How Mergers & Acquisitions Strategy Works

Companies execute M&A through:

1. **Identifying Strategic Targets** – Finding firms that align with business goals.

2. **Valuation & Due Diligence** – Assessing financials, risks, and cultural fit.

3. **Negotiation & Deal Structuring** – Determining acquisition terms and financing options.

4. **Integration Planning** – Merging operations, systems, and teams for smooth transition.

5. **Post-Merger Optimization** – Aligning strategies to extract synergies and maximize value.

For example, **Amazon's acquisition of Whole Foods integrated brick-and-mortar retail with its e-commerce ecosystem**, improving logistics and customer engagement.

Application of Mergers & Acquisitions Strategy

Businesses use M&A to:

- **Expand into new industries** – Facebook acquired Oculus to enter the virtual reality market.

- **Eliminate competition** – Uber acquired Careem to dominate the Middle Eastern ride-hailing sector.

- **Gain technological capabilities** – Apple acquires AI and chip-making companies to enhance its ecosystem.

- **Enhance product portfolios** – Nestlé acquired Blue Bottle Coffee to strengthen its premium beverage segment.

For instance, **Nike acquired Converse to maintain control over sports footwear and prevent competition from gaining ground**.

Key Insights on Mergers & Acquisitions Strategy

- **Cultural integration is crucial** – Many M&As fail due to mismatched corporate cultures.

- **Due diligence determines success** – Poorly evaluated deals can lead to financial losses.

- **Execution must be strategic** – M&As require detailed planning for smooth transitions.

- **Not all acquisitions create value** – Some deals destroy shareholder value due to overvaluation.

- **Regulatory scrutiny is increasing** – Governments monitor large M&As to prevent monopolies.

When executed correctly, a **Mergers & Acquisitions Strategy accelerates growth, strengthens market dominance, and creates lasting competitive advantages**, making it a powerful expansion tool for businesses.

23. Market Penetration Strategy

Market Penetration Strategy: A Comprehensive Breakdown

Theory Behind Market Penetration Strategy

A **Market Penetration Strategy** is a business approach where a company increases sales of existing products or services in its current market to gain a larger market share. This strategy focuses on **maximizing revenue from existing customers, attracting competitors' customers, and deepening market dominance without expanding into new markets or developing new products**.

Market penetration is one of the four growth strategies in the **Ansoff Matrix**, which outlines business expansion tactics:

1. **Market Penetration** – Selling more in an existing market.
2. **Market Development** – Entering new markets.
3. **Product Development** – Creating new products for existing markets.
4. **Diversification** – Expanding into new products and markets.

Companies use market penetration to **outperform competitors, optimize sales efficiency, and increase customer loyalty**. It is often implemented in industries like **retail, technology, consumer goods, and fast food**, where capturing market share is essential for profitability.

Example of Market Penetration Strategy

A strong example is **McDonald's**, which continuously increases market penetration by:

- **Promotions & Discounts** – Limited-time offers (e.g., "$1 menu") encourage frequent purchases.
- **Loyalty Programs** – McDonald's Rewards incentivizes repeat business.
- **Expansion of Delivery Services** – Partnering with Uber Eats and DoorDash increases accessibility.

Another example is **Apple**, which grows its iPhone sales in existing markets by:

- **Trade-in Programs** – Encouraging existing users to upgrade.
- **Bundling Services** – Offering Apple One (Music, iCloud, TV) to retain customers.
- **Retail & Online Expansion** – Increasing store locations and online presence.

Both companies **focus on maximizing customer retention and sales growth within their current markets** rather than expanding geographically.

Why Market Penetration Strategy Works

A **Market Penetration Strategy** is effective because:

- **Lower Risk Than Expansion** – Selling existing products in familiar markets is safer than entering new territories.

- **Increases Customer Loyalty** – Strengthens relationships with existing buyers through engagement.

- **Drives Sales Without Heavy R&D Costs** – Focuses on marketing and sales optimization rather than developing new products.

- **Takes Market Share from Competitors** – Competitive pricing and aggressive marketing attract rival customers.

- **Enhances Brand Recognition** – Higher market presence reinforces brand dominance.

For instance, **Netflix expanded its market penetration by enhancing content recommendations, improving streaming quality, and launching lower-priced ad-supported plans**.

How Market Penetration Strategy Works

Businesses implement market penetration by:

1. **Increasing Marketing & Promotions** – Running targeted ads, discounts, and referral programs.

2. **Enhancing Product Accessibility** – Expanding distribution channels and optimizing pricing strategies.

3. **Improving Customer Engagement** – Leveraging loyalty programs, personalized content, and excellent customer service.

4. **Aggressive Pricing & Bundling** – Offering value deals to increase purchase frequency.

5. **Leveraging Competitive Intelligence** – Monitoring competitors and adjusting strategies accordingly.

For example, **Coca-Cola maintains its dominance by constantly running advertising campaigns, entering more stores, and offering bulk discounts to retailers.**

Application of Market Penetration Strategy

Businesses use this strategy to:

- **Increase sales in competitive industries** – Starbucks expands its loyalty program to retain customers.

- **Dominate retail and e-commerce markets** – Amazon offers Prime membership benefits to encourage repeat purchases.

- **Improve customer lifetime value** – Spotify keeps users engaged with exclusive content and personalized playlists.

- **Expand in local markets before international growth** – Domino's perfected its home delivery strategy before expanding globally.

For instance, **Samsung increases its smartphone market penetration by offering trade-in deals, financing options, and software updates to keep users engaged**.

Key Insights on Market Penetration Strategy

- **Customer retention is as important as acquisition** – Repeat customers drive long-term profitability.

- **Price wars can be risky** – Lowering prices too much may reduce profitability.

- **Innovation isn't required, but optimization is** – Businesses must refine marketing, sales, and distribution efforts.

- **Competitor responses must be anticipated** – Aggressive penetration can provoke price competition.

- **Market saturation can be a limit** – Companies must eventually consider product innovation or market expansion.

When executed effectively, a **Market Penetration Strategy helps businesses increase revenue, strengthen customer relationships, and build a dominant position in their industry**, making it a powerful growth tool.

24. Market Development Strategy

Market Development Strategy: A Comprehensive Breakdown

Theory Behind Market Development Strategy

A **Market Development Strategy** is a business approach where a company expands its customer base by **entering new markets with existing products or services**. Instead of creating new products, businesses **identify new customer segments, geographical areas, or industry applications** to drive growth.

This strategy is one of the four growth options in the **Ansoff Matrix**, which includes:

1. **Market Penetration** – Selling more of an existing product in an existing market.
2. **Market Development** – Selling an existing product in a new market.
3. **Product Development** – Selling a new product in an existing market.
4. **Diversification** – Selling a new product in a new market.

Market development is often used by businesses in **retail, technology, pharmaceuticals, and consumer goods** looking to expand their reach without the costs of new product development.

Example of Market Development Strategy

A strong example is **Tesla**, which initially targeted high-income consumers but expanded into **new customer segments** by launching more affordable models like the Model 3. This shift:

- Increased Tesla's market reach beyond luxury buyers.
- Made electric vehicles accessible to a wider audience.
- Strengthened its competitive position in the global automotive industry.

Another example is **McDonald's**, which used market development by:

- Expanding internationally into **Asia, the Middle East, and Africa**.
- Adapting its menu to local tastes (e.g., the McSpicy Paneer in India).
- Establishing **new store formats** such as drive-thrus and delivery-only locations.

Both companies **leveraged their existing offerings to attract new customer groups and expand geographically**.

Why Market Development Strategy Works

A **Market Development Strategy** is effective because:

- **Creates New Revenue Streams** – Expands business without relying solely on existing markets.
- **Leverages Existing Strengths** – Uses current products and brand equity to enter new territories.
- **Increases Competitive Edge** – Early entry into new markets provides first-mover advantages.
- **Diversifies Risk** – Reduces dependence on a single market, protecting against economic downturns.
- **Boosts Brand Recognition** – Exposure to new audiences strengthens global brand positioning.

For instance, **Netflix expanded internationally by localizing content and pricing, gaining a dominant position in non-U.S. markets.**

How Market Development Strategy Works

Companies implement market development by:

1. **Geographic Expansion** – Entering new regions, countries, or global markets.
2. **Targeting New Customer Segments** – Adjusting marketing strategies to appeal to different demographics.

3. **Exploring New Use Cases** – Finding alternative applications for existing products (e.g., baking soda as a cleaning agent).
4. **Expanding Distribution Channels** – Using online platforms, retail partnerships, or direct sales models.
5. **Adapting Marketing Strategies** – Customizing messaging, branding, and pricing for new audiences.

For example, **Apple's entry into China involved opening flagship stores, partnering with local telecom companies, and launching region-specific promotions.**

Application of Market Development Strategy

Businesses use market development to:

- **Expand internationally** – Starbucks grows by localizing products and store designs in new regions.
- **Attract new demographics** – Nike targets different sports communities beyond running and basketball.
- **Find alternative industry uses** – Microsoft repurposed its cloud technology for government and healthcare clients.
- **Grow through strategic partnerships** – Airbnb collaborated with local tourism boards to promote travel.

For instance, **Coca-Cola expanded into health-conscious markets by launching sugar-free variants like Diet Coke and Coke Zero.**

Key Insights on Market Development Strategy

- **Not all markets respond the same way** – Cultural, economic, and regulatory factors impact success.

- **Requires strong brand adaptation** – Localization is key to winning new customers.

- **Competition will react** – Entering new markets invites direct competition from local players.

- **Market research is critical** – Businesses must analyse demand, pricing, and consumer behaviour before expansion.

- **Customer education may be needed** – In some cases, companies must introduce and explain their product's value to new audiences.

When executed effectively, a **Market Development Strategy helps businesses scale, diversify risk, and tap into new revenue streams**, making it a powerful tool for sustainable growth.

25. Product Development Strategy

Product Development Strategy: A Comprehensive Breakdown

Theory Behind Product Development Strategy

A **Product Development Strategy** is a business approach where a company creates **new or improved products** to serve its existing markets. Instead of expanding into new geographical locations or customer segments, businesses **innovate, refine, or extend their product lines** to drive growth and meet evolving consumer needs.

This strategy is part of the **Ansoff Matrix**, which outlines four growth strategies:

1. **Market Penetration** – Selling more of an existing product in an existing market.
2. **Market Development** – Expanding an existing product into a new market.
3. **Product Development** – Introducing a new or improved product to an existing market.
4. **Diversification** – Creating a new product for a new market.

Product development is common in **technology, automotive, consumer goods, and pharmaceuticals**, where innovation is essential for staying competitive.

Example of Product Development Strategy

A well-known example is **Apple**, which continuously improves its product lineup:

- **The iPhone evolves annually** with new features (better cameras, faster chips, improved battery life).

- **Apple Watch and AirPods expanded its ecosystem**, introducing new product categories.

- **MacBooks transitioned to Apple's M1 and M2 chips**, improving performance and efficiency.

Another example is **Coca-Cola**, which expanded its product line with:

- **Diet Coke and Coke Zero**, targeting health-conscious consumers.

- **Flavoured and premium beverages**, such as Coca-Cola Energy and Smartwater.

- **Sustainable packaging initiatives**, responding to environmental concerns.

Both companies use product development to **retain customers, differentiate from competitors, and maintain market leadership.**

Why Product Development Strategy Works

A **Product Development Strategy** is effective because:

- **Increases Customer Retention** – Offering new products keeps customers engaged with the brand.

- **Differentiates from Competitors** – Innovation creates unique selling points and pricing advantages.

- **Expands Market Share** – New features attract new customer segments within existing markets.

- **Drives Brand Loyalty** – Consistently evolving products strengthen customer relationships.

- **Boosts Revenue Growth** – Frequent updates encourage repeat purchases and higher spending.

For instance, **Netflix transitioned from DVD rentals to online streaming, then expanded into original content, continuously evolving to stay ahead.**

How Product Development Strategy Works

Companies implement product development by:

1. **Investing in R&D** – Continuous innovation through research, prototyping, and testing.

2. **Customer-Centric Design** – Gathering feedback to align new products with consumer needs.

3. **Product Line Extensions** – Expanding variations, such as new Flavors, sizes, or premium versions.

4. **Technology Integration** – Enhancing features with digital advancements (AI, automation, smart tech).

5. **Sustainability and Trends** – Aligning new products with market shifts, such as eco-friendly initiatives.

For example, **Tesla constantly updates its software, adding new features to vehicles even after purchase.**

Application of Product Development Strategy

Businesses use this strategy to:

- **Keep up with industry trends** – Fashion brands release seasonal collections to stay relevant.

- **Expand offerings in competitive markets** – Fast-food chains introduce limited-time menu items.

- **Capitalize on emerging technologies** – Tech firms invest in AI, blockchain, and smart devices.

- **Satisfy changing consumer preferences** – Personal care brands develop natural and organic product lines.

For instance, **Nike innovates with new shoe materials and self-lacing technology to maintain leadership in sportswear.**

Key Insights on Product Development Strategy

- **Innovation must be continuous** – Stagnation leads to market decline.

- **Customer feedback is crucial** – Understanding needs ensures product success.

- **R&D investments can be high** – Success depends on well-managed research and execution.

- **Competitors will imitate successful products** – Speed to market is key.

- **Not every new product succeeds** – Businesses must test, adapt, and refine based on performance.

When executed effectively, a **Product Development Strategy helps businesses drive innovation, strengthen brand loyalty, and sustain long-term growth**, making it essential in fast-evolving industries.

26. Blue Ocean Expansion

Blue Ocean Expansion Strategy in Product Development

Theory Behind Blue Ocean Expansion Strategy in Product Development

A **Blue Ocean Expansion Strategy in Product Development** is a business approach where companies create entirely new markets (Blue Oceans) rather than competing in saturated, highly competitive markets (Red Oceans). This strategy focuses on **innovation, differentiation, and value creation** to open up untapped demand.

The **Blue Ocean Strategy**, developed by **W. Chan Kim and Renée Mauborgne**, emphasizes:

1. **Value Innovation** – Creating a product that is both high-value and cost-efficient.

2. **Breaking Industry Norms** – Challenging traditional assumptions to redefine market boundaries.

3. **Uncontested Market Space** – Avoiding direct competition by offering something unique.

4. **Customer-Centric Approach** – Focusing on non-customers and expanding demand.

By applying this to product development, companies **introduce groundbreaking products that transform industries**, rather than making incremental improvements in existing markets.

Example of Blue Ocean Expansion Strategy in Product Development

A strong example is **Nintendo's Wii**, which disrupted the gaming industry by:

- **Focusing on casual gamers instead of hardcore players.**
- **Introducing motion-sensing controls**, making gaming more interactive.
- **Lowering hardware specs** to keep prices affordable while offering a unique experience.

Another example is **Tesla**, which:

- **Repositioned electric vehicles (EVs) as premium, high-performance cars.**
- **Integrated software updates**, making cars continuously improve after purchase.
- **Expanded the EV ecosystem** by building a Supercharger network.

Both companies **created new demand by redefining customer expectations and expanding their market reach**.

Why Blue Ocean Expansion Strategy Works

A **Blue Ocean Expansion Strategy in Product Development** is effective because:

- **Eliminates Price Wars** – By creating a unique market, companies don't need to compete on cost.

- **Attracts Non-Customers** – It focuses on untapped audiences, increasing demand.

- **Encourages Innovation** – New products redefine industries and set new standards.

- **Creates Strong Brand Loyalty** – Customers associate the company with pioneering innovation.

- **Generates High Profit Margins** – Unique products justify premium pricing.

For example, **Airbnb created a new lodging market by offering unique stays in private homes, rather than competing with hotels.**

How Blue Ocean Expansion Strategy Works

Businesses implement this strategy by:

1. **Identifying Unmet Needs** – Understanding gaps in current offerings.

2. **Redefining Market Boundaries** – Creating products that challenge industry assumptions.

3. **Combining Innovation with Affordability** – Offering superior value at a reasonable price.

4. **Developing a New Customer Base** – Targeting those ignored by existing solutions.

5. **Scaling with Ecosystem Support** – Building infrastructure to sustain the new market (e.g., Tesla's charging network).

For example, **Spotify transformed music consumption by shifting from ownership (buying songs) to access (streaming), revolutionizing the industry.**

Application of Blue Ocean Expansion Strategy

Businesses use this strategy to:

- **Create new demand** – Cirque du Soleil reinvented the circus by combining theatre and acrobatics.
- **Differentiate in crowded markets** – Apple's iPad defined the tablet industry before competitors reacted.
- **Shift customer expectations** – Uber changed transportation by offering an app-based ride service.
- **Expand beyond traditional customers** – Peloton attracted non-gym-goers by offering immersive, at-home fitness.

For instance, **Netflix evolved from DVD rentals to streaming, then into original content, continuously expanding into Blue Oceans.**

Key Insights on Blue Ocean Expansion Strategy in Product Development

- **Innovation must create both value and affordability** – A breakthrough product must be desirable and accessible.

- **Timing is crucial** – Entering too early may result in a lack of demand; too late, and competitors might adapt.

- **Customer adoption requires education** – Companies must communicate why their product is a game-changer.

- **Sustainability is key** – Once a Blue Ocean is created, companies must defend and expand it.

- **Not every attempt succeeds** – Risk is involved, but well-executed strategies redefine industries.

When applied effectively, a **Blue Ocean Expansion Strategy in Product Development leads to market dominance, customer loyalty, and industry disruption**, making it a powerful approach for long-term success.

27. Growth Hacking Strategy

Growth Hacking Strategy: A Comprehensive Breakdown

Theory Behind Growth Hacking Strategy

A **Growth Hacking Strategy** is a business approach focused on achieving rapid, scalable growth through **data-driven experimentation, creative marketing, and automation**. Unlike traditional marketing, which often relies on large budgets and broad campaigns, growth hacking is about **leveraging low-cost, high-impact strategies to accelerate user acquisition, engagement, and retention**.

The concept was introduced by **Sean Ellis**, who defined a growth hacker as **"a person whose true north is growth."** Growth hacking is commonly used by **startups, digital platforms, and tech companies** that need to scale quickly with limited resources.

Key elements of growth hacking include:

1. **Data-Driven Decisions** – Using analytics to test and optimize strategies.
2. **Viral & Referral Loops** – Encouraging users to bring in new customers.
3. **Product-Led Growth** – Designing features that naturally drive adoption.
4. **Automation & Scalability** – Leveraging technology to maximize efficiency.

5. **Rapid Experimentation** – Constantly testing different approaches to identify what works.

Growth hacking is **not just about marketing**—it integrates product development, user experience, and psychology to drive sustainable growth.

Example of Growth Hacking Strategy

A classic example is **Dropbox**, which achieved explosive growth by:

- **Offering extra storage for referrals**, turning existing users into brand ambassadors.
- **Gamifying user engagement**, rewarding actions like file uploads and app installations.
- **Optimizing onboarding**, making sign-up seamless and inviting collaboration.

Another example is **Airbnb**, which used:

- **Craigslist integration** to attract early users, tapping into an existing marketplace.
- **Personalized email campaigns** to re-engage inactive users.
- **Social proof & urgency tactics**, such as showing limited availability and recent bookings.

Both companies **leveraged low-cost, high-impact tactics to scale rapidly** without relying on traditional advertising.

Why Growth Hacking Strategy Works

A **Growth Hacking Strategy** is effective because:

- **Maximizes Growth with Minimal Spend** – Relies on viral mechanics, automation, and data rather than large marketing budgets.

- **Focuses on User Acquisition & Retention** – Prioritizes rapid scaling and user engagement.

- **Encourages Virality** – Referral programs, shareable content, and network effects accelerate adoption.

- **Iterates Quickly** – Continuous testing and improvement ensure strategies evolve.

- **Integrates Marketing & Product Development** – Growth hacking blends marketing, technology, and psychology for maximum impact.

For instance, **TikTok's algorithm-driven content discovery keeps users engaged and increases organic sharing, fuelling exponential growth.**

How Growth Hacking Strategy Works

Businesses implement growth hacking through:

1. **Identifying Growth Loops** – Designing features that drive continuous user acquisition (e.g., referrals, shareable content).

2. **A/B Testing & Optimization** – Running experiments to refine conversion rates and engagement.

3. **Leveraging Data & Automation** – Using AI, analytics, and automation tools to scale efficiently.

4. **Building a Community** – Encouraging user-generated content, discussions, and brand advocacy.

5. **Creating Urgency & Exclusivity** – Using scarcity tactics like limited-time offers and waitlists.

For example, **LinkedIn's growth hack involved making profiles public by default, boosting SEO rankings and attracting organic traffic.**

Application of Growth Hacking Strategy

Businesses use growth hacking to:

- **Scale fast with limited resources** – Startups like Stripe grew by offering seamless developer integrations.

- **Create viral referral programs** – PayPal paid users to invite friends, fuelling its early adoption.

- **Optimize conversion funnels** – Spotify refines its onboarding process to increase subscriptions.

- **Boost user engagement** – Instagram uses push notifications and AI-powered feeds to retain users.

For instance, **Zoom gained massive adoption by making video conferencing frictionless, with one-click meeting access and viral product-led growth**.

Key Insights on Growth Hacking Strategy

- **Experimentation is key** – Growth hackers must constantly test, iterate, and optimize.

- **Not all tactics work forever** – What scales one company may not work for another.

- **Product virality drives sustainable growth** – Features that encourage sharing lead to organic expansion.

- **User experience matters** – Growth hacking works best when the product naturally attracts and retains users.

- **Data should guide every decision** – Metrics like retention rate, churn, and LTV (lifetime value) determine success.

When executed correctly, a **Growth Hacking Strategy enables businesses to scale rapidly, attract loyal users, and outpace competitors**, making it a vital approach for modern digital businesses.

28. Freemium Strategy

Freemium Strategy: A Comprehensive Breakdown

Theory Behind Freemium Strategy

A **Freemium Strategy** is a business model where companies offer a basic version of their product or service for free, while charging for premium features, upgrades, or additional services. This model **attracts a large user base, encourages engagement, and converts a percentage of users into paying customers**.

The freemium model is based on the **principles of behavioural economics** and customer psychology, where:

1. **Low Entry Barrier** – Free access lowers resistance to trying a product.

2. **Value Perception** – Users experience the product's benefits before committing to payment.

3. **Network Effects** – More free users increase brand visibility and encourage organic growth.

4. **Upsell Opportunities** – Premium features create incentives for users to upgrade.

This strategy is commonly used in **software, SaaS (Software as a Service), gaming, digital media, and mobile apps**, where ongoing engagement leads to higher monetization potential.

Example of Freemium Strategy

A prime example is **Spotify**, which:

- Offers **free, ad-supported streaming** with limitations.
- Provides **Premium subscriptions** that remove ads, allow offline listening, and enhance audio quality.
- Uses **personalized recommendations and AI-driven playlists** to increase user retention and encourage upgrades.

Another example is **Dropbox**, which:

- Gives **free cloud storage** with limited space.
- Offers **paid plans** for more storage, file sharing, and business tools.
- Uses **referral incentives** (extra storage for inviting friends) to grow its user base.

Both companies successfully convert free users into paying customers by **demonstrating clear value and providing strong incentives for upgrades.**

Why Freemium Strategy Works

A **Freemium Strategy** is effective because:

- **Attracts a Large User Base** – Free access encourages mass adoption.

- **Reduces Customer Acquisition Costs (CAC)** – Users discover the product organically.
- **Increases Customer Retention** – Continuous use builds habit formation.
- **Enables Viral Growth** – Free users promote the product through word-of-mouth.
- **Provides Data-Driven Insights** – User behaviour analytics help optimize conversion strategies.

For example, **Zoom's freemium model (limited free meetings) drove rapid adoption during the pandemic, leading to strong enterprise conversions**.

How Freemium Strategy Works

Companies implement freemium by:

1. **Creating a Valuable Free Tier** – Ensuring the basic version is useful but has limitations.
2. **Optimizing the Upgrade Path** – Designing premium features that solve specific pain points.
3. **Leveraging Network Effects** – Encouraging user referrals, collaboration, and social sharing.
4. **Implementing Usage-Based Triggers** – Reminding users of limitations and benefits of upgrading.
5. **Personalizing Marketing & Offers** – Using AI to target users with relevant upgrade incentives.

For example, **LinkedIn offers a free professional networking platform but charges for premium features like advanced search and resume insights.**

Application of Freemium Strategy

Businesses use freemium to:

- **Drive mass adoption** – Canva's free design tools attract millions before upselling premium templates.

- **Enhance retention & engagement** – Duolingo keeps users hooked with gamification, then monetizes with subscriptions.

- **Create premium brand positioning** – YouTube Premium removes ads and adds exclusive content.

- **Monetize network effects** – Slack's free team collaboration tool leads to enterprise upgrades.

For instance, **Evernote built a loyal user base with free note-taking, then monetized through paid plans with advanced features.**

Key Insights on Freemium Strategy

- **Balancing free vs. premium is crucial** – If the free version is too good, users won't upgrade; if too limited, they won't stay.

- **Conversion rates vary** – Industry benchmarks suggest **2-5% of freemium users convert to paid**, but strong upsell strategies can increase this.

- **Customer experience drives upgrades** – If users love the free product, they are more likely to pay for extras.

- **Retention is key** – Freemium success depends on engaging users long enough to see value in upgrading.

- **Data analysis is a competitive advantage** – Tracking user behaviour helps optimize pricing, features, and upgrade triggers.

When executed effectively, a **Freemium Strategy enables businesses to scale rapidly, acquire loyal users, and drive sustainable revenue**, making it one of the most effective modern digital business models.

29. Cross-Selling & Upselling Strategy

Cross-Selling & Upselling Strategy: A Comprehensive Breakdown

Theory Behind Cross-Selling & Upselling Strategy

A **Cross-Selling & Upselling Strategy** is a business approach used to **maximize revenue per customer by encouraging additional or higher-value purchases**. Instead of focusing solely on acquiring new customers, this strategy increases the lifetime value (LTV) of existing customers by offering complementary or upgraded products.

The two techniques differ in execution:

1. **Cross-Selling** – Encouraging customers to buy related or complementary products (e.g., Amazon suggesting a phone case when buying a smartphone).

2. **Upselling** – Persuading customers to buy a higher-priced or premium version of a product (e.g., Apple recommending a MacBook Pro instead of a MacBook Air).

Cross-selling and upselling are rooted in **consumer psychology**, leveraging principles such as:

- **Convenience & Bundling** – Customers prefer one-stop solutions.

- **Perceived Value** – Higher-tier products often provide better quality or features.

- **Loss Aversion** – Highlighting what customers miss by not upgrading encourages higher spending.

These strategies are widely used in **e-commerce, SaaS, financial services, hospitality, and retail**, where customer relationships drive profitability.

Example of Cross-Selling & Upselling Strategy

A leading example is **Amazon**, which:

- Uses **"Frequently Bought Together" suggestions** to cross-sell complementary products.
- **Recommends upgraded versions** of products based on customer preferences.
- **Offers Amazon Prime**, an upsell that enhances shopping experience with free shipping and exclusive content.

Another example is **McDonald's**, which:

- **Cross-sells by suggesting fries and drinks with burgers** ("Would you like fries with that?").
- **Upsells by offering larger meal sizes or premium menu items** (e.g., "Go Large" option).

Both companies successfully increase **average order value (AOV) and customer retention** by integrating these strategies into the buying journey.

Why Cross-Selling & Upselling Strategy Works

This strategy is effective because it:

- **Boosts Revenue Without Increasing Customer Acquisition Costs (CAC)** – Encouraging existing customers to spend more is more cost-effective than acquiring new ones.

- **Improves Customer Experience** – Providing relevant recommendations enhances convenience and satisfaction.

- **Increases Customer Lifetime Value (CLV)** – Higher spending over time maximizes long-term profits.

- **Enhances Brand Loyalty** – Personalized upselling and cross-selling build deeper customer relationships.

- **Creates Competitive Differentiation** – Businesses offering tailored product suggestions stand out in crowded markets.

For example, **Spotify cross-sells audiobooks and podcasts, while upselling with premium subscription plans** to improve user engagement.

How Cross-Selling & Upselling Strategy Works

Companies implement these strategies by:

1. **Personalizing Product Recommendations** – Using AI and data analytics to suggest relevant cross-sells and upsells.

2. **Bundling Products** – Offering discounts on combined purchases (e.g., laptop + accessories).

3. **Using Limited-Time Offers** – Creating urgency around upgrades or add-ons.

4. **Incorporating Upsells During Checkout** – Prompting customers with higher-tier versions before finalizing purchases.

5. **Enhancing Customer Support Interactions** – Training sales teams to recommend complementary or premium solutions.

For instance, **Apple Store employees guide customers toward higher-spec devices based on needs, making upselling feel natural and beneficial.**

Application of Cross-Selling & Upselling Strategy

Businesses use these strategies to:

- **Increase AOV in E-commerce** – Shopify stores recommend "Customers Also Bought" products.

- **Boost SaaS Revenue** – Netflix upsells higher-tier plans with 4K streaming and more screens.

- **Enhance Hospitality Sales** – Hotels cross-sell spa packages and upsell room upgrades.

- **Maximize Financial Services Profits** – Banks cross-sell credit cards and upsell premium account tiers.

For instance, **Tesla cross-sells software upgrades and autopilot features, while upselling longer-range battery options**.

Key Insights on Cross-Selling & Upselling Strategy

- **Timing is crucial** – Upselling works best during decision-making, while cross-selling fits post-purchase recommendations.

- **Relevance is key** – Irrelevant suggestions annoy customers; data-driven personalization enhances effectiveness.

- **Customer experience should come first** – The goal is to add value, not just increase sales.

- **Too much upselling can backfire** – Excessive prompts may lead to abandoned purchases.

- **Data & AI enhance strategy** – Smart algorithms optimize recommendations based on user behaviour.

When executed correctly, a **Cross-Selling & Upselling Strategy increases revenue, improves customer satisfaction, and strengthens brand loyalty**, making it a vital tool for long-term business success.

30. Localization Strategy

Localization Strategy: A Comprehensive Breakdown

Theory Behind Localization Strategy

A **Localization Strategy** is a business approach where companies adapt their products, services, marketing, and operations to fit the specific needs, preferences, and cultural norms of different geographic markets. Rather than using a **one-size-fits-all** global approach, localization ensures that offerings are **relevant, accessible, and appealing to local consumers**.

Localization goes beyond just **language translation**—it includes:

1. **Cultural Adaptation** – Adjusting messaging, visuals, and branding to align with local customs and values.

2. **Product Customization** – Modifying features, packaging, or design to meet local needs.

3. **Regulatory Compliance** – Ensuring adherence to local laws, taxes, and business regulations.

4. **Localized Pricing & Payment Options** – Adapting costs and payment methods to align with local economic conditions.

5. **Market-Specific Marketing Strategies** – Using regionally relevant advertising channels, influencers, and campaigns.

This strategy is essential for **global businesses, e-commerce, fast food chains, consumer electronics, and media companies**, where cultural differences greatly impact customer preferences.

Example of Localization Strategy

A prime example is **McDonald's**, which localizes its menu based on regional tastes:

- **India** – Offers the McAloo Tikki (potato-based burger) and removed beef products due to cultural sensitivities.
- **Japan** – Introduced the Teriyaki Burger and shrimp-based meals catering to local tastes.
- **Middle East** – Uses Halal-certified ingredients to meet religious dietary laws.

Another example is **Netflix**, which:

- **Creates region-specific content** (e.g., "Money Heist" for Spanish audiences, "Squid Game" for South Korea).
- **Adjusts its interface and subtitles for different languages.**
- **Uses localized marketing campaigns** featuring regionally popular actors and influencers.

Both companies successfully expand into new markets by **respecting local cultures, tastes, and consumer behaviours**.

Why Localization Strategy Works

A **Localization Strategy** is effective because:

- **Enhances Customer Experience** – Users connect better with products that feel tailored to their culture.

- **Increases Market Penetration** – Adapting to local preferences attracts a broader audience.

- **Strengthens Brand Loyalty** – Customers appreciate brands that respect and reflect their identity.

- **Reduces Market Entry Barriers** – Aligning with local regulations and expectations prevents operational challenges.

- **Improves Competitive Advantage** – Companies that localize effectively outperform global competitors using generic strategies.

For instance, **Coca-Cola modifies its marketing messages and Flavors for different regions, ensuring strong customer affinity worldwide.**

How Localization Strategy Works

Businesses implement localization through:

1. **Market Research** – Analyzing local consumer behaviour, trends, and cultural nuances.

2. **Product & Service Adaptation** – Customizing features, ingredients, or pricing models.

3. **Language & Branding Adjustments** – Translating marketing content while maintaining cultural sensitivity.

4. **Strategic Partnerships** – Collaborating with local influencers, distributors, and agencies.

5. **Compliance & Logistics Alignment** – Adapting operations to local regulations, supply chains, and payment systems.

For example, **Apple's iPhones in China integrate WeChat Pay and use localized software features tailored to Chinese users.**

Application of Localization Strategy

Businesses use localization to:

- **Expand into international markets** – Airbnb localized its website, currency, and customer support for different countries.

- **Improve customer engagement** – Starbucks adjusts store designs and menu items to reflect local cultures.

- **Comply with government regulations** – Google modifies its search algorithms to meet country-specific laws.

- **Enhance brand perception** – IKEA adapts store layouts based on regional shopping behaviours.

For instance, **KFC succeeded in China by introducing rice-based meals and tea drinks, aligning with local dining habits.**

Key Insights on Localization Strategy

- **One strategy does not fit all markets** – Customization is key to global success.

- **Cultural sensitivity is crucial** – Brands that ignore local norms risk backlash or rejection.

- **Market research is non-negotiable** – Understanding local consumer behaviour is the foundation of effective localization.

- **Regulatory compliance matters** – Ignoring local laws can lead to bans or restrictions.

- **Localization requires ongoing adaptation** – Consumer preferences evolve, so strategies must be continuously refined.

When executed effectively, a **Localization Strategy enables businesses to build trust, expand globally, and increase long-term profitability by delivering market-specific experiences that resonate with diverse audiences.**

Marketing & Branding Strategies

31. Content Marketing Strategy

Content Marketing Strategy: A Comprehensive Breakdown

Theory Behind Content Marketing Strategy

A **Content Marketing Strategy** is a business approach focused on creating, distributing, and optimizing valuable, relevant, and engaging content to attract, retain, and convert customers. Unlike traditional advertising, which directly promotes products, content marketing aims to **educate, inform, or entertain audiences**, building long-term relationships and brand trust.

The theory behind content marketing is based on:

1. **Inbound Marketing** – Attracting customers naturally through helpful content rather than pushing ads.

2. **Brand Authority & Thought Leadership** – Establishing credibility by providing expertise and insights.

3. **SEO & Organic Reach** – Driving website traffic through search engine optimization (SEO).

4. **Engagement & Community Building** – Encouraging audience interaction and brand loyalty.

5. **Lead Generation & Conversion** – Using content to nurture prospects through the sales funnel.

This strategy is widely used in **B2B, e-commerce, SaaS, media, and personal branding**, where long-term trust and engagement drive purchasing decisions.

Example of Content Marketing Strategy

A strong example is **HubSpot**, which:

- **Publishes educational blogs, e-books, and webinars** on marketing, sales, and CRM topics.
- **Offers free tools and templates** to attract and nurture potential customers.
- **Uses SEO-driven content** to rank highly on Google, bringing in organic traffic.

Another example is **Red Bull**, which:

- **Creates high-energy video content and extreme sports documentaries** rather than traditional beverage ads.
- **Hosts Red Bull-sponsored events** that align with its brand identity.
- **Engages audiences through social media storytelling**.

Both companies successfully use content marketing to **build brand affinity and maintain strong customer engagement.**

Why Content Marketing Strategy Works

A **Content Marketing Strategy** is effective because:

- **Builds Long-Term Trust** – Valuable content fosters credibility and brand loyalty.

- **Reduces Customer Acquisition Costs (CAC)** – Organic traffic and inbound leads lower reliance on paid advertising.

- **Increases Brand Awareness** – High-quality content gets shared, extending reach.

- **Boosts SEO & Organic Growth** – Search-optimized content drives consistent, sustainable website traffic.

- **Encourages Customer Engagement** – Interactive and informative content keeps audiences involved.

For example, **Nike's storytelling-driven marketing connects with consumers emotionally, reinforcing brand loyalty.**

How Content Marketing Strategy Works

Businesses implement content marketing by:

1. **Identifying Audience Needs** – Conducting research to understand customer pain points and interests.

2. **Creating High-Value Content** – Producing blogs, videos, infographics, podcasts, and case studies.

3. **Optimizing for SEO & Social Sharing** – Using keywords, backlinks, and social media promotion.

4. **Building a Distribution Plan** – Leveraging email marketing, social media, and partnerships to maximize reach.

5. **Tracking & Refining Performance** – Analyzing engagement metrics and optimizing content accordingly.

For instance, **LinkedIn's content marketing strategy involves publishing thought leadership articles and professional insights to engage business audiences.**

Application of Content Marketing Strategy

Businesses use content marketing to:

- **Educate & nurture leads** – Salesforce provides in-depth industry reports and whitepapers.

- **Drive traffic & SEO rankings** – Moz creates SEO guides that attract marketers.

- **Enhance social media engagement** – GoPro shares user-generated action videos.

- **Support product launches** – Apple creates sleek product videos and blog content to build anticipation.

For instance, **Coca-Cola's "Share a Coke" campaign personalized its product, leading to massive user-generated content and engagement.**

Key Insights on Content Marketing Strategy

- **Quality over quantity** – A few well-crafted pieces outperform mass-produced, low-value content.

- **Consistency is key** – Regular publishing maintains audience engagement.

- **SEO is a long-term investment** – Ranking high on search engines takes time but drives sustained traffic.

- **Storytelling increases impact** – Emotional connections drive deeper audience engagement.

- **Content should align with business goals** – Every piece should serve a strategic purpose (awareness, conversion, loyalty).

When executed effectively, a **Content Marketing Strategy builds brand authority, attracts customers organically, and drives sustainable business growth**, making it a critical tool for modern marketing success.

32. Influencer Marketing Strategy

Influencer Marketing Strategy: A Comprehensive Breakdown

Theory Behind Influencer Marketing Strategy

An **Influencer Marketing Strategy** is a business approach where brands collaborate with individuals who have a dedicated audience to **promote products, increase brand awareness, and drive engagement.** Instead of relying on traditional advertising, companies use influencers' credibility, trust, and authority to connect with consumers authentically.

The theory behind influencer marketing is based on:

1. **Social Proof & Trust** – Consumers trust recommendations from people they admire.
2. **Word-of-Mouth Effect** – Influencers amplify brand messages through their established communities.
3. **Targeted Audience Reach** – Brands can connect with niche markets effectively.
4. **Engagement & Authenticity** – Influencer-driven content feels more genuine than direct brand promotions.
5. **Virality & Shareability** – Influencers create content that spreads organically.

This strategy is widely used in **fashion, beauty, technology, fitness, food, and lifestyle industries**, where personal recommendations strongly influence purchasing decisions.

Example of Influencer Marketing Strategy

A leading example is **Daniel Wellington**, a watch brand that:

- **Partnered with micro-influencers on Instagram**, offering free watches in exchange for promotion.
- **Used unique discount codes**, allowing influencers to drive direct sales.
- **Created a viral brand presence**, growing from a startup to a globally recognized watch brand.

Another example is **Gymshark**, which:

- **Collaborated with fitness influencers and athletes** to promote its activewear.
- **Encouraged user-generated content**, making customers part of its community.
- **Leveraged social media challenges** to boost engagement.

Both brands successfully built **global recognition and strong brand loyalty** by using influencer-driven marketing.

Why Influencer Marketing Strategy Works

An **Influencer Marketing Strategy** is effective because:

- **Builds Trust & Authenticity** – Consumers believe recommendations from influencers more than traditional ads.

- **Increases Engagement & Reach** – Influencers drive likes, shares, and comments, amplifying brand exposure.
- **Boosts Conversion Rates** – Personalized recommendations lead to higher purchase intent.
- **Targets Niche Audiences Effectively** – Brands can partner with influencers who align with specific demographics.
- **Maximizes ROI Compared to Traditional Ads** – Influencer marketing often yields higher engagement at lower costs.

For example, **Tesla leverages tech influencers and YouTubers instead of traditional advertising, generating organic buzz around its products.**

How Influencer Marketing Strategy Works

Companies implement influencer marketing by:

1. **Identifying the Right Influencers** – Selecting those whose audience aligns with the brand's target market.
2. **Defining Campaign Goals** – Establishing whether the focus is on brand awareness, engagement, or conversions.
3. **Creating Authentic Collaborations** – Encouraging influencers to share personal experiences with the brand.
4. **Tracking Performance Metrics** – Measuring reach, engagement, and sales impact.

5. **Scaling Successful Campaigns** – Expanding partnerships with high-performing influencers.

For example, **Nike works with athletes and fitness influencers to promote its products in a way that resonates with sports enthusiasts.**

Application of Influencer Marketing Strategy

Businesses use influencer marketing to:

- **Launch new products** – Apple gives early access to tech influencers for product reviews.
- **Drive sales through discount codes** – Fashion Nova provides influencers with custom discount links.
- **Increase social media presence** – Starbucks partners with lifestyle influencers to showcase new drinks.
- **Strengthen community engagement** – L'Oréal collaborates with beauty bloggers for tutorial content.

For instance, **Coca-Cola's #ShareACoke campaign leveraged influencers to encourage user-generated content and global participation.**

Key Insights on Influencer Marketing Strategy

- **Micro-influencers (10K–100K followers) often have higher engagement rates than celebrities.**

- **Authenticity is crucial** – Forced or overly promotional content can alienate audiences.

- **Long-term partnerships work better than one-off promotions** – Consistency strengthens brand association.

- **Influencer selection matters** – The right influencer must align with brand values and audience demographics.

- **Regulations must be followed** – Sponsored posts must disclose partnerships (e.g., #ad, #sponsored).

When executed effectively, an **Influencer Marketing Strategy helps businesses build credibility, expand reach, and drive customer engagement**, making it a powerful tool for modern digital marketing.

33. SEO Strategy

SEO Strategy: A Comprehensive Breakdown

Theory Behind SEO Strategy

A **Search Engine Optimization (SEO) Strategy** is a business approach designed to increase a website's visibility on search engines like Google, Bing, and Yahoo. The goal is to **optimize content, structure, and performance** so that search engines rank the website higher for relevant queries, resulting in more organic (non-paid) traffic.

SEO is based on **Google's search algorithms** and revolves around three core pillars:

1. **On-Page SEO** – Optimizing content, keywords, headings, metadata, and internal links.

2. **Off-Page SEO** – Building backlinks, social signals, and external authority.

3. **Technical SEO** – Improving site speed, mobile-friendliness, and structured data.

The strategy aligns with **Google's E-E-A-T principles (Experience, Expertise, Authoritativeness, Trustworthiness)**, which determine content credibility and ranking potential.

SEO is essential for **content marketing, e-commerce, SaaS, local businesses, and digital publishing**, where high search rankings directly impact traffic and sales.

Example of SEO Strategy

A leading example is **HubSpot**, which:

- **Publishes in-depth, keyword-rich blog content** targeting industry-specific queries.
- **Uses internal linking and pillar pages** to enhance website structure.
- **Earns backlinks from authoritative sites**, boosting domain authority.

Another example is **Amazon**, which dominates search rankings by:

- **Optimizing product pages with relevant keywords and descriptions.**
- **Using customer reviews to add fresh, user-generated content.**
- **Leveraging AI-driven recommendations to enhance engagement.**

Both companies achieve **high organic visibility and increased customer acquisition** through strategic SEO efforts.

Why SEO Strategy Works

A **SEO Strategy** is effective because:

- **Increases Organic Traffic** – Ranking higher on Google leads to continuous, free website visitors.

- **Builds Long-Term Credibility** – Appearing at the top of search results increases brand authority.

- **Improves User Experience** – Faster load times, mobile optimization, and structured content enhance engagement.

- **Boosts Conversion Rates** – Visitors from search engines often have strong purchase intent.

- **Reduces Marketing Costs** – Unlike paid ads, organic traffic does not require ongoing investment.

For example, **The New York Times uses SEO-driven content strategies to dominate news-related search queries, maintaining a steady influx of organic visitors**.

How SEO Strategy Works

Companies implement SEO by:

1. **Conducting Keyword Research** – Identifying high-traffic, low-competition search terms.

2. **Optimizing Content & Metadata** – Writing structured, keyword-rich articles with compelling titles and meta descriptions.

3. **Building Quality Backlinks** – Gaining references from authoritative sites to boost domain authority.

4. **Improving Site Performance** – Enhancing speed, mobile compatibility, and user experience.

5. **Analyzing & Adapting** – Using tools like Google Analytics and Search Console to refine SEO efforts.

For example, **Moz builds a content-rich blog and offers free SEO tools, attracting millions of organic visitors and reinforcing its industry leadership.**

Application of SEO Strategy

Businesses use SEO to:

- **Drive sales in e-commerce** – Shopify stores optimize product listings to rank higher in search results.

- **Increase local visibility** – Restaurants and retailers use local SEO (Google My Business, local keywords).

- **Enhance blog traffic** – Travel blogs like Lonely Planet use SEO to attract adventure seekers.

- **Strengthen SaaS growth** – Companies like SEMrush dominate search results for digital marketing tools.

For instance, **Tesla optimizes its website for electric vehicle-related keywords, ensuring it ranks highly in relevant searches**.

Key Insights on SEO Strategy

- **SEO is a long-term investment** – Results take time but offer lasting benefits.

- **Content quality matters more than keyword stuffing** – Google prioritizes value-driven content.

- **Mobile & voice search are growing** – Optimizing for mobile and conversational queries is crucial.

- **Backlinks are still essential** – High-quality inbound links improve domain authority.

- **SEO is always evolving** – Google's algorithm updates require ongoing strategy adjustments.

When executed effectively, an **SEO Strategy drives sustainable growth, increases online visibility, and enhances brand credibility**, making it a fundamental pillar of modern digital marketing.

34. Viral Marketing Strategy

Viral Marketing Strategy: A Comprehensive Breakdown

Theory Behind Viral Marketing Strategy

A **Viral Marketing Strategy** is a business approach that leverages **word-of-mouth, social sharing, and organic engagement** to rapidly spread a brand message, product, or campaign. The goal is to create content so compelling that people **share it voluntarily**, amplifying its reach without requiring significant advertising spend.

The theory behind viral marketing is rooted in **psychology, social behaviour, and digital media dynamics**, focusing on:

1. **Emotional Triggers** – Content that evokes strong emotions (joy, surprise, nostalgia, awe) is more likely to be shared.

2. **Social Currency** – People share content that enhances their status, identity, or credibility.

3. **Ease of Sharing** – Content must be simple to distribute (click-to-share, hashtags, challenges).

4. **Memorable & Unique Messaging** – Viral campaigns are often distinct, controversial, or entertaining.

5. **Network Effects** – The more people share, the faster the reach multiplies.

This strategy is widely used in **social media, digital marketing, consumer goods, and entertainment industries**, where engagement and mass visibility drive business success.

Example of Viral Marketing Strategy

A classic example is **Old Spice's "The Man Your Man Could Smell Like" campaign**, which:

- Used humour and a charismatic character to engage audiences.
- Encouraged sharing with its quirky, unpredictable style.
- Generated millions of views and significantly boosted sales.

Another example is **Ice Bucket Challenge (ALS Awareness)**, which:

- Leveraged social participation, encouraging influencers and celebrities to take part.
- Created a viral loop where nominees challenged others to participate.
- Raised over $115 million for ALS research due to its widespread visibility.

Both examples demonstrate how **viral campaigns create massive brand exposure with minimal advertising investment.**

Why Viral Marketing Strategy Works

A **Viral Marketing Strategy** is effective because:

- **Expands Reach Rapidly** – A single viral campaign can attract millions of viewers.
- **Reduces Advertising Costs** – Organic shares lower the need for paid promotions.
- **Boosts Brand Awareness** – Viral content spreads brand recognition instantly.
- **Engages Audiences** – Interactive and entertaining content keeps users engaged.
- **Creates Long-Lasting Impact** – A successful viral campaign can leave a cultural or industry imprint.

For example, **Dove's "Real Beauty Sketches" campaign went viral by addressing self-perception and emotional storytelling, increasing brand loyalty and engagement.**

How Viral Marketing Strategy Works

Businesses implement viral marketing by:

1. **Creating Highly Engaging Content** – Crafting videos, memes, challenges, or campaigns that resonate emotionally.
2. **Leveraging Influencers & Trendsetters** – Partnering with social media figures to amplify reach.

3. **Encouraging Participation & Sharing** – Using hashtags, challenges, and user-generated content.

4. **Optimizing for Social Media Algorithms** – Ensuring content is mobile-friendly and platform-optimized.

5. **Tracking Performance & Engagement** – Using analytics to measure shares, views, and conversion rates.

For example, **TikTok challenges like the #InMyFeelings dance challenge went viral because they encouraged user participation and easy sharing.**

Application of Viral Marketing Strategy

Businesses use viral marketing to:

- **Launch new products** – Apple uses teaser campaigns that spark social media conversations.

- **Increase social media presence** – Wendy's Twitter engagement strategy turned witty comebacks into viral interactions.

- **Encourage user-generated content** – Starbucks' #RedCupContest allows customers to showcase their coffee art.

- **Raise awareness for social causes** – Nike's Colin Kaepernick ad sparked discussions and massive brand engagement.

For instance, **Netflix uses viral memes and interactive social content to promote its shows, creating anticipation and audience buzz.**

Key Insights on Viral Marketing Strategy

- **Viral success is unpredictable** – Even great content doesn't always go viral; testing is essential.

- **Timing and trends matter** – Aligning with cultural moments increases virality potential.

- **Authenticity is key** – Overly promotional content rarely goes viral; relatability wins.

- **Simplicity drives shares** – Content should be easy to consume and spread.

- **Emotion fuels engagement** – Campaigns that evoke strong emotions (joy, inspiration, nostalgia) perform best.

When executed effectively, a **Viral Marketing Strategy generates massive brand exposure, customer engagement, and long-term business growth**, making it one of the most cost-effective marketing tactics.

35. Brand Differentiation Strategy

Brand Differentiation Strategy: A Comprehensive Breakdown

Theory Behind Brand Differentiation Strategy

A **Brand Differentiation Strategy** is a business approach where companies create a unique identity, value proposition, or customer experience to stand out from competitors. Instead of competing solely on price, differentiated brands **emphasize unique features, superior quality, emotional connections, or niche positioning** to attract and retain customers.

Brand differentiation is based on **perception and positioning**—the way consumers see and relate to a brand. The key elements of differentiation include:

1. **Product Quality & Innovation** – Offering superior features or unique technology.

2. **Brand Storytelling & Values** – Creating emotional connections with consumers.

3. **Customer Experience & Service** – Providing exceptional customer engagement and loyalty programs.

4. **Aesthetic & Design** – Unique branding, packaging, and user experience.

5. **Market Positioning** – Catering to a niche or underserved market segment.

This strategy is common in **luxury, fashion, technology, automotive, and consumer goods**, where customer perception influences purchasing decisions.

Example of Brand Differentiation Strategy

A prime example is **Apple**, which differentiates itself through:

- **Premium product design** – Sleek aesthetics and high-quality materials.
- **Ecosystem integration** – Seamless connectivity across iPhones, iPads, Macs, and services.
- **Strong brand storytelling** – Marketing that emphasizes creativity, privacy, and exclusivity.
- **Superior customer experience** – Personalized in-store service and AppleCare support.

Another example is **Tesla**, which:

- **Positions itself as a premium electric vehicle brand** with high-performance models.
- **Leverages sustainable innovation** as a core brand differentiator.
- **Uses direct-to-consumer sales**, eliminating dealerships for a unique buying experience.

Both brands dominate their industries by offering **distinctive value beyond product features alone**.

Why Brand Differentiation Strategy Works

A **Brand Differentiation Strategy** is effective because:

- **Reduces Price Sensitivity** – Customers are willing to pay a premium for unique value.

- **Creates Customer Loyalty** – Emotional connections lead to repeat business and advocacy.

- **Strengthens Market Positioning** – Standing out makes competition less direct.

- **Enhances Perceived Value** – Consumers see differentiated brands as higher quality or status-driven.

- **Encourages Word-of-Mouth Marketing** – Unique experiences and storytelling drive organic brand promotion.

For example, **Nike's brand differentiation through innovation (self-lacing shoes, performance tech) and emotional marketing (Just Do It campaign) keeps it ahead of competitors.**

How Brand Differentiation Strategy Works

Companies implement differentiation by:

1. **Defining Unique Brand Values** – Establishing what makes the brand distinct.

2. **Creating a Consistent Brand Identity** – Using a recognizable logo, voice, and aesthetic.

3. **Focusing on Customer Experience** – Enhancing service, support, and engagement.

4. **Developing Exclusive Features** – Adding functionalities competitors don't offer.

5. **Telling a Compelling Brand Story** – Connecting with consumers emotionally through advertising and content.

For example, **Patagonia differentiates itself with sustainability, ethical production, and a strong environmental mission.**

Application of Brand Differentiation Strategy

Businesses use brand differentiation to:

- **Compete in saturated markets** – Lush Cosmetics stands out with handmade, cruelty-free products.

- **Build long-term customer relationships** – Starbucks creates a premium café experience with customization and ambiance.

- **Drive product desirability** – Rolex maintains exclusivity through craftsmanship and heritage.

- **Enhance digital presence** – Netflix differentiates through exclusive original content and AI-driven recommendations.

For instance, **Coca-Cola differentiates itself not just through taste but through emotional branding ("Happiness in a Bottle") and global campaigns.**

Key Insights on Brand Differentiation Strategy

- **Authenticity matters** – Consumers see through forced differentiation; brands must be genuine.

- **Emotional connection is powerful** – People buy into **stories, values, and experiences** more than just products.

- **Differentiation must be sustainable** – Unique selling points should be hard for competitors to copy.

- **Consistency builds trust** – Branding must remain recognizable across all touchpoints.

- **Innovation fuels differentiation** – Staying ahead requires continuous product and service improvements.

When executed effectively, a **Brand Differentiation Strategy creates long-term competitive advantage, fosters customer loyalty, and drives premium brand positioning**, making it essential for businesses seeking sustained market success.

36. Loyalty Program Strategy

Loyalty Program Strategy: A Comprehensive Breakdown

Theory Behind Loyalty Program Strategy

A **Loyalty Program Strategy** is a business approach designed to **increase customer retention, engagement, and lifetime value** by offering rewards for repeat purchases or interactions. Instead of focusing only on acquiring new customers, loyalty programs encourage existing customers to stay engaged, increasing their spending and reducing churn.

The strategy is based on **behavioural economics and psychology**, emphasizing:

1. **Reciprocity** – Customers feel obligated to return loyalty when rewarded.
2. **Loss Aversion** – Users fear losing accumulated points or benefits.
3. **Gamification** – Points, levels, and milestones create motivation to engage.
4. **Personalization** – Tailored rewards and experiences enhance customer satisfaction.
5. **Social Proof & Exclusivity** – VIP tiers and referral bonuses encourage participation.

Loyalty programs are widely used in **retail, hospitality, travel, e-commerce, and SaaS**, where repeat business is essential for profitability.

Example of Loyalty Program Strategy

A prime example is **Starbucks Rewards**, which:

- **Offers stars (points) for every purchase**, redeemable for free drinks and food.
- **Provides personalized offers** based on purchase history.
- **Uses tier-based incentives**, where frequent buyers get premium benefits.

Another example is **Amazon Prime**, which:

- **Encourages loyalty through free shipping, exclusive deals, and Prime Video access**.
- **Increases spending frequency** by making shopping more convenient.
- **Creates a subscription model** where customers feel invested in using Amazon services.

Both programs **successfully increase retention, average order value (AOV), and customer satisfaction**.

Why Loyalty Program Strategy Works

A **Loyalty Program Strategy** is effective because:

- **Encourages Repeat Purchases** – Customers prefer brands where they accumulate benefits.

- **Reduces Customer Churn** – Exclusive perks make switching to competitors less appealing.
- **Boosts Revenue & AOV** – Rewards incentivize customers to spend more.
- **Enhances Customer Engagement** – Gamification elements keep users actively involved.
- **Provides Valuable Customer Data** – Helps personalize marketing and offers.

For example, **Nike's "NikePlus" rewards members with early product access, exclusive content, and training programs, fostering strong brand loyalty.**

How Loyalty Program Strategy Works

Companies implement loyalty programs by:

1. **Defining Program Goals** – Increasing retention, boosting spending, or improving engagement.
2. **Selecting the Right Model** – Points-based, tiered, paid membership, or cashback programs.
3. **Personalizing Rewards** – Offering relevant incentives based on customer behaviour.
4. **Gamifying the Experience** – Encouraging participation through milestones, challenges, or social sharing.
5. **Tracking & Optimizing Performance** – Analyzing data to refine program effectiveness.

For example, **Delta Airlines' SkyMiles program rewards frequent travellers with free flights and elite status upgrades, encouraging long-term brand loyalty.**

Application of Loyalty Program Strategy

Businesses use loyalty programs to:

- **Drive long-term customer retention** – Sephora's "Beauty Insider" gives members exclusive perks.

- **Increase brand advocacy & referrals** – Tesla rewards customers who refer new buyers.

- **Enhance digital engagement** – McDonald's "MyMcDonald's Rewards" integrates app-based incentives.

- **Encourage higher spending** – Hotels like Marriott Bonvoy offer free stays to loyal guests.

For instance, **Apple's ecosystem loyalty isn't points-based but is built on seamless product integration, ensuring customers stay within the Apple brand.**

Key Insights on Loyalty Program Strategy

- **Simplicity increases participation** – Complicated programs deter users.

- **Personalization enhances effectiveness** – Tailored offers boost engagement.

- **Loyalty is more than discounts** – Emotional and experiential rewards work best.

- **Retention is more cost-effective than acquisition** – Keeping a customer is cheaper than acquiring a new one.

- **Ongoing optimization is key** – Regularly refining benefits keeps users engaged.

When executed effectively, a **Loyalty Program Strategy strengthens customer relationships, increases lifetime value, and drives sustainable revenue growth**, making it an essential tool for modern businesses.

37. Personalization Strategy

Personalization Strategy: A Comprehensive Breakdown

Theory Behind Personalization Strategy

A **Personalization Strategy** is a business approach where companies tailor products, services, and marketing efforts to individual customer preferences, behaviours, and needs. Instead of using a one-size-fits-all approach, personalization **leverages data and AI-driven insights** to enhance customer experiences, improve engagement, and drive conversions.

This strategy is rooted in **behavioural psychology, AI-driven decision-making, and customer experience (CX) optimization**, with key principles including:

1. **Customer-Centric Approach** – Delivering relevant, customized experiences that add value.

2. **Data-Driven Insights** – Using analytics, browsing history, and past behaviour to personalize content.

3. **Predictive Personalization** – Leveraging AI to anticipate customer needs before they express them.

4. **Omnichannel Integration** – Ensuring personalized experiences across multiple touchpoints (web, mobile, email, in-store).

5. **Adaptive Learning** – Continuously refining recommendations based on user interactions.

Personalization is widely used in **e-commerce, technology, media, healthcare, and finance**, where customized experiences drive customer satisfaction and loyalty.

Example of Personalization Strategy

A prime example is **Netflix**, which:

- **Uses AI algorithms to recommend shows and movies based on viewing history.**
- **Personalizes content thumbnails and descriptions** to increase engagement.
- **Sends tailored notifications and email recommendations** to keep users engaged.

Another example is **Amazon**, which:

- **Suggests products based on past purchases and browsing behaviour.**
- **Uses dynamic pricing and personalized deals to enhance conversion rates.**
- **Customizes homepage content and ads for each customer.**

Both companies successfully **increase user engagement, retention, and sales through hyper-personalized experiences.**

Why Personalization Strategy Works

A **Personalization Strategy** is effective because:

- **Enhances Customer Experience** – Users feel valued when experiences are tailored to them.

- **Increases Engagement & Retention** – Personalized interactions encourage customers to return.

- **Boosts Conversions & Revenue** – Relevant recommendations drive higher purchase rates.

- **Reduces Decision Fatigue** – AI-driven suggestions simplify choices for customers.

- **Builds Long-Term Loyalty** – Stronger emotional connections lead to brand advocacy.

For example, **Spotify's personalized playlists (Discover Weekly, Release Radar) keep users engaged and prevent churn**.

How Personalization Strategy Works

Companies implement personalization by:

1. **Collecting & Analyzing Customer Data** – Using cookies, purchase history, and AI to understand preferences.

2. **Segmenting Audiences** – Grouping users based on behaviour, interests, and demographics.

3. **Tailoring Content & Recommendations** – Delivering personalized messaging, promotions, and product suggestions.

4. **Implementing AI & Machine Learning** – Automating and refining personalization efforts based on real-time interactions.

5. **Ensuring Privacy & Data Security** – Balancing personalization with ethical data usage and compliance (e.g., GDPR, CCPA).

For instance, **Nike uses personalization in its NikePlus app, offering customized workouts, product recommendations, and exclusive member deals**.

Application of Personalization Strategy

Businesses use personalization to:

- **Enhance e-commerce experiences** – Shopify stores provide dynamic product recommendations.
- **Improve email marketing** – Airbnb sends personalized travel suggestions based on past searches.
- **Drive customer engagement in media** – YouTube's AI-powered homepage adapts to user preferences.
- **Personalize financial services** – Banks tailor loan offers and investment advice based on spending habits.

For instance, **Coca-Cola's "Share a Coke" campaign personalized bottles with customer names, boosting engagement and sales.**

Key Insights on Personalization Strategy

- **Relevance is key** – Over-personalization can feel invasive; balance is needed.

- **Real-time personalization drives engagement** – AI-powered recommendations create instant value.

- **Data privacy must be prioritized** – Transparency builds trust in personalized experiences.

- **Omnichannel consistency is crucial** – Personalization should be seamless across web, mobile, and physical stores.

- **AI and automation improve efficiency** – Scalable personalization increases business impact.

When executed effectively, a **Personalization Strategy enhances customer relationships, increases conversions, and builds long-term brand loyalty**, making it a crucial tool in modern business growth.

38. Nostalgia Marketing Strategy

Nostalgia Marketing Strategy: A Comprehensive Breakdown

Theory Behind Nostalgia Marketing Strategy

A **Nostalgia Marketing Strategy** is a business approach where brands tap into consumers' emotions by evoking memories from the past. Instead of focusing solely on innovation or trends, this strategy **leverages nostalgia to create deep emotional connections, enhance brand loyalty, and drive engagement.**

Nostalgia marketing is rooted in **consumer psychology and emotional branding**, with key principles including:

1. **Emotional Resonance** – Triggering fond memories to create positive brand associations.
2. **Cultural & Generational Connection** – Targeting specific age groups by referencing their childhood or youth.
3. **Revivals & Reboots** – Bringing back discontinued products, retro designs, or classic brand elements.
4. **Storytelling & Brand Heritage** – Reinforcing trust by celebrating a brand's history and legacy.
5. **Social & Viral Appeal** – Encouraging organic sharing by invoking shared cultural moments.

This strategy is particularly effective in **consumer goods, fashion, entertainment, food & beverage, and tech**, where emotional attachment influences purchasing behaviour.

Example of Nostalgia Marketing Strategy

A classic example is **Nintendo's relaunch of the NES Classic Edition**, which:

- **Revived a beloved gaming console from the 1980s** with modern features.
- **Targeted Millennials and Gen X, who grew up playing NES games.**
- **Sold out quickly due to strong nostalgia-driven demand.**

Another example is **Coca-Cola's "New Coke" revival**, where:

- The brand **temporarily reintroduced its failed 1985 formula** as a limited-edition product.
- The campaign **capitalized on the popularity of the Netflix series "Stranger Things"**, set in the 1980s.
- The move **generated massive social media engagement and press coverage**.

Both examples show how **brands use nostalgia to reignite customer interest and drive sales**.

Why Nostalgia Marketing Strategy Works

A **Nostalgia Marketing Strategy** is effective because:

- **Creates Strong Emotional Bonds** – Consumers feel comforted by familiar memories.

- **Enhances Brand Trust & Loyalty** – Nostalgic branding reinforces long-standing customer relationships.

- **Differentiates from Competitors** – Retro themes stand out in a digital-heavy market.

- **Encourages Social Sharing & Engagement** – People love to reminisce and discuss nostalgic moments online.

- **Drives Impulse Purchases** – Limited-time nostalgic releases trigger urgency and excitement.

For example, **McDonald's frequently brings back the McRib and old-school Happy Meal toys, creating excitement among loyal customers.**

How Nostalgia Marketing Strategy Works

Companies implement nostalgia marketing by:

1. **Identifying Cultural & Generational Trends** – Researching which past trends resonate with their target audience.

2. **Reintroducing Classic Products or Branding** – Bringing back vintage logos, packaging, or old product versions.

3. **Collaborating with Pop Culture & Media** – Aligning campaigns with retro-themed shows, movies, or music.

4. **Using Storytelling & Visual Elements** – Leveraging familiar colours, fonts, and jingles that evoke nostalgia.

5. **Encouraging Community Engagement** – Inviting customers to share memories and experiences.

For example, **Pepsi reintroduced its retro logo and design, aligning it with 1990s pop culture references** to appeal to Millennials.

Application of Nostalgia Marketing Strategy

Businesses use nostalgia marketing to:

- **Boost seasonal sales** – Starbucks' holiday cups and Flavors trigger nostalgic holiday memories.
- **Revive legacy products** – Adidas re-releases classic sneaker designs to attract long-time fans.
- **Leverage pop culture trends** – Burger King revived its 90s logo to appeal to Gen Z and Millennials.
- **Reinforce brand heritage** – Levi's markets its jeans as timeless, celebrating decades of style.

For instance, **Netflix capitalized on 80s and 90s nostalgia with "Stranger Things," incorporating music, fashion, and pop culture references.**

Key Insights on Nostalgia Marketing Strategy

- **Authenticity is crucial** – Forced nostalgia can feel gimmicky; brands must stay true to their legacy.
- **Timing matters** – Aligning nostalgia with anniversaries or cultural moments increases impact.

- **Multigenerational appeal enhances success** – While Millennials love 90s throwbacks, Gen Z resonates with early 2000s nostalgia.

- **Limited editions drive urgency** – Time-sensitive nostalgic campaigns create high demand.

- **Social media amplifies nostalgia** – Encouraging user-generated content strengthens community engagement.

When executed effectively, a **Nostalgia Marketing Strategy rekindles emotional connections, strengthens brand loyalty, and creates highly shareable content**, making it a powerful tool for long-term brand success.

39. Storytelling Strategy

Storytelling Strategy: A Comprehensive Breakdown

Theory Behind Storytelling Strategy

A **Storytelling Strategy** is a business approach where brands use compelling narratives to connect with their audience emotionally, build trust, and differentiate themselves in the market. Instead of focusing solely on product features, companies leverage **engaging, relatable, and memorable stories** to create deeper customer relationships.

Storytelling is based on **psychology, brand positioning, and consumer behaviour**, with key elements including:

1. **Emotional Connection** – Stories evoke feelings, making brands more relatable and memorable.

2. **Hero's Journey Framework** – Using a protagonist (customer, brand, or product) who overcomes challenges.

3. **Authenticity & Transparency** – Sharing real experiences builds trust and credibility.

4. **Brand Identity & Purpose** – Defining why the brand exists beyond selling products.

5. **Consistent Narrative Across Channels** – Ensuring storytelling aligns across social media, ads, and customer interactions.

This strategy is commonly used in **luxury, technology, hospitality, sports, and personal branding**, where differentiation and emotional engagement drive customer loyalty.

Example of Storytelling Strategy

A prime example is **Nike's "Just Do It" campaign**, which:

- **Focuses on personal triumph and perseverance** rather than just selling shoes.
- **Features real athletes overcoming challenges**, making the brand inspiring and relatable.
- **Uses cinematic ads and social media content** to reinforce its message.

Another example is **Airbnb**, which:

- **Tells host and traveller stories** to highlight unique, human-centred experiences.
- **Uses customer testimonials and UGC (user-generated content)** to make its service feel personal.
- **Builds trust by showcasing real people's experiences**, making travellers feel at home anywhere in the world.

Both brands successfully **create emotional connections that go beyond transactions, fostering strong customer loyalty.**

Why Storytelling Strategy Works

A **Storytelling Strategy** is effective because:

- **Enhances Emotional Engagement** – People remember stories more than facts or features.

- **Differentiates the Brand** – Unique narratives create distinct brand identities.

- **Builds Brand Loyalty & Trust** – Authentic storytelling fosters deeper customer relationships.

- **Encourages Word-of-Mouth & Sharing** – Engaging stories are more likely to be shared organically.

- **Increases Conversion Rates** – Compelling narratives help customers visualize product benefits.

For example, **Apple's marketing doesn't just highlight product specs—it tells stories about how its devices empower creativity and human connection.**

How Storytelling Strategy Works

Companies implement storytelling by:

1. **Identifying a Core Brand Narrative** – Defining the brand's purpose, mission, and values.

2. **Creating Relatable Protagonists** – Showcasing customers, employees, or brand ambassadors.

3. **Structuring Stories with Conflict & Resolution** – Demonstrating transformation and success.

4. **Using Multiple Content Formats** – Leveraging video, blog posts, podcasts, and social media.

5. **Maintaining Consistency Across Touchpoints** – Ensuring a unified message across marketing channels.

For example, **Coca-Cola's holiday ads use storytelling to evoke nostalgia, warmth, and togetherness, reinforcing its brand identity as a symbol of happiness.**

Application of Storytelling Strategy

Businesses use storytelling to:

- **Launch & position brands** – Tesla's story of innovation and sustainability differentiates it from traditional car manufacturers.

- **Strengthen emotional branding** – Dove's "Real Beauty" campaign tells empowering stories about self-acceptance.

- **Enhance social media engagement** – Red Bull's adventure storytelling aligns with extreme sports culture.

- **Build personal brands** – Elon Musk and Richard Branson use storytelling to shape their business legacies.

For instance, **LEGO transformed from a toy company into a storytelling brand by creating movies, comics, and branded content that inspire creativity.**

Key Insights on Storytelling Strategy

- **Authenticity is non-negotiable** – Forced or exaggerated storytelling can harm credibility.

- **Visual storytelling amplifies impact** – Videos, images, and animations enhance engagement.

- **Customer-centric stories resonate more** – Making the customer the hero of the story strengthens emotional appeal.

- **Consistency matters** – The narrative should align with brand values across all channels.

- **Great stories inspire action** – Effective storytelling doesn't just entertain; it motivates audiences to engage with the brand.

When executed effectively, a **Storytelling Strategy transforms brands from mere sellers into meaningful, relatable entities, fostering long-term loyalty, engagement, and business growth**.

40. Omnichannel Strategy

Omnichannel Strategy: A Comprehensive Breakdown

Theory Behind Omnichannel Strategy

An **Omnichannel Strategy** is a business approach that integrates multiple customer touchpoints—both online and offline—into a seamless, consistent experience. Unlike multichannel marketing, which simply involves using different platforms, omnichannel focuses on **synchronization across all channels**, ensuring that a customer can transition smoothly between them.

The strategy is rooted in **customer experience (CX), digital transformation, and integrated marketing**, with key principles including:

1. **Seamless Integration** – Ensuring all platforms (e-commerce, physical stores, mobile apps, social media) are connected.
2. **Personalized Experience** – Using data to tailor interactions based on customer behaviour.
3. **Consistency Across Channels** – Maintaining uniform branding, messaging, and product availability.
4. **Real-Time Synchronization** – Updating inventory, promotions, and interactions in real time.
5. **Customer-Centric Approach** – Prioritizing convenience, flexibility, and engagement.

Omnichannel is widely used in **retail, banking, hospitality, e-commerce, and service industries**, where **customer interactions occur across multiple platforms.**

Example of Omnichannel Strategy

A prime example is **Nike**, which:

- **Synchronizes its website, app, and physical stores**, allowing customers to browse online and pick up in-store.

- **Uses the Nike app to offer personalized product recommendations**, driving digital engagement.

- **Connects loyalty programs across all channels**, ensuring rewards can be redeemed anywhere.

Another example is **Starbucks**, which:

- **Links its mobile app, website, and in-store experience**, allowing users to order ahead and pay via mobile.

- **Integrates its rewards program**, so customers earn and redeem points whether online or offline.

- **Uses AI-powered personalization**, sending customized offers based on buying behaviour.

Both companies successfully **enhance customer convenience, personalization, and engagement** through a fully integrated omnichannel experience.

Why Omnichannel Strategy Works

An **Omnichannel Strategy** is effective because:

- **Improves Customer Experience** – Customers enjoy seamless interactions across platforms.

- **Boosts Engagement & Retention** – Personalized interactions increase loyalty.

- **Increases Sales & Conversions** – Customers who interact across multiple channels tend to spend more.

- **Enhances Brand Consistency** – Uniform messaging reinforces brand identity.

- **Optimizes Operational Efficiency** – Real-time data integration reduces errors and improves service.

For example, **Apple's omnichannel approach ensures that customers can start shopping on their phone, book an in-store appointment, and receive product support across all touchpoints**.

How Omnichannel Strategy Works

Companies implement omnichannel strategies by:

1. **Unifying Customer Data** – Using CRM and AI to track interactions across all platforms.

2. **Connecting Online & Offline Channels** – Offering services like "buy online, pick up in-store" (BOPIS).

3. **Personalizing Customer Journeys** – Delivering relevant product recommendations and promotions.

4. **Ensuring Cross-Platform Consistency** – Aligning branding, pricing, and messaging across all channels.

5. **Leveraging Automation & AI** – Using chatbots, smart assistants, and predictive analytics to enhance CX.

For example, **Amazon's omnichannel ecosystem includes e-commerce, Prime membership benefits, Alexa voice shopping, and physical stores (Whole Foods, Amazon Go), creating an interconnected shopping experience.**

Application of Omnichannel Strategy

Businesses use omnichannel strategies to:

- **Enhance retail experiences** – Sephora integrates in-store beauty services with digital product recommendations.

- **Streamline banking services** – Chase allows customers to manage accounts seamlessly across mobile, web, and ATMs.

- **Strengthen hospitality engagement** – Marriott personalizes guest experiences across its website, app, and hotel services.

- **Optimize healthcare services** – Telemedicine platforms connect patients with doctors via apps, websites, and in-person visits.

For instance, **Disney's omnichannel strategy enables users to book trips online, use the MagicBand for park access, and receive real-time updates via its app.**

Key Insights on Omnichannel Strategy

- **Customer expectations drive omnichannel success** – Consumers demand seamless, personalized experiences.

- **Technology & data integration are essential** – AI, CRM, and cloud-based solutions power real-time synchronization.

- **Omnichannel isn't just about sales** – It enhances customer support, loyalty programs, and brand engagement.

- **Consistency is key** – Disjointed experiences across platforms can frustrate customers.

- **Scalability matters** – Businesses must continuously refine and expand their omnichannel efforts as technology evolves.

When executed effectively, an **Omnichannel Strategy enhances customer loyalty, maximizes convenience, and drives long-term business growth**, making it a must-have for modern businesses.

Pricing Strategies

41. Penetration Pricing Strategy

Penetration Pricing Strategy: A Comprehensive Breakdown

Theory Behind Penetration Pricing Strategy

A **Penetration Pricing Strategy** is a business approach where a company introduces a new product or service at a **low initial price** to quickly attract customers, gain market share, and establish brand loyalty. The strategy relies on **psychological pricing, demand stimulation, and competitive disruption** to gain traction in price-sensitive markets.

Key principles behind penetration pricing include:

1. **Low Price to Drive Rapid Adoption** – Encouraging trial and building a strong customer base.

2. **Economies of Scale** – As demand increases, production costs decrease, allowing sustainable pricing.

3. **Market Share Over Immediate Profits** – Prioritizing customer acquisition over short-term revenue.

4. **Customer Lock-In Effect** – Once customers adopt a product, switching becomes less likely.

5. **Competitive Disruption** – Challenging competitors by undercutting prices and establishing dominance.

Penetration pricing is widely used in **consumer goods, SaaS, subscription services, technology, and fast-moving retail**, where capturing customers quickly is essential for long-term profitability.

Example of Penetration Pricing Strategy

A well-known example is **Netflix's early pricing strategy**, which:

- **Launched with lower subscription fees than traditional cable services.**
- **Offered free trials to hook customers into the platform.**
- **Gradually increased prices once it established a loyal user base.**

Another example is **Amazon Prime**, which:

- **Started with a low-cost annual membership** to encourage sign-ups.
- **Bundled services like Prime Video and fast shipping to add value.**
- **Increased prices over time while retaining strong customer loyalty.**

Both companies successfully **disrupted traditional markets by offering an unbeatable price-to-value ratio, ensuring rapid adoption and long-term dominance.**

Why Penetration Pricing Strategy Works

A **Penetration Pricing Strategy** is effective because:

- **Drives Quick Market Entry** – A lower price attracts early adopters, building initial traction.

- **Increases Customer Loyalty** – Once users integrate a product into their routine, they're less likely to switch.

- **Forces Competitor Adjustments** – Established players must react, often leading to price wars or innovation shifts.

- **Enhances Brand Recognition** – A large customer base strengthens brand positioning.

- **Encourages Word-of-Mouth Growth** – More users mean more organic recommendations.

For example, **Spotify offered an extended free trial period to lure customers away from Apple Music and paid competitors, solidifying itself as a top streaming service.**

How Penetration Pricing Strategy Works

Companies implement penetration pricing by:

1. **Setting an Aggressive Introductory Price** – Lower than competitors to capture early demand.

2. **Building Customer Trust & Dependence** – Encouraging users to experience the product's full value.

3. **Gradually Increasing Prices** – Once customer loyalty is established, prices can rise without significant churn.

4. **Expanding Product Offerings** – Adding premium features, bundles, or upgrades for long-term monetization.

5. **Monitoring Market Response** – Adjusting pricing strategy based on competition and customer behaviour.

For example, **Disney+ launched at a lower price than Netflix, attracting millions of subscribers before gradually adjusting pricing and adding premium content.**

Application of Penetration Pricing Strategy

Businesses use penetration pricing to:

- **Break into competitive industries** – Xiaomi enters new smartphone markets with affordable, feature-packed devices.

- **Encourage subscriptions & memberships** – Adobe transitioned to a subscription model with initially low Creative Cloud pricing.

- **Expand in emerging markets** – Uber used aggressive pricing in new cities to establish market dominance.

- **Disrupt traditional industries** – Dollar Shave Club undercut Gillette by offering razor subscriptions at a fraction of the cost.

For instance, **Samsung uses penetration pricing for new smartphone models in price-sensitive regions, gaining a foothold against competitors like Apple.**

Key Insights on Penetration Pricing Strategy

- **Low prices must be sustainable** – If prices are too low for too long, profit margins suffer.

- **Gradual price increases should be well-timed** – Raising prices too soon can lead to customer loss.

- **Brand differentiation is crucial** – Companies must offer more than just low prices to retain customers.

- **Competitor reactions can be unpredictable** – Some may match prices, making differentiation essential.

- **Customer loyalty must be nurtured** – Engaging users through rewards, exclusive offers, or superior service prevents churn.

When executed effectively, a **Penetration Pricing Strategy drives rapid market entry, establishes brand presence, and builds a strong foundation for long-term profitability**, making it a powerful tool for companies looking to scale quickly.

42. Premium Pricing Strategy

Premium Pricing Strategy: A Comprehensive Breakdown

Theory Behind Premium Pricing Strategy

A **Premium Pricing Strategy** is a business approach where companies price their products or services **higher than competitors** to create a perception of superior quality, exclusivity, and status. This strategy is not based on low costs or mass appeal but on **brand positioning, perceived value, and customer experience**.

Key principles behind premium pricing include:

1. **Perceived Value & Luxury Positioning** – Customers associate higher prices with higher quality and status.

2. **Brand Equity & Exclusivity** – Premium brands maintain strong reputations and limited accessibility.

3. **Superior Product Differentiation** – High-end features, craftsmanship, or technology justify the price.

4. **Exceptional Customer Experience** – Personalized service and exclusivity enhance customer loyalty.

5. **Targeting Affluent Consumers** – Focusing on a niche audience that values quality over cost.

This strategy is widely used in **luxury goods, technology, fashion, automobiles, hospitality, and high-end services**, where branding plays a crucial role in customer decision-making.

Example of Premium Pricing Strategy

A prime example is **Apple**, which:

- **Prices its products higher than competitors** despite offering similar hardware specifications.
- **Justifies pricing through sleek design, branding, and a seamless ecosystem.**
- **Maintains exclusivity through limited product launches and high-end retail experiences.**

Another example is **Rolex**, which:

- **Uses premium pricing to establish its watches as symbols of status and craftsmanship.**
- **Limits production to maintain exclusivity and desirability.**
- **Focuses on long-term brand equity rather than short-term discounts or promotions.**

Both brands successfully **leverage high pricing to reinforce their premium positioning and create strong customer loyalty.**

Why Premium Pricing Strategy Works

A **Premium Pricing Strategy** is effective because:

- **Enhances Brand Perception** – High prices create an aura of exclusivity and quality.

- **Builds Customer Loyalty** – Buyers feel emotionally connected to premium brands.

- **Drives Higher Profit Margins** – Fewer sales at higher prices can generate substantial revenue.

- **Limits Competition** – Competitors struggle to match quality, service, and branding.

- **Reduces Price Sensitivity** – Affluent consumers prioritize value and experience over cost.

For example, **Tesla's high pricing reinforces its image as an innovative, luxury EV brand, differentiating it from mass-market competitors.**

How Premium Pricing Strategy Works

Companies implement premium pricing by:

1. **Establishing a Strong Brand Identity** – Investing in high-quality materials, craftsmanship, and storytelling.

2. **Enhancing Customer Experience** – Offering personalized service, VIP treatment, and exclusive perks.

3. **Maintaining Limited Availability** – Creating scarcity to increase perceived value.

4. **Leveraging Emotional & Status-Based Marketing** – Positioning products as aspirational.

5. **Avoiding Discounting & Price Wars** – Preserving brand prestige by resisting price reductions.

For example, **Louis Vuitton never holds sales, reinforcing its luxury positioning by maintaining consistent high pricing.**

Application of Premium Pricing Strategy

Businesses use premium pricing to:

- **Create luxury brand identity** – Chanel and Prada maintain elite fashion status.

- **Monetize exclusivity** – Ferrari produces limited-edition models for ultra-high-end customers.

- **Justify innovation & R&D costs** – Dyson's premium vacuum cleaners highlight advanced technology.

- **Expand into affluent markets** – High-end hotels like The Ritz-Carlton target luxury travellers.

For instance, **Montblanc's expensive pens reinforce their brand as a symbol of success and status, making them desirable for executives and collectors.**

Key Insights on Premium Pricing Strategy

- **Perception is as important as product quality** – Customers pay for brand prestige, not just functionality.

- **Consistency builds trust** – Frequent discounting can damage premium brand credibility.

- **Exclusivity increases desirability** – Limited releases and VIP experiences enhance demand.

- **Customer experience must match the price** – High prices require superior service and attention to detail.

- **Marketing should emphasize status, craftsmanship, and heritage** – Storytelling reinforces the brand's premium image.

When executed effectively, a **Premium Pricing Strategy elevates brand positioning, enhances profitability, and creates lasting customer loyalty**, making it a powerful approach for businesses targeting affluent markets.

43. Dynamic Pricing Strategy

Dynamic Pricing Strategy: A Comprehensive Breakdown

Theory Behind Dynamic Pricing Strategy

A **Dynamic Pricing Strategy** is a business approach where prices continuously adjust in real-time based on factors like **demand, competitor pricing, market conditions, customer behaviour, and inventory levels**. Unlike fixed pricing, dynamic pricing allows businesses to **maximize revenue, optimize inventory, and stay competitive** by changing prices based on real-time data.

Dynamic pricing is based on **economic principles and artificial intelligence (AI)-driven analytics**, with key components including:

1. **Price Elasticity** – Adjusting prices according to customer willingness to pay.

2. **Demand-Based Pricing** – Higher prices during peak demand, lower during off-peak times.

3. **Competitor-Based Pricing** – Adapting pricing based on competitor rates.

4. **Segmented Pricing** – Charging different prices for different customer segments.

5. **Algorithmic & AI-Driven Pricing** – Using data analytics to automate real-time price adjustments.

This strategy is commonly used in **e-commerce, travel, hospitality, ride-sharing, event ticketing, and retail**, where fluctuating demand requires flexible pricing.

Example of Dynamic Pricing Strategy

A prime example is **Uber's surge pricing**, which:

- **Increases ride fares during peak hours or high demand periods** to balance supply and demand.

- **Encourages more drivers to be available** by making it financially attractive.

- **Automatically adjusts fares in real-time using AI algorithms** based on traffic, weather, and rider demand.

Another example is **Amazon**, which:

- **Changes product prices multiple times a day** based on demand, competitor pricing, and buying trends.

- **Uses machine learning to analyse customer behaviour and adjust discounts accordingly.**

- **Offers personalized pricing and deals to repeat customers based on shopping history.**

Both companies successfully **maximize revenue, optimize supply-demand balance, and improve competitiveness through dynamic pricing.**

Why Dynamic Pricing Strategy Works

A **Dynamic Pricing Strategy** is effective because:

- **Maximizes Revenue & Profitability** – Businesses capture higher margins during peak demand.

- **Optimizes Inventory Management** – Discounts help clear excess stock while premium pricing capitalizes on scarcity.

- **Increases Competitive Advantage** – Real-time price adjustments prevent being undercut by competitors.

- **Enhances Customer Segmentation** – Different customers see different prices based on their behaviour and demand patterns.

- **Encourages Behavioural Shifts** – Incentivizes customers to buy during off-peak times with lower prices.

For example, **airlines like Delta and Emirates adjust flight ticket prices dynamically based on seasonality, time of booking, and seat availability, ensuring maximum seat occupancy and profitability.**

How Dynamic Pricing Strategy Works

Companies implement dynamic pricing by:

1. **Collecting Real-Time Market Data** – Monitoring demand, competition, and customer behaviour.

2. **Using AI & Algorithms for Price Adjustments** – Automating price changes based on pre-set rules.

3. **Segmenting Customers** – Offering personalized pricing based on customer loyalty, browsing history, and purchase patterns.

4. **A/B Testing Pricing Models** – Experimenting with different pricing levels to determine optimal price points.

5. **Ensuring Transparency & Compliance** – Avoiding unethical pricing practices that could lead to customer distrust.

For example, **hotel chains like Marriott and Hilton use dynamic pricing to adjust room rates based on seasonality, booking time, and occupancy levels.**

Application of Dynamic Pricing Strategy

Businesses use dynamic pricing to:

- **Increase profitability in high-demand industries** – Streaming services like Netflix test regional pricing models.

- **Attract customers during off-peak times** – Movie theatres offer cheaper tickets for matinee showings.

- **React to competitor pricing changes instantly** – Walmart automatically adjusts online product prices to remain competitive.

- **Optimize supply & demand** – Airlines use yield management to adjust ticket prices dynamically.

For instance, **Google Ads uses a bidding-based dynamic pricing system, where ad placements become more expensive based on advertiser competition and search demand.**

Key Insights on Dynamic Pricing Strategy

- **AI & automation are essential** – Real-time adjustments require advanced data analytics.

- **Customer perception matters** – Overpricing during high demand can cause backlash if not justified.

- **Industry type determines pricing flexibility** – Travel and e-commerce benefit most from dynamic pricing.

- **Transparency is key** – Customers should understand why prices change to maintain trust.

- **Regulatory compliance is necessary** – Some industries face legal restrictions on frequent price fluctuations.

When executed effectively, a **Dynamic Pricing Strategy enhances revenue, improves market positioning, and allows businesses to stay agile in response to real-time market conditions**, making it a powerful tool for modern commerce.

44. Loss Leader Strategy

Loss Leader Strategy: A Comprehensive Breakdown

Theory

The **Loss Leader Strategy** is a pricing tactic where a company deliberately sells a product at a loss (below cost) to attract customers, with the goal of making a profit through subsequent purchases of higher-margin products or services. This strategy is based on the concept of **customer acquisition and lifetime value (LTV)**—the idea that attracting a customer initially at a loss can lead to long-term profitability through repeat purchases or complementary goods.

The psychology behind this approach relies on **consumer behaviour theories**, particularly the **foot-in-the-door technique**, where customers who make an initial purchase are more likely to return and buy more. It also leverages the **bait-and-hook model**, where a basic product (the bait) is sold cheaply, but complementary goods (the hook) generate profit.

This strategy is common in industries where products have strong **cross-selling opportunities** or where repeat purchases are expected. By lowering the price of a key item, businesses increase foot traffic or brand loyalty, enabling them to profit from additional purchases.

Example

A classic example of the Loss Leader Strategy is **video game consoles** like the PlayStation or Xbox. Companies such as Sony and Microsoft often sell gaming consoles at a loss or at breakeven prices, but they recoup their investment through **game sales, subscriptions (PlayStation Plus, Xbox Game Pass), and accessories**. Once a customer has purchased the console, they are locked into the ecosystem, leading to long-term profitability.

Another common example is **supermarkets selling milk or eggs below cost** to bring customers into the store, where they are likely to purchase additional items with higher profit margins.

Why It Works

1. **Increases Customer Traffic:** By offering a high-demand product at an attractive price, businesses can draw more customers to their stores or platforms.

2. **Encourages Additional Purchases:** Once customers are engaged, they are more likely to buy higher-margin complementary products.

3. **Builds Brand Loyalty:** Customers may return for repeat purchases, increasing their lifetime value.

4. **Creates Entry Barriers for Competitors:** Smaller businesses may struggle to match the pricing strategy, allowing dominant players to capture market share.

How It Works

1. **Identify a High-Demand Product:** Businesses choose a product with broad appeal that complements other profitable items.

2. **Price It Below Cost:** The product is sold at a loss or very low profit margin to attract customers.

3. **Leverage Cross-Selling & Upselling:** Customers are encouraged to buy additional products that compensate for the initial loss.

4. **Retain Customers for Future Sales:** Loyalty programs, subscriptions, and personalized marketing ensure continued purchases.

Application

- **Retail & E-commerce:** Amazon often uses loss leaders like books or electronics to encourage customers to shop for other higher-margin items.

- **Technology & Software:** Printers are sold at a low price, but ink cartridges (where the profit lies) are expensive.

- **Subscription Services:** Streaming platforms like Netflix or Spotify offer free trials (a type of loss leader) to hook users into paying subscriptions.

- **Restaurants & Hospitality:** Fast-food chains may offer discounted combo meals to increase footfall and generate upsell opportunities.

Key Insights

1. **Works Best with Strong Cross-Selling Opportunities:** The strategy is only effective if customers buy additional, profitable products.

2. **Not Sustainable Without a Profit Mechanism:** A loss leader without a clear path to profitability can damage a company's financial health.

3. **Best Used by Established Businesses:** Larger companies with capital reserves can afford short-term losses to gain long-term market dominance.

4. **Can Create Legal and Ethical Concerns:** In some cases, regulators may view aggressive loss leader strategies as predatory pricing, which can harm smaller competitors.

5. **Understanding Consumer Psychology is Key:** The success of this strategy hinges on how customers perceive value and how they respond to pricing incentives.

Conclusion

The **Loss Leader Strategy** is a powerful tool in business strategy, effectively used across industries to attract customers, build loyalty, and drive long-term profitability. While it carries risks, when executed correctly with complementary high-margin products, it becomes an effective method for growth and competitive advantage.

45. Bundling Strategy

Bundling Strategy: A Comprehensive Breakdown

Theory

The **Bundling Strategy** is a business approach where multiple products or services are packaged together and sold at a combined price, often at a discount compared to purchasing each item separately. This strategy is used to increase perceived value, enhance sales volume, and drive customer retention.

Bundling is rooted in **behavioural economics**, particularly the **perception of value**—customers are more likely to perceive a bundle as a better deal even if individual components may not be needed. This strategy also leverages **price discrimination**, where businesses can capture different customer segments who may not purchase each item separately but find the bundled price appealing.

There are two main types of bundling:

1. **Pure Bundling** – Products are only available as a package (e.g., cable TV plans where channels cannot be purchased individually).
2. **Mixed Bundling** – Customers can buy items separately or as a bundle at a discount (e.g., fast-food combo meals).

This strategy helps businesses **increase revenue per customer, reduce inventory, and enhance the perceived value** of less popular products by pairing them with high-demand items.

Example

A well-known example of bundling is **Microsoft Office**. Instead of selling Word, Excel, and PowerPoint separately, Microsoft bundles them into an Office suite at a lower total price than if purchased individually. This encourages users to buy the full package rather than just one application, increasing overall revenue.

Another example is **McDonald's meal combos**. Instead of selling a burger, fries, and a drink separately, they offer a value meal at a lower combined price, encouraging customers to buy more than they originally intended.

Why It Works

1. **Increases Perceived Value:** Customers feel they are getting more for their money, leading to increased purchase likelihood.

2. **Encourages Higher Spending:** Customers are more likely to spend more when products are bundled together, increasing average order value.

3. **Simplifies Decision-Making:** Bundles reduce decision fatigue by providing a pre-selected package, making it easier for customers to choose.

4. **Improves Sales of Low-Demand Products:** Bundling less popular products with high-demand ones helps move

inventory and generate revenue from otherwise slow-moving items.

How It Works

1. **Identify Complementary Products:** Businesses choose products that naturally go together (e.g., a laptop and a carrying case).

2. **Set an Attractive Price:** The bundle price should be lower than the sum of individual prices but still profitable.

3. **Market the Bundle Effectively:** Businesses highlight the convenience, cost savings, and added value of the bundle.

4. **Monitor Performance:** Companies track sales data to adjust bundling strategies based on customer behaviour and demand trends.

Application

- **Technology & Software:** Adobe Creative Cloud offers a bundle of design tools instead of selling them individually.

- **Retail & E-commerce:** Amazon offers "Frequently Bought Together" bundles to encourage upselling.

- **Telecommunications:** Internet providers bundle services like broadband, TV, and phone plans.

- **Health & Beauty:** Skincare brands offer product kits (e.g., cleanser, toner, moisturizer) for a complete regimen.

Key Insights

1. **Bundling Works Best When Products Are Complementary:** A well-structured bundle increases the perceived value and justifies the combined purchase.

2. **Not All Bundles Are Effective:** Poorly designed bundles with unrelated items may deter customers instead of attracting them.

3. **It Can Increase Customer Lock-In:** Subscription services use bundling to make it less attractive for customers to switch to competitors.

4. **Discounts Should Be Strategic:** If the price reduction is too steep, bundling may erode profit margins rather than increase overall revenue.

5. **Customization Can Enhance Effectiveness:** Allowing customers to choose elements within a bundle can further increase sales and satisfaction.

Conclusion

The **Bundling Strategy** is an effective business tactic for increasing sales, enhancing customer value, and boosting profitability. When executed correctly, it not only drives higher revenue but also strengthens brand loyalty by simplifying purchasing decisions and maximizing perceived savings.

46. Pay-What-You-Want Strategy

Pay-What-You-Want Strategy: A Comprehensive Breakdown

Theory

The **Pay-What-You-Want (PWYW) Strategy** is a pricing model where customers decide how much they are willing to pay for a product or service. Unlike traditional fixed pricing, this strategy relies on **consumer goodwill, reciprocity, and perceived value** to generate revenue.

PWYW is based on **behavioural economics**, particularly the **fairness principle**—customers want to pay a fair price, especially when they perceive value in a product or service. It also leverages **reciprocity**, where people feel an obligation to pay something when given the freedom to choose their price. Additionally, **social influence** plays a role; when others are paying, individuals may feel pressure to contribute appropriately.

This strategy works well when the cost of production is low, the product has a high perceived value, or there is a strong emotional connection between the consumer and the seller. It is often used as a marketing tool to attract new customers, create buzz, and build brand loyalty.

Example

A well-known example is **Radiohead's 2007 album "In Rainbows."** The band released the album under a PWYW model, allowing fans to download it and pay whatever they wanted—

including nothing. Despite the risk, the strategy was highly successful, generating millions in revenue and increasing fan engagement.

Another example is **Panera Bread's "Panera Cares" Cafés,** where customers could pay whatever they wanted for meals. While some people paid more than the suggested price, others paid less, creating a mixed financial outcome. Though the initiative eventually closed, it demonstrated the power of PWYW in fostering community goodwill and social responsibility.

Why It Works

1. **Encourages Customer Goodwill:** People appreciate businesses that trust them to decide a fair price, which can build long-term loyalty.

2. **Creates Marketing Buzz:** The novelty of PWYW generates media attention, social sharing, and word-of-mouth marketing.

3. **Increases Accessibility:** Customers who might not afford a product at a fixed price can still access it, potentially leading to future purchases.

4. **Taps into Psychological Drivers:** The desire to be fair, avoid guilt, and reciprocate generosity encourages people to pay rather than exploit the model.

How It Works

1. **Define the Offer:** Businesses select a product or service where PWYW pricing is feasible, often with low production costs.

2. **Communicate Value Clearly:** To encourage fair payment, businesses highlight the effort, quality, or social impact of the product.

3. **Suggest Reference Prices (Optional):** Some businesses provide a suggested price or show what others are paying to guide customer decisions.

4. **Leverage Social and Ethical Pressure:** Businesses can tie payments to charitable causes or social responsibility to encourage generosity.

5. **Analyse Data & Adjust:** Companies track revenue trends to see if the model is sustainable or needs modification.

Application

- **Music & Entertainment:** Artists release albums, movies, or books under PWYW to attract more fans and increase visibility.

- **Restaurants & Cafés:** Some eateries allow customers to pay as they wish, often with a suggested donation amount.

- **Digital Products & Services:** Software companies and online content creators use PWYW to attract users while relying on voluntary contributions.

- **Charity & Fundraising:** Non-profits use this model to encourage donations while providing value to supporters.

Key Insights

1. **Works Best When Trust is High:** Customers need to feel a connection to the brand or cause for PWYW to be effective.

2. **Perceived Value Drives Success:** The higher the value customers see in a product, the more they are willing to pay.

3. **Risk of Undervaluation:** Some customers may exploit the model, making profitability uncertain without safeguards.

4. **Social Proof & Anchoring Help:** Providing reference prices or showing what others paid can guide customer decisions.

5. **Best Used as a Short-Term or Promotional Strategy:** PWYW is often more effective for limited-time offers rather than a long-term pricing model.

Conclusion

The **Pay-What-You-Want Strategy** is an innovative pricing approach that leverages consumer psychology, trust, and goodwill to drive sales and engagement. While it carries risks, it can be highly effective when used strategically, particularly in industries where customer relationships, brand loyalty, and social influence play a key role.

47. Subscription Model Strategy

Subscription Model Strategy: A Comprehensive Breakdown

Theory

The **Subscription Model Strategy** is a business approach where customers pay a recurring fee—weekly, monthly, or annually—to access a product or service. This model provides businesses with **predictable revenue streams, enhanced customer retention, and long-term customer relationships.**

The strategy is based on **customer lifetime value (CLV)** rather than one-time purchases, ensuring continuous revenue from each customer. It aligns with the **access over ownership trend**, where consumers prefer access to services rather than owning products outright (e.g., Netflix for entertainment, Spotify for music, and SaaS tools for software).

Subscription models thrive on the principles of **habit formation and convenience.** Customers benefit from regular access without the hassle of repeated purchasing decisions, and businesses gain steady income while building strong brand loyalty.

There are several types of subscription models:

1. **Fixed Subscriptions** – A set price for continuous access (e.g., Amazon Prime, Netflix).
2. **Usage-Based Subscriptions** – Pricing based on consumption levels (e.g., AWS cloud services).

3. **Freemium-to-Paid Models** – A free tier with optional paid upgrades (e.g., Spotify, LinkedIn Premium).
4. **Curation Subscriptions** – Handpicked products delivered regularly (e.g., Birchbox, meal kit services).

Example

A standout example of the subscription model is **Netflix.** Instead of selling individual movies or TV shows, Netflix offers a flat-rate subscription for unlimited access to a vast library of content. This model disrupted the traditional pay-per-rental approach and revolutionized the entertainment industry.

Another example is **Amazon Prime,** which bundles multiple services (free shipping, Prime Video, Prime Music) under a single subscription, increasing customer loyalty and boosting additional Amazon purchases.

Why It Works

1. **Predictable Revenue:** Businesses can forecast earnings accurately, enabling better financial planning and investment.
2. **Customer Retention & Loyalty:** Long-term subscriptions increase engagement and reduce churn compared to one-time purchases.

3. **Lower Customer Acquisition Costs:** Retaining an existing subscriber is cheaper than acquiring a new customer, making the model highly cost-effective.

4. **Convenience & Habit Formation:** Customers appreciate the ease of continuous access without repeated purchasing decisions.

5. **Upselling & Cross-Selling Opportunities:** Businesses can introduce premium features or additional services, increasing overall revenue.

How It Works

1. **Define the Core Value Proposition:** Identify what makes the subscription offering valuable and sustainable for customers.

2. **Choose a Pricing Structure:** Decide between tiered, usage-based, or fixed pricing based on market demand and competitive analysis.

3. **Offer a Free Trial or Entry-Level Plan:** Many companies provide a freemium model or trial period to attract users before converting them into paying customers.

4. **Ensure a Seamless Customer Experience:** The onboarding process, user interface, and renewal system should be frictionless to retain subscribers.

5. **Monitor Metrics & Reduce Churn:** Businesses track key performance indicators (KPIs) like churn rate, customer

acquisition cost (CAC), and lifetime value (LTV) to optimize growth strategies.

Application

- **Streaming Services:** Netflix, Disney+, and Spotify provide unlimited access to content for a monthly fee.
- **Software as a Service (SaaS):** Adobe Creative Cloud, Microsoft 365, and Zoom use subscription models for cloud-based tools.
- **E-commerce & Retail:** Amazon Prime, subscription box services (e.g., Dollar Shave Club, Birchbox).
- **Fitness & Health:** Peloton, online workout platforms, and meal kit subscriptions (e.g., HelloFresh).
- **News & Publications:** The New York Times, The Wall Street Journal, and Substack offer digital subscriptions for exclusive content.

Key Insights

1. **Retention is More Important Than Acquisition:** The success of a subscription model depends on keeping customers engaged and minimizing churn.
2. **Value Delivery Must Be Continuous:** Customers must see ongoing benefits to justify the recurring cost.

3. **Personalization Enhances Loyalty:** Tailoring content, features, or recommendations improves engagement and reduces cancellations.

4. **Pricing Strategy is Crucial:** Offering multiple tiers or bundling services can maximize revenue from different customer segments.

5. **Churn Management is Essential:** Monitoring customer behaviour, sending renewal reminders, and offering incentives can reduce subscription cancellations.

Conclusion

The **Subscription Model Strategy** is a powerful way to build sustainable revenue, improve customer relationships, and increase lifetime value. When executed correctly, it provides businesses with a **stable income stream** and gives customers **continuous value, convenience, and personalization.** However, maintaining engagement and minimizing churn are critical for long-term success.

48. Skimming Pricing Strategy

Skimming Pricing Strategy: A Comprehensive Breakdown

Theory

The **Skimming Pricing Strategy** is a pricing approach where a business sets an initially high price for a new or innovative product and then gradually lowers it over time. This strategy is often used when launching cutting-edge products to maximize profits from early adopters before making the product accessible to a broader market.

Skimming pricing is based on **price discrimination** and the **product life cycle theory**. It targets customers willing to pay a premium for exclusivity or early access, then systematically reduces the price to attract more price-sensitive consumers.

This strategy works well in industries where products become obsolete or face rapid competition, allowing businesses to recover research and development (R&D) costs quickly. It also establishes a **perceived value of exclusivity** before mass adoption.

There are key conditions for skimming pricing to be effective:

1. **Strong Product Differentiation** – The product must be innovative or unique to justify the high price.

2. **Inelastic Demand Among Early Adopters** – Consumers must be willing to pay a premium for early access.

3. **Limited or Delayed Competition** – If competitors enter too quickly, a high price may not be sustainable.

4. **Gradual Price Reduction Strategy** – The business must lower prices carefully to maintain profitability while expanding the market.

Example

A classic example of the skimming strategy is **Apple's iPhone launches.** Every new iPhone starts at a high price, targeting tech enthusiasts and brand-loyal customers. Over time, prices decrease as newer models are introduced, making older models more affordable for price-sensitive buyers.

Another example is **Sony's PlayStation consoles,** which debut at high prices to capture demand from hardcore gamers. As the technology ages and competition intensifies, Sony lowers prices to attract a broader audience, extending the product's life cycle.

Why It Works

1. **Maximizes Early Profits:** Companies capture high margins from early adopters willing to pay a premium.

2. **Recovers R&D Costs Quickly:** Helps businesses recoup investments before competitors drive prices down.

3. **Establishes a High-Value Perception:** Consumers associate higher prices with premium quality and exclusivity.

4. **Allows for Market Segmentation:** The strategy targets different customer segments over time, from innovators to mass-market consumers.

5. **Provides Flexibility in Pricing:** Businesses can adjust prices strategically as competition and demand evolve.

How It Works

1. **Introduce the Product at a High Price:** The product is marketed as premium, appealing to early adopters.

2. **Leverage Early Sales to Recover Costs:** High margins in the initial phase help cover development and marketing expenses.

3. **Monitor Market Demand & Competitor Activity:** Businesses track sales trends and competitive responses.

4. **Gradually Reduce the Price to Expand the Market:** The price is lowered strategically to attract more cost-conscious buyers.

5. **Sustain Profitability Through Differentiation:** Companies maintain brand loyalty and profitability by continuously innovating.

Application

- **Technology & Electronics:** Smartphones, gaming consoles, and new gadgets often follow this model.

- **Pharmaceuticals:** New prescription drugs are introduced at high prices before generics enter the market.

- **Luxury Goods:** High-end brands introduce exclusive collections at premium prices before expanding accessibility.

- **Entertainment & Media:** Movie streaming platforms often charge more for early access to new releases.

- **Automotive Industry:** New car models start with high introductory prices before discounts and financing options become available.

Key Insights

1. **Works Best for Innovative or Premium Products:** The strategy is effective when customers perceive significant value in exclusivity.

2. **Pricing Must Be Managed Carefully:** Lowering prices too quickly can alienate early adopters, while waiting too long can allow competitors to take market share.

3. **Brand Perception is Critical:** A successful skimming strategy reinforces the product's premium status and quality.

4. **Market Timing is Crucial:** Businesses must anticipate when to adjust prices based on demand, competition, and product life cycle.

5. **Competition Can Limit Effectiveness:** If competitors release similar products at lower prices early on, skimming pricing may fail to gain traction.

Conclusion

The **Skimming Pricing Strategy** is an effective approach for maximizing early profits, recovering development costs, and reinforcing a premium brand image. When executed correctly, it allows businesses to capture value from early adopters before expanding to a larger market. However, **careful timing and price adjustments** are essential to sustain profitability and stay ahead of competitors.

49. Psychological Pricing Strategy

Psychological Pricing Strategy: A Comprehensive Breakdown

Theory

The **Psychological Pricing Strategy** is a pricing approach that leverages consumer psychology to influence purchasing decisions. Instead of setting prices purely based on cost or competition, businesses use **pricing tactics that appeal to emotions, perceptions, and cognitive biases** to make prices seem more attractive.

This strategy is grounded in **behavioural economics and consumer psychology**, particularly in how people perceive value. Rather than making purely rational decisions, customers are influenced by **price presentation, numbers, and mental shortcuts (heuristics)** when assessing whether a price is a good deal.

There are several common types of psychological pricing:

1. **Charm Pricing (Odd Pricing):** Setting prices just below a round number (e.g., $9.99 instead of $10) makes the price seem lower due to the "left-digit effect."

2. **Prestige Pricing:** Higher prices create a perception of exclusivity and luxury (e.g., Rolex, Louis Vuitton).

3. **Anchor Pricing:** Showing a higher original price next to a discounted price makes the deal seem more valuable.

4. **Bundle Pricing:** Grouping products together at a lower total price (e.g., "Buy 1 Get 1 Free") increases perceived savings.

5. **Decoy Pricing:** Introducing a higher-priced, less attractive option to make another option look like a better deal.

6. **Scarcity Pricing:** Using limited-time discounts or "only a few left" messages triggers urgency and fear of missing out (FOMO).

By applying these techniques, businesses can subtly **steer consumer behaviour, increase conversion rates, and enhance sales volume** without significantly changing actual costs.

Example

A classic example of psychological pricing is **Apple's use of charm pricing.** The company often prices products at **$999 instead of $1,000**, making them appear significantly cheaper despite a minimal difference.

Another example is **Black Friday sales**, where retailers show original prices next to steep discounts to create the illusion of major savings. Even if the original price was inflated, customers feel they're getting a great deal due to the contrast effect.

Why It Works

1. **Influences Perception of Value:** Consumers focus on the first number they see, making $9.99 feel much cheaper than $10.

2. **Creates a Sense of Urgency:** Limited-time deals and scarcity tactics encourage impulsive purchases.

3. **Enhances Price Justification:** Higher prices feel more reasonable when compared to an even higher "original" price.

4. **Simplifies Decision-Making:** Consumers rely on mental shortcuts, like assuming higher prices equal higher quality.

5. **Maximizes Emotional Impact:** Pricing can evoke feelings of exclusivity (prestige pricing) or excitement (discounts, bundles).

How It Works

1. **Analyse Consumer Behaviour:** Understand how customers perceive pricing and what influences their buying decisions.

2. **Select the Right Pricing Technique:** Choose a strategy based on the target audience, product type, and brand positioning.

3. **Test & Optimize Pricing:** A/B test different pricing structures to determine which psychological techniques drive the most sales.

4. **Use Strategic Pricing Presentation:** Ensure pricing is displayed in a way that enhances perceived value (e.g., original vs. discounted price, pricing in small font for discounts).

5. **Monitor Market Response & Adjust Accordingly:** Track customer reactions and sales data to refine pricing tactics over time.

Application

- **Retail & E-commerce:** Amazon uses anchor pricing by showing discounted prices alongside original prices.
- **Luxury Brands:** Rolex and Chanel use prestige pricing to maintain an aura of exclusivity.
- **Fast Food & Restaurants:** McDonald's uses bundle pricing (e.g., meal combos) to increase perceived savings.
- **Tech Industry:** Apple and Samsung use charm pricing and decoy pricing to make higher-end models seem more appealing.
- **Travel & Hospitality:** Airlines and hotels use scarcity pricing (e.g., "Only 2 seats left at this price!") to drive bookings.

Key Insights

1. **Perception Matters More Than Reality:** Customers often base decisions on how a price *feels* rather than its actual value.

2. **Psychological Pricing is Versatile:** It can be applied across industries, from luxury goods to budget-friendly products.

3. **Discounts Should Be Carefully Positioned:** Too many discounts can harm perceived brand value, while strategic markdowns increase appeal.

4. **Numbers Play a Powerful Role:** Small numerical tweaks, such as ending a price in .99 or showing a higher anchor price, can significantly impact purchasing behaviour.

5. **Testing & Data Are Essential:** What works for one audience may not work for another—continuous testing ensures pricing remains effective.

Conclusion

The **Psychological Pricing Strategy** is a powerful tool for influencing consumer perception and driving sales. By understanding how customers interpret prices, businesses can strategically adjust pricing to maximize profitability, increase perceived value, and enhance customer engagement. When applied correctly, **psychological pricing can make products more desirable, increase conversion rates, and boost long-term revenue.**

50. Geographical Pricing Strategy

Geographical Pricing Strategy: A Comprehensive Breakdown

Theory

The **Geographical Pricing Strategy** is a pricing approach where businesses set different prices for the same product or service based on the customer's location. This strategy considers **regional demand, economic conditions, shipping costs, local competition, and purchasing power** to optimize pricing for different markets.

This pricing strategy is based on **market segmentation** and **cost-based pricing principles**. Businesses recognize that customers in different regions have varying willingness and ability to pay, which allows them to maximize revenue and profitability by adjusting prices accordingly.

Key factors influencing geographical pricing include:

1. **Cost of Doing Business:** Taxes, import duties, and operational expenses vary across regions.
2. **Local Demand & Competition:** A product may be more in demand in one location, justifying a higher price.

3. **Economic Conditions:** Prices are often adjusted based on the purchasing power of consumers in different areas.

4. **Logistics & Distribution Costs:** Shipping and handling costs differ depending on the region, affecting final pricing.

There are several types of geographical pricing strategies:

- **Zone Pricing:** Different price zones are created based on distance or market characteristics.

- **Freight Absorption Pricing:** The seller absorbs shipping costs for competitive advantage.

- **FOB (Free on Board) Pricing:** The buyer pays for shipping from the seller's location.

- **Local Market Pricing:** Prices are adjusted based on local demand and competitor pricing.

- **International Pricing:** Different pricing structures are used in global markets due to currency fluctuations, tariffs, and local regulations.

Example

A common example of geographical pricing is **gasoline prices.** The same fuel brand may be priced differently across cities and states based on local taxes, transportation costs, and market competition.

Another example is **Apple's iPhone pricing.** The same model can have different prices in the U.S., Europe, and India due to import duties, local regulations, and differences in consumer purchasing power.

Why It Works

1. **Maximizes Revenue Based on Local Market Conditions:** Businesses can charge higher prices in wealthier areas while remaining competitive in lower-income markets.

2. **Balances Supply Chain Costs:** Companies can adjust prices to reflect varying transportation and distribution costs.

3. **Adapts to Regional Competition:** Prices can be set higher in areas with less competition and lowered where competition is intense.

4. **Enhances Global Market Penetration:** By adjusting pricing internationally, businesses can appeal to local consumers while maintaining profitability.

5. **Encourages Efficient Logistics Management:** Companies can optimize pricing to account for shipping and operational expenses, ensuring sustainable profits.

How It Works

1. **Analyse Regional Demand & Purchasing Power:** Companies research consumer income levels, spending habits, and market conditions in different locations.

2. **Segment Markets by Geography:** Pricing zones or categories are created based on factors like distance, economy, and competition.

3. **Adjust Prices Accordingly:** Companies modify product pricing based on costs, competitive landscape, and local willingness to pay.

4. **Monitor & Optimize Pricing Strategy:** Businesses track sales data, competitor prices, and market trends to refine their geographical pricing.

5. **Use Technology for Dynamic Pricing Adjustments:** Many companies use AI and data analytics to adjust pricing in real time based on location-based demand fluctuations.

Application

- **Retail & E-commerce:** Amazon adjusts prices based on regional supply and demand conditions.

- **Airline & Travel Industry:** Ticket prices fluctuate based on the departure location and local demand.

- **Automotive Industry:** Car manufacturers price vehicles differently based on local import taxes and consumer income levels.

- **Fast Food Chains:** McDonald's adjusts menu prices depending on local living costs and market conditions.

- **Subscription Services & Software:** Netflix and Spotify charge different prices in different countries based on affordability and market competition.

Key Insights

1. **Understanding Local Markets is Crucial:** Businesses must analyse consumer behaviour, competition, and economic conditions before setting regional prices.

2. **Pricing Must Be Justified:** Consumers may react negatively to large price discrepancies if they do not perceive a valid reason.

3. **Technology Enables Smarter Pricing Adjustments:** AI-driven pricing models can help businesses set optimal prices based on real-time market data.

4. **Legal & Ethical Considerations Matter:** Companies must ensure compliance with local pricing regulations and avoid perceived price discrimination.

5. **Geographical Pricing Can Be a Competitive Advantage:** If done correctly, it allows businesses to expand into diverse markets while maintaining profitability.

Conclusion

The **Geographical Pricing Strategy** allows businesses to optimize pricing based on location-specific factors like demand, costs, and competition. It is particularly useful for companies operating across multiple regions or countries, as it helps them maximize revenue, enhance competitiveness, and manage logistical costs effectively. However, businesses must carefully research and monitor pricing strategies to ensure they align with local market conditions and consumer expectations.

Operational & Supply Chain Strategies Enhancing efficiency, productivity, and logistics:

51. Lean Manufacturing Strategy

Lean Manufacturing Strategy: A Comprehensive Breakdown

Theory

The **Lean Manufacturing Strategy** is a production methodology focused on minimizing waste while maximizing efficiency and value. Originally developed by **Toyota in the mid-20th century** as the **Toyota Production System (TPS),** lean manufacturing seeks to optimize resources, streamline operations, and continuously improve processes.

At its core, lean manufacturing revolves around **eliminating waste (Muda), standardizing workflows, and improving quality.** The strategy is based on five key principles:

1. **Identify Value:** Define what customers consider valuable and eliminate non-essential processes.

2. **Map the Value Stream:** Analyse the entire production process to identify areas of waste.

3. **Create Flow:** Ensure smooth, uninterrupted production by removing bottlenecks.

4. **Establish Pull Systems:** Produce only when there is demand, reducing excess inventory.

5. **Pursue Perfection:** Implement a culture of continuous improvement (**Kaizen**) to enhance productivity over time.

Types of waste targeted in lean manufacturing include **overproduction, waiting time, unnecessary transportation, excess inventory, motion inefficiencies, defects, and underutilized talent.** By eliminating these inefficiencies, businesses can improve cost savings, increase output, and enhance customer satisfaction.

Example

A famous example of lean manufacturing is **Toyota's Production System (TPS).** Toyota implemented just-in-time (JIT) production, where parts are manufactured and delivered only when needed, reducing excess inventory and costs. They also used **Kaizen (continuous improvement)** and **Kanban (visual workflow management)** to optimize efficiency and maintain consistent quality.

Another example is **Amazon's fulfilment centres.** Amazon uses lean principles to streamline warehouse operations, reduce packaging waste, and enhance order fulfilment speed, ensuring cost-effective and efficient deliveries.

Why It Works

1. **Reduces Waste & Costs:** Eliminating unnecessary steps and materials lowers production costs.

2. **Increases Efficiency:** Standardized workflows and optimized processes enhance productivity.

3. **Improves Product Quality:** Continuous improvement methods ensure higher quality and fewer defects.

4. **Enhances Customer Satisfaction:** Faster production cycles and improved quality lead to better customer experiences.

5. **Creates a Competitive Advantage:** Businesses that adopt lean manufacturing can produce goods faster and cheaper than competitors.

How It Works

1. **Analyse the Current Workflow:** Businesses assess their production processes to identify inefficiencies and areas of waste.

2. **Implement Just-in-Time (JIT) Production:** Materials and components are ordered and used only when needed, reducing inventory costs.

3. **Use Visual Management Tools:** Techniques like **Kanban boards** help track progress and improve workflow transparency.

4. **Adopt Continuous Improvement (Kaizen):** Employees at all levels are encouraged to suggest small but impactful improvements.

5. **Empower Employees & Standardize Workflows:** Workers are trained to follow standardized procedures while having the flexibility to identify and resolve inefficiencies.

Application

- **Automotive Industry:** Toyota, Ford, and Tesla use lean manufacturing to optimize production and reduce waste.
- **Electronics:** Companies like Apple and Dell use lean strategies for efficient supply chain management.
- **Retail & E-commerce:** Amazon uses lean logistics to speed up order fulfilment and reduce costs.
- **Healthcare:** Hospitals implement lean principles to improve patient flow and reduce wait times.
- **Food & Beverage:** Fast-food chains like McDonald's standardize operations to minimize waste and improve efficiency.

Key Insights

1. **Lean is a Mindset, Not Just a Process:** Businesses must embrace a culture of continuous improvement and efficiency.

2. **Employee Involvement is Essential:** Frontline workers play a crucial role in identifying inefficiencies and suggesting improvements.

3. **Technology Enhances Lean Practices:** Automation, AI, and data analytics improve tracking and optimization efforts.

4. **Flexibility & Adaptability Are Crucial:** Lean manufacturing requires businesses to adjust quickly based on demand and market conditions.

5. **Not One-Size-Fits-All:** While lean principles can be applied broadly, businesses must customize strategies to their specific industry and operational needs.

Conclusion

The **Lean Manufacturing Strategy** is a powerful approach for optimizing production, reducing costs, and enhancing efficiency. By focusing on **waste elimination, process improvement, and value creation,** businesses can gain a significant competitive advantage. While lean requires a cultural shift and continuous effort, the long-term benefits of **higher efficiency, lower costs, and improved quality** make it a cornerstone of modern manufacturing success.

52. Just-in-Time (JIT) Strategy

Just-in-Time (JIT) Strategy: A Comprehensive Breakdown

Theory

The **Just-in-Time (JIT) Strategy** is a lean production method where materials, components, and goods are acquired and produced only as needed to meet customer demand, rather than being stockpiled in advance. This approach minimizes inventory costs, reduces waste, and enhances operational efficiency.

JIT was pioneered by **Toyota in the mid-20th century** as part of its **Toyota Production System (TPS)** to optimize manufacturing and supply chain processes. The core idea is to **synchronize production with demand, ensuring that each step in the production process operates smoothly without excessive stock or idle time.**

The key principles of JIT include:

1. **Demand-Driven Production:** Items are only produced when there is an actual demand for them.

2. **Minimized Inventory:** Reducing storage costs by keeping minimal raw materials and finished goods.

3. **Elimination of Waste (Muda):** Removing inefficiencies such as overproduction, excess transportation, and waiting time.

4. **Continuous Improvement (Kaizen):** Encouraging employees to identify and eliminate inefficiencies in real-time.

5. **Strong Supplier Relationships:** Reliable, quick-response suppliers are essential for timely deliveries.

By implementing JIT, businesses can enhance productivity, improve cash flow, and reduce risks associated with excess inventory and product obsolescence.

Example

One of the most well-known examples of JIT is **Toyota's manufacturing system.** Toyota produces vehicles based on actual customer orders rather than making cars in bulk. Parts and materials arrive exactly when needed in the assembly process, reducing storage costs and improving efficiency.

Another example is **McDonald's "Made for You" system.** Instead of preparing large quantities of food in advance, McDonald's restaurants prepare meals only when customers place orders, ensuring freshness while minimizing food waste.

Why It Works

1. **Reduces Inventory Costs:** Storing excess stock ties up capital and increases storage expenses. JIT minimizes these costs by keeping inventory levels low.

2. **Enhances Efficiency:** By streamlining production, JIT reduces delays, excess labour, and unnecessary resource use.

3. **Improves Cash Flow:** Less money is locked in unsold inventory, allowing businesses to allocate capital more effectively.

4. **Reduces Waste & Defects:** Continuous improvement and quality control help eliminate unnecessary materials and defective products.

5. **Increases Responsiveness to Demand:** Businesses can quickly adapt to market changes, avoiding overproduction or shortages.

How It Works

1. **Assess Customer Demand:** Businesses analyse real-time sales data and forecasts to determine production needs.

2. **Establish Reliable Supply Chains:** Companies work closely with suppliers to ensure timely delivery of materials.

3. **Implement Lean Production Processes:** Streamlined workflows reduce waste and inefficiencies in production.

4. **Use Kanban Systems for Inventory Management:** Visual scheduling tools help track material flow and ensure just-in-time replenishment.

5. **Train Employees in Continuous Improvement:** Workers are encouraged to identify bottlenecks and propose efficiency improvements.

Application

- **Automotive Industry:** Toyota, Ford, and Honda use JIT to reduce excess inventory and optimize assembly line efficiency.

- **Retail & E-commerce:** Companies like **Zara** use JIT to produce and distribute fast fashion based on current trends, reducing unsold inventory.

- **Restaurants & Food Industry:** McDonald's and Starbucks prepare food and beverages only when ordered, ensuring freshness and reducing waste.

- **Technology & Electronics:** Dell uses JIT to build customized computers based on customer orders rather than pre-manufacturing large quantities.

- **Healthcare:** Hospitals and clinics use JIT to manage medical supplies efficiently, ensuring that critical items are available without overstocking.

Key Insights

1. **JIT Requires Strong Supplier Relationships:** Businesses need **reliable and responsive suppliers** to prevent production delays.

2. **Technology Enhances JIT Efficiency: AI, automation, and real-time tracking systems** help manage demand fluctuations.

3. **JIT is Best for Stable Demand Environments:** Industries with unpredictable demand may struggle with stock shortages under JIT.

4. **Risk of Supply Chain Disruptions:** Any delay in materials delivery can **halt production,** making JIT vulnerable to external disruptions.

5. **Continuous Monitoring & Improvement is Essential:** To maintain JIT efficiency, businesses must **regularly assess processes and make incremental improvements.**

Conclusion

The **Just-in-Time (JIT) Strategy** is a highly effective approach for minimizing waste, improving efficiency, and reducing inventory costs. When properly implemented, JIT enhances profitability by aligning production with actual demand. However, it requires **strong supplier coordination, real-time data tracking, and a commitment to continuous improvement** to maintain seamless operations. Businesses that successfully adopt JIT can gain a **competitive advantage through cost savings, increased responsiveness, and improved product quality.**

53. Six Sigma Strategy

Six Sigma Strategy: A Comprehensive Breakdown

Theory

The **Six Sigma Strategy** is a data-driven approach to improving business processes by minimizing errors, reducing variability, and enhancing efficiency. Originally developed by **Motorola in the 1980s**, Six Sigma focuses on **continuous quality improvement** through statistical analysis and problem-solving methodologies.

At its core, Six Sigma aims to **achieve near-perfection in business operations**, with a goal of **no more than 3.4 defects per million opportunities (DPMO)**. This level of precision ensures high product quality, increased efficiency, and better customer satisfaction.

Six Sigma follows two primary methodologies:

1. **DMAIC (Define, Measure, Analyse, Improve, Control):** Used for improving existing processes by identifying inefficiencies and implementing solutions.

2. **DMADV (Define, Measure, Analyse, Design, Verify):** Used for developing new processes or products that meet Six Sigma quality standards.

The strategy relies on **key roles within an organization,** including Six Sigma **Green Belts, Black Belts, and Master Black Belts**, who lead process improvement initiatives.

By applying Six Sigma, businesses can eliminate waste, standardize processes, and enhance profitability through **statistical analysis, process optimization, and customer-focused improvements.**

Example

A well-known example of Six Sigma in action is **General Electric (GE)** under the leadership of **Jack Welch** in the 1990s. GE implemented Six Sigma across all divisions, resulting in **$12 billion in savings over five years**, improved product quality, and increased operational efficiency.

Another example is **Amazon,** which applies Six Sigma techniques to optimize its supply chain, reduce shipping errors, and improve warehouse efficiency, ensuring fast and accurate order fulfilment.

Why It Works

1. **Reduces Defects & Errors:** By identifying and eliminating process variations, Six Sigma improves product and service quality.

2. **Enhances Customer Satisfaction:** Fewer defects lead to better reliability, increasing customer trust and loyalty.

3. **Improves Efficiency & Productivity:** Streamlined processes reduce waste, rework, and downtime.

4. **Data-Driven Decision Making:** Six Sigma relies on statistical analysis to implement measurable improvements rather than guesswork.

5. **Increases Profitability:** By reducing defects and improving efficiency, businesses lower costs and maximize revenue.

How It Works

1. **Define the Problem:** Identify a process that needs improvement and set clear objectives.

2. **Measure Performance:** Collect data to understand the current process and baseline performance.

3. **Analyse Root Causes:** Use statistical tools like **Fishbone Diagrams and Pareto Charts** to identify inefficiencies and defects.

4. **Implement Improvements:** Apply process changes, automation, or redesign to enhance efficiency and reduce errors.

5. **Control & Sustain Improvements:** Monitor performance and establish controls to maintain Six Sigma standards.

Application

- **Manufacturing:** Toyota and Ford use Six Sigma to minimize defects in automotive production.
- **Healthcare:** Hospitals apply Six Sigma to reduce medical errors and improve patient outcomes.
- **Finance & Banking:** Banks like Bank of America use Six Sigma to streamline loan processing and reduce transaction errors.
- **Retail & E-commerce:** Amazon applies Six Sigma to optimize inventory management and supply chain efficiency.
- **Telecommunications:** AT&T improves network reliability and customer service through Six Sigma methodologies.

Key Insights

1. **Six Sigma is a Long-Term Strategy:** It requires continuous monitoring and commitment from leadership to sustain improvements.
2. **Employee Training is Crucial:** Companies must invest in Six Sigma training for employees to successfully implement the methodology.
3. **Not Just for Manufacturing:** While Six Sigma originated in manufacturing, it is widely applicable across **service industries, healthcare, and IT.**

4. **Combining Six Sigma with Lean Principles Enhances Results:** Many businesses adopt **Lean Six Sigma**, integrating waste reduction with process optimization.

5. **Success Depends on Data & Execution:** Effective implementation relies on **accurate data collection, statistical analysis, and disciplined execution** rather than assumptions.

Conclusion

The **Six Sigma Strategy** is a proven methodology for **enhancing quality, reducing waste, and improving operational efficiency** across industries. By applying statistical analysis and structured problem-solving techniques, businesses can achieve **near-zero defects, increased customer satisfaction, and higher profitability**. Though Six Sigma requires rigorous implementation and training, its long-term benefits make it an invaluable strategy for companies committed to **continuous improvement and operational excellence**.

54. Outsourcing Strategy

Outsourcing Strategy: A Comprehensive Breakdown

Theory

The **Outsourcing Strategy** is a business approach where a company delegates certain functions, services, or processes to external vendors instead of handling them in-house. This strategy is often used to **reduce costs, improve efficiency, access specialized skills, and focus on core competencies**.

Outsourcing is rooted in the principles of **comparative advantage and cost efficiency**. Businesses leverage external expertise to **lower operational expenses, enhance service quality, and increase flexibility**. It allows organizations to allocate resources strategically while external providers handle non-core functions.

There are different types of outsourcing:

1. **Business Process Outsourcing (BPO):** Delegating back-office or customer-facing processes (e.g., HR, call centres).

2. **IT Outsourcing:** Contracting external vendors for software development, IT support, or cloud computing services.

3. **Manufacturing Outsourcing:** Using third-party manufacturers to produce goods (e.g., Apple outsourcing iPhone production to Foxconn).

4. **Knowledge Process Outsourcing (KPO):** Outsourcing high-value tasks like market research, data analytics, or financial consulting.

5. **Offshoring vs. Nearshoring vs. Onshoring:** Companies may outsource work overseas (offshoring), to nearby countries (nearshoring), or within their own country (onshoring) depending on costs and convenience.

By outsourcing, companies **gain access to global talent, reduce capital expenditures, and scale operations more effectively.** However, it also presents risks like loss of control, quality concerns, and potential security issues.

Example

A well-known example of outsourcing is **Apple's supply chain strategy.** Apple designs its products in-house but outsources manufacturing to companies like **Foxconn and TSMC**, which handle production at a lower cost and higher efficiency. This allows Apple to focus on product innovation and marketing rather than factory management.

Another example is **Netflix outsourcing its cloud infrastructure to Amazon Web Services (AWS).** Instead of maintaining its own data centres, Netflix uses AWS to **handle streaming services, data storage, and scalability**, enabling seamless global operations.

Why It Works

1. **Cost Reduction:** Outsourcing eliminates the need for large investments in infrastructure, labour, and technology.

2. **Focus on Core Competencies:** Companies can direct resources to innovation, strategy, and business growth instead of non-essential functions.

3. **Access to Specialized Skills:** External providers offer expertise that may not be available in-house.

4. **Scalability & Flexibility:** Businesses can quickly adjust operations based on demand fluctuations without hiring or firing employees.

5. **Increased Efficiency & Speed:** External firms often have optimized processes, leading to faster turnaround times and higher quality output.

How It Works

1. **Identify Functions to Outsource:** Companies determine which tasks can be delegated to external providers.

2. **Select a Reliable Vendor:** Businesses choose outsourcing partners based on cost, expertise, reputation, and scalability.

3. **Establish Clear Agreements:** Service-level agreements (SLAs) define quality expectations, timelines, and performance metrics.

4. **Integrate & Monitor Performance:** Companies implement communication tools and tracking systems to ensure quality control.

5. **Adapt & Optimize:** Continuous evaluation of outsourcing partnerships ensures alignment with business goals.

Application

- **Technology & IT:** Companies outsource software development, cybersecurity, and cloud management.
- **Manufacturing:** Automakers like **Tesla and BMW** outsource components production to suppliers.
- **Customer Support: Amazon and Microsoft** use BPO firms for call centres and technical support.
- **Finance & Accounting:** Many businesses outsource payroll, tax preparation, and financial auditing.
- **Healthcare:** Hospitals outsource medical billing, telehealth services, and data processing.

Key Insights

1. **Outsourcing Should Align with Business Goals:** Companies must evaluate which functions can be effectively outsourced without compromising quality.

2. **Vendor Selection is Critical:** The right outsourcing partner ensures reliability, efficiency, and alignment with company culture.

3. **Communication & Collaboration Are Essential:** Strong coordination between internal teams and external providers is key to success.

4. **Risk Management is Necessary:** Outsourcing can introduce security and compliance risks that must be carefully managed.

5. **Long-Term Strategy Matters:** Businesses should periodically reassess outsourcing arrangements to ensure continued cost savings and efficiency.

Conclusion

The **Outsourcing Strategy** is a powerful tool for businesses seeking **cost efficiency, specialized expertise, and operational flexibility**. When implemented correctly, it allows companies to **scale efficiently, focus on core strengths, and improve productivity.** However, outsourcing requires **careful vendor selection, strong management oversight, and risk mitigation strategies** to ensure long-term success.

55. Vertical Supply Chain Control Strategy

Vertical Supply Chain Control Strategy: A Comprehensive Breakdown

Theory

The **Vertical Supply Chain Control Strategy** refers to a business approach where a company **controls multiple stages of its supply chain**, from raw material sourcing to manufacturing, distribution, and retail. This strategy allows firms to **increase efficiency, reduce costs, and ensure quality control** throughout the production and distribution process.

Vertical supply chain control is based on **vertical integration**, which is categorized into two main types:

1. **Backward Integration:** A company takes control of its suppliers or raw materials (e.g., a car manufacturer acquiring a steel production company).

2. **Forward Integration:** A company gains control over distribution, retail, or after-sales service (e.g., a clothing brand opening its own stores instead of selling through third parties).

By implementing vertical control, businesses reduce their dependence on external suppliers and distributors, which helps **improve stability, manage costs, and protect proprietary processes or technology**. However, this strategy requires significant investment and operational expertise to manage various aspects of the supply chain effectively.

Example

A well-known example of vertical supply chain control is **Tesla**. Unlike traditional automakers that rely on third-party suppliers for key components, Tesla **manufactures its own batteries (via Gigafactories), develops proprietary software, and sells cars directly to consumers through its own stores.** This strategy allows Tesla to **control costs, optimize production, and enhance customer experience** while reducing reliance on external vendors.

Another example is **Apple**, which owns the hardware design, software development, chip production (Apple Silicon), and even operates its own retail stores. By controlling these aspects, Apple ensures **high product quality, seamless integration, and better profit margins**.

Why It Works

1. **Greater Control Over Quality & Production:** Companies can maintain strict standards across the entire supply chain.

2. **Cost Reduction in the Long Run:** Eliminating intermediaries reduces markups and improves profit margins.

3. **Increased Supply Chain Stability:** Reduced dependency on external suppliers minimizes risks from disruptions.

4. **Better Coordination & Efficiency:** A fully integrated supply chain streamlines logistics, inventory management, and production planning.

5. **Competitive Advantage:** Controlling the supply chain allows companies to innovate faster, protect proprietary technology, and differentiate from competitors.

How It Works

1. **Analyse the Current Supply Chain:** Businesses identify which stages of the supply chain they should control for better efficiency and cost savings.

2. **Invest in Infrastructure & Capabilities:** Companies acquire suppliers, open manufacturing plants, or establish direct distribution channels.

3. **Implement Advanced Supply Chain Management Systems:** AI and data analytics help optimize inventory, demand forecasting, and logistics.

4. **Enhance Supplier & Customer Relationships:** Direct control allows for better coordination with both raw material providers and end consumers.

5. **Continuously Improve & Expand Control:** Businesses refine processes and explore new areas for vertical integration over time.

Application

- **Automotive Industry:** Tesla and Ford control key parts of their supply chains, from battery production to vehicle sales.
- **Technology & Electronics:** Apple and Samsung develop components in-house instead of relying on third-party manufacturers.
- **Retail & E-commerce:** Amazon owns warehouses, delivery networks (Amazon Logistics), and cloud computing services (AWS).
- **Food & Beverage:** Starbucks sources its own coffee beans and operates its own cafes instead of using third-party retailers.
- **Fashion & Apparel:** Zara controls design, production, and retail through vertically integrated operations, allowing for fast fashion cycles.

Key Insights

1. **Vertical Integration Requires Large Capital Investment:** Businesses must be financially prepared for infrastructure, acquisitions, and operational costs.

2. **Not Every Business Needs Full Control:** Companies should evaluate which supply chain segments provide the highest value when integrated.

3. **Flexibility is Crucial:** Over-integration can limit a company's ability to adapt to market changes if it becomes too rigid.

4. **Technology Enhances Supply Chain Control:** AI, automation, and real-time data analytics improve efficiency and decision-making.

5. **Strategic Partnerships Can Complement Integration:** In some cases, selective outsourcing still plays a role while maintaining key supply chain control points.

Conclusion

The **Vertical Supply Chain Control Strategy** is a powerful approach for **enhancing efficiency, reducing costs, and gaining a competitive edge** by managing multiple supply chain stages. Companies like Tesla, Apple, and Amazon have demonstrated how controlling production and distribution can **improve profitability, increase quality assurance, and drive innovation**. However, businesses must weigh the **financial and operational complexities** before fully committing to this strategy.

56. Automation Strategy

Automation Strategy: A Comprehensive Breakdown

Theory

The **Automation Strategy** is a business approach that focuses on using **technology, software, and robotics** to streamline operations, reduce costs, and improve efficiency. Automation eliminates manual processes, reducing human intervention in repetitive or labour-intensive tasks, allowing businesses to focus on higher-value activities.

The strategy is based on **process optimization, artificial intelligence (AI), and machine learning (ML)** to improve accuracy, reduce errors, and enhance productivity. Automation can be categorized into:

1. **Robotic Process Automation (RPA):** Software bots perform repetitive tasks like data entry and transaction processing.

2. **Industrial Automation:** Machines and robotics automate manufacturing and assembly line operations.

3. **AI & Machine Learning:** Predictive algorithms help optimize decision-making, customer interactions, and supply chain logistics.

4. **Business Process Automation (BPA):** Automates administrative workflows such as HR onboarding, invoicing, and customer support.

By integrating automation, companies achieve **higher efficiency, lower operational costs, and improved accuracy** while freeing employees to focus on innovation and problem-solving.

Example

A leading example of automation is **Amazon's fulfilment centres**. Amazon uses **robotic arms, AI-driven warehouse management systems, and automated picking & packing robots** to handle inventory, reducing processing time and labour costs while increasing order accuracy.

Another example is **Tesla's Gigafactories**, where robotic automation assembles electric vehicle components with **minimal human intervention**, significantly reducing production time and defects.

Why It Works

1. **Increases Efficiency & Productivity:** Automated systems work faster and without breaks, significantly improving output.

2. **Reduces Human Error:** Software bots and AI-powered decision-making minimize mistakes, improving accuracy.

3. **Lowers Operational Costs:** Automation reduces labour costs, energy consumption, and material waste.

4. **Enhances Customer Experience:** AI-driven chatbots and automation in customer service ensure faster and more accurate responses.

5. **Scalability & Flexibility:** Businesses can scale operations without increasing workforce size, adapting quickly to demand fluctuations.

How It Works

1. **Identify Repetitive & High-Cost Processes:** Companies analyse operations to determine which tasks can be automated for maximum efficiency gains.

2. **Implement the Right Automation Tools:** Businesses deploy software bots, AI, or industrial robots based on process requirements.

3. **Integrate Automation with Existing Systems:** Ensuring compatibility with ERP, CRM, and other digital platforms optimizes workflow continuity.

4. **Monitor & Optimize Performance:** Continuous evaluation helps refine automation processes for efficiency improvements.

5. **Train Employees for Strategic Roles:** Workers transition from manual tasks to supervisory, analytical, or problem-solving roles.

Application

- **Retail & E-commerce:** Amazon and Walmart use warehouse automation and AI-driven recommendation engines.
- **Manufacturing:** Tesla and BMW automate car production with robotics and AI-driven quality control.
- **Finance & Banking:** JP Morgan and PayPal use AI for fraud detection and automated transaction processing.
- **Healthcare:** Hospitals automate patient records, diagnostics, and robotic-assisted surgeries.
- **Customer Service:** AI chatbots like **ChatGPT-powered assistants** handle customer inquiries efficiently.

Key Insights

1. **Automation Should Complement Human Labor:** Instead of replacing jobs, automation should enhance efficiency while employees handle creative or complex tasks.

2. **Security & Compliance Must Be Prioritized:** Businesses must ensure **data protection, cybersecurity, and regulatory compliance** when implementing automation.

3. **Automation Requires Continuous Optimization:** AI models, bots, and systems must be **regularly updated** to maintain accuracy and efficiency.

4. **Initial Investment Can Be High:** While automation reduces long-term costs, upfront expenses for technology and system integration can be significant.

5. **Not All Processes Should Be Automated:** Businesses must evaluate which tasks benefit most from automation while maintaining a balance with human oversight.

Conclusion

The **Automation Strategy** is a transformative approach that enables businesses to **streamline operations, reduce costs, and improve efficiency** through robotics, AI, and intelligent software. Companies like Amazon and Tesla have demonstrated how automation enhances scalability and accuracy while freeing human workers to focus on innovation. However, businesses must strategically implement automation to ensure **long-term sustainability, security, and seamless integration** with existing workflows.

57. Reshoring Strategy

Reshoring Strategy: A Comprehensive Breakdown

Theory

The **Reshoring Strategy** is a business approach where companies **bring back manufacturing, production, or services to their home country** after previously outsourcing them to foreign locations. This strategy is the opposite of offshoring and is often driven by factors like rising overseas labour costs, supply chain disruptions, quality control issues, and government incentives.

Reshoring aligns with **economic protectionism, supply chain risk management, and national economic policies** aimed at strengthening domestic industries. The key drivers of reshoring include:

1. **Increasing Labor Costs Abroad:** Wages in countries like China and India have risen, reducing the cost advantage of offshoring.

2. **Supply Chain Disruptions:** Global events like **COVID-19, geopolitical tensions, and shipping delays** have highlighted the vulnerabilities of relying on foreign supply chains.

3. **Quality & Innovation Control:** Companies can ensure **better product quality, intellectual property protection, and faster innovation cycles** when production is closer to home.

4. **Government Incentives & Tariffs:** Tax breaks, subsidies, and trade policies encourage companies to relocate operations domestically.

5. **Consumer & National Preference:** Many consumers prefer **"Made in [Home Country]"** products, boosting demand for locally produced goods.

By reshoring, businesses **reduce risk, improve supply chain resilience, and contribute to local job creation** while maintaining greater control over production.

Example

A key example of reshoring is **Apple's decision to shift some manufacturing back to the U.S.** While Apple still produces most of its devices in China, the company has invested in **chip manufacturing in Arizona** and **Mac assembly in Texas** to reduce dependence on overseas suppliers.

Another example is **General Electric (GE),** which moved appliance manufacturing from China and Mexico back to

Kentucky. This allowed GE to **reduce shipping costs, shorten lead times, and improve product quality** while supporting the U.S. economy.

Why It Works

1. **Reduces Supply Chain Risks:** Eliminates reliance on distant suppliers, reducing vulnerability to global disruptions.

2. **Enhances Quality Control:** Local production ensures stricter **oversight, better compliance with regulations, and faster issue resolution.**

3. **Improves Speed to Market:** Shorter supply chains allow businesses to **respond faster to demand changes and customization needs.**

4. **Boosts Brand Reputation:** Consumers favour businesses that **support local economies and jobs.**

5. **Capitalizes on Government Support:** Tax breaks, grants, and tariffs on imports make reshoring financially attractive.

How It Works

1. **Evaluate Total Costs & Risks of Offshoring:** Companies analyse expenses beyond labour, including **logistics, tariffs, quality control, and geopolitical risks.**

2. **Assess Domestic Infrastructure & Workforce:** Businesses must ensure they have the necessary **facilities, skilled labour, and automation technology** to support production.

3. **Implement Advanced Manufacturing Techniques:** Automation, AI, and robotics help **offset higher domestic labour costs** while improving efficiency.

4. **Redesign Supply Chain for Local Sourcing:** Businesses identify domestic suppliers to reduce dependency on foreign components.

5. **Leverage Government Incentives & Partnerships:** Companies work with policymakers to secure **tax incentives, grants, and subsidies** for reshoring.

Application

- **Automotive Industry: Ford and Tesla** reshored some manufacturing to improve supply chain resilience and meet **domestic EV production goals.**
- **Electronics: Intel and TSMC** are investing in **U.S. chip factories** to reduce reliance on Asian semiconductor supply chains.

- **Pharmaceuticals: Pfizer and Moderna** have expanded domestic production of vaccines and essential drugs.

- **Apparel & Retail: Nike and Adidas** are using **localized manufacturing and 3D printing** to produce goods closer to major markets.

- **Consumer Goods: GE and Whirlpool** moved home appliance manufacturing back to North America for **better quality control and logistics.**

Key Insights

1. **Reshoring is Not Just About Labor Costs:** Businesses must consider **automation, infrastructure, logistics, and government incentives** when evaluating reshoring feasibility.

2. **Technology Can Offset Higher Domestic Wages:** Investing in **AI, robotics, and lean manufacturing** makes domestic production competitive.

3. **Reshoring Requires Strong Supplier Networks:** Businesses need reliable **local sourcing options** to avoid dependence on foreign suppliers.

4. **Consumer Demand for Local Products is Rising:** Companies can **leverage "Made in [Home Country]" branding** to attract customers.

5. **Policy & Economic Conditions Matter:** Reshoring is most viable when supported by **government policies, stable**

labour markets, and advanced manufacturing ecosystems.

Conclusion

The **Reshoring Strategy** is a growing business trend driven by **supply chain resilience, quality control, and economic factors.** While it requires **investment in domestic manufacturing, workforce development, and technology adoption,** reshoring offers **long-term cost savings, risk reduction, and competitive advantages.** Companies that strategically implement reshoring can benefit from **greater control, faster innovation cycles, and stronger brand loyalty.**

58. Green Supply Chain Strategy

Green Supply Chain Strategy: A Comprehensive Breakdown

Theory

The **Green Supply Chain Strategy** is a business approach that integrates **environmentally sustainable practices** into supply chain management, from raw material sourcing to product disposal. This strategy focuses on **reducing carbon footprints, minimizing waste, optimizing resource efficiency, and ensuring compliance with environmental regulations.**

The strategy is built on the principles of **sustainability, circular economy, and corporate social responsibility (CSR).** Companies adopting this strategy aim to **reduce environmental impact while maintaining profitability and efficiency.**

Key elements of a green supply chain include:

1. **Sustainable Sourcing:** Procuring raw materials from eco-friendly and ethical suppliers.

2. **Energy Efficiency:** Using renewable energy and optimizing production processes to reduce emissions.

3. **Eco-Friendly Logistics:** Implementing low-emission transportation and smart distribution networks.

4. **Waste Reduction & Recycling:** Adopting a **circular economy approach**, where waste is minimized, and materials are reused.

5. **Green Packaging:** Reducing plastic use and shifting to biodegradable or recyclable materials.

6. **Compliance with Environmental Regulations:** Adhering to sustainability laws and industry standards.

By implementing a **Green Supply Chain Strategy**, businesses not only **reduce environmental harm** but also enhance **brand reputation, comply with regulations, and improve long-term cost efficiency.**

Example

A leading example of a green supply chain strategy is **Patagonia**, the outdoor apparel company. Patagonia has committed to **sustainable material sourcing, reducing carbon emissions, and implementing a circular economy approach** through its **Worn Wear program**, which encourages customers to repair and reuse clothing instead of discarding it.

Another example is **Tesla**, which has integrated a **low-carbon supply chain by producing electric vehicles (EVs), using solar** energy, and sourcing sustainable battery materials to minimize environmental impact. Tesla's supply chain focuses on **reducing emissions, recycling batteries, and improving energy efficiency in manufacturing.**

Why It Works

1. **Regulatory Compliance:** Governments worldwide are enforcing stricter environmental laws, and green supply chains ensure compliance, avoiding legal penalties.

2. **Cost Savings in the Long Run:** Energy-efficient production and waste reduction lead to **lower operational costs over time.**

3. **Enhanced Brand Image & Customer Loyalty:** Consumers are increasingly choosing **eco-conscious brands**, leading to stronger brand reputation and market preference.

4. **Risk Mitigation:** Reducing reliance on **non-renewable resources and polluting practices** minimizes exposure to future regulatory and economic risks.

5. **Competitive Advantage:** Companies with sustainable supply chains attract **eco-conscious investors, partners, and consumers.**

How It Works

1. **Assess Current Supply Chain Impact:** Businesses evaluate their **carbon footprint, energy consumption, and waste generation.**

2. **Adopt Sustainable Procurement Practices:** Sourcing raw materials from **certified sustainable and ethical suppliers.**

3. **Invest in Energy-Efficient Technologies:** Implementing **renewable energy, AI-driven logistics, and smart manufacturing** to reduce emissions.

4. **Optimize Transportation & Logistics:** Using **electric vehicles, biofuels, and efficient routing systems** to minimize environmental impact.

5. **Encourage Recycling & Reusability:** Implementing a **closed-loop supply chain** where materials are reused or upcycled.

6. **Monitor & Improve Performance:** Tracking sustainability metrics and continuously improving processes to enhance green initiatives.

Application

- **Retail & Fashion:** Patagonia and H&M use recycled materials and promote circular fashion.

- **Automotive Industry:** Tesla and Toyota develop **low-emission vehicles and sustainable production systems.**

- **Food & Beverage:** Starbucks and Nestlé invest in **ethical sourcing, sustainable packaging, and carbon reduction initiatives.**

- **Technology & Electronics:** Apple uses **recycled aluminium and carbon-neutral suppliers** in product manufacturing.

- **Logistics & Shipping:** Companies like **DHL and UPS** invest in electric fleets and carbon-neutral shipping.

Key Insights

1. **Sustainability is No Longer Optional:** Regulatory, consumer, and investor pressure is pushing businesses toward **eco-friendly supply chains.**

2. **Technology Enhances Green Supply Chains:** AI, blockchain, and IoT improve **energy efficiency, tracking, and waste reduction.**

3. **Collaboration with Suppliers is Critical:** Businesses must work with **eco-conscious vendors** to achieve sustainability goals.

4. **Cost Savings Come Over Time:** While initial investments in green supply chains can be high, **long-term savings in energy and waste reduction** outweigh the costs.

5. **Consumer Preferences Are Shifting:** Eco-conscious consumers are willing to **pay a premium for sustainable products,** driving demand for green supply chains.

Conclusion

The **Green Supply Chain Strategy** is a **sustainable, cost-effective, and forward-thinking** approach to business operations. By integrating **environmental responsibility into procurement, production, and logistics**, companies can **reduce waste, comply with regulations, and strengthen brand reputation**. While transitioning to a **fully green supply chain requires investment and planning**, the **long-term benefits—lower costs, risk reduction, and stronger customer loyalty—make it a vital strategy for future success.

59. Agile Manufacturing Strategy

Agile Manufacturing Strategy: A Comprehensive Breakdown

Theory

The **Agile Manufacturing Strategy** is a business approach that focuses on **flexibility, speed, and adaptability** in production processes to quickly respond to changing market demands. Unlike traditional manufacturing, which relies on rigid systems and economies of scale, agile manufacturing emphasizes **customization, rapid innovation, and lean operations** to maintain a competitive edge.

Agile manufacturing is rooted in **lean production, just-in-time (JIT) principles, and digital transformation**. It integrates **automation, artificial intelligence (AI), cloud computing, and real-time data analytics** to optimize supply chain management and production efficiency.

Key characteristics of agile manufacturing include:

1. **Customer-Centric Approach:** Rapidly adjusting production to meet specific customer needs and market shifts.

2. **Flexibility & Adaptability:** Quick reconfiguration of production lines and supply chains in response to demand fluctuations.

3. **Technology Integration:** Using **IoT, AI, robotics, and cloud-based systems** to enhance efficiency and decision-making.

4. **Collaboration Across Networks:** Working closely with suppliers, partners, and even competitors to drive innovation and responsiveness.

5. **Lean & Waste Reduction:** Minimizing waste and inefficiencies while maintaining high product quality.

Agile manufacturing allows companies to **respond swiftly to disruptions, launch new products faster, and maintain competitive advantages in dynamic industries.**

Example

A leading example of agile manufacturing is **Tesla**. Unlike traditional automakers, Tesla continuously updates its vehicle software **over-the-air (OTA)** and quickly reconfigures production lines to adapt to **market trends and supply chain challenges**. During the global chip shortage, Tesla adjusted its software to use **alternative semiconductors**, demonstrating agility in manufacturing.

Another example is **Zara**, the fast-fashion retailer that **designs, produces, and distributes new clothing styles within weeks** based on real-time consumer demand. By using **small-batch production and local manufacturing**, Zara avoids overproduction and quickly adapts to changing fashion trends.

Why It Works

1. **Faster Response to Market Changes:** Companies can pivot quickly to meet evolving consumer demands.

2. **Reduced Lead Times:** Agile systems enable faster production cycles, ensuring products reach customers sooner.

3. **Minimized Inventory Costs:** Just-in-time production reduces excess stock and storage costs.

4. **Enhanced Customization & Innovation:** Companies can offer personalized products and implement new technologies faster.

5. **Competitive Advantage in Uncertain Markets:** Agility allows businesses to adapt to economic disruptions, supply chain issues, and technological advancements.

How It Works

1. **Adopt Digital Technologies:** Businesses implement **IoT sensors, AI-driven analytics, and automation** to enhance production agility.

2. **Develop Modular & Flexible Production Lines:** Equipment and processes are designed to be **easily reconfigurable** for different product variations.

3. **Implement Cross-Functional Teams:** Employees work in **collaborative, adaptable teams** to improve innovation and efficiency.

4. **Use Data-Driven Decision-Making:** AI and cloud computing help analyse **real-time demand trends** for better production planning.

5. **Collaborate with Suppliers & Customers:** Agile businesses work closely with **partners and consumers** to forecast demand and reduce waste.

Application

- **Automotive Industry: Tesla and Toyota** use agile principles for **rapid software updates and adaptable supply chains.**

- **Fast Fashion: Zara and H&M** leverage **real-time demand tracking and quick production cycles.**

- **Electronics & Tech: Apple and Dell** use **modular design and just-in-time manufacturing** to adjust production based on new technology trends.

- **Aerospace & Defence: Boeing and SpaceX** apply agile methods to **optimize aircraft and spacecraft manufacturing.**

- **Pharmaceuticals: Pfizer and Moderna** adapted quickly during the COVID-19 pandemic to **accelerate vaccine production.**

Key Insights

1. **Agility is Not Just Speed—It's Smart Adaptability:** Companies must balance **fast production with strategic decision-making.**

2. **Technology is the Backbone of Agile Manufacturing:** Businesses that **embrace AI, automation, and IoT** gain a significant edge.

3. **Cross-Functional Collaboration is Essential:** Agile manufacturing **breaks down silos** and fosters teamwork across departments.

4. **Agility Requires a Culture of Continuous Improvement:** Employees must be trained in **adaptability, problem-solving, and lean methodologies.**

5. **Supply Chain Flexibility is Key:** Companies must develop **strong supplier relationships** and **diverse sourcing strategies** to minimize disruptions.

Conclusion

The **Agile Manufacturing Strategy** is a game-changing approach that enables companies to **stay ahead in fast-changing industries.** By leveraging **digital technology, lean processes, and flexible production systems,** businesses can **respond faster, reduce waste, and enhance customization.** However, true agility requires **investment in innovation, strong leadership, and a company-wide commitment to adaptability and efficiency.**

60. Vendor-Managed Inventory (VMI) Strategy

Vendor-Managed Inventory (VMI) Strategy: A Comprehensive Breakdown

Theory

The **Vendor-Managed Inventory (VMI) Strategy** is a supply chain management approach in which the **supplier (vendor) is responsible for managing inventory levels at the customer's location.** Instead of the customer placing orders, the vendor monitors stock levels and replenishes inventory as needed. This strategy aims to **reduce stockouts, minimize holding costs, and improve supply chain efficiency.**

VMI is based on **collaborative supply chain management and demand forecasting**, where both parties share real-time data for better inventory optimization. By shifting inventory control to the vendor, businesses can focus on **core operations while ensuring a steady supply of products.**

Key components of VMI include:

1. **Data Sharing & Transparency:** Vendors access **real-time inventory data** from the customer's warehouse or store.
2. **Demand Forecasting & Replenishment:** The vendor predicts **future demand** and restocks inventory **before shortages occur.**
3. **Automated Ordering Systems:** Inventory is **automatically replenished** based on usage patterns and sales data.
4. **Reduced Inventory Holding Costs:** Customers maintain **lower safety stock levels** while ensuring consistent product availability.
5. **Strengthened Vendor-Customer Relationships:** Long-term collaboration leads to better efficiency and cost savings for both parties.

By implementing VMI, businesses achieve **leaner supply chains, lower inventory risks, and improved customer satisfaction.**

Example

A well-known example of **VMI in action** is **Walmart's partnership with Procter & Gamble (P&G).** Instead of Walmart placing orders, P&G **monitors inventory levels in Walmart's warehouses and automatically replenishes stock.** This approach ensures **on-**

time product availability, reduces excess inventory, and minimizes logistics costs.

Another example is **Boeing and its aircraft parts suppliers.** Boeing uses VMI to ensure critical parts are **always available** for production without maintaining excessive stock, improving efficiency in the aerospace industry.

Why It Works

1. **Minimizes Stockouts & Overstocking:** Vendors replenish inventory based on **real-time demand**, ensuring optimal stock levels.

2. **Reduces Administrative Burden:** Customers **no longer need to manage inventory orders manually**, saving time and effort.

3. **Lowers Holding & Warehousing Costs:** Companies maintain **leaner inventories** while ensuring uninterrupted supply.

4. **Improves Forecast Accuracy:** Vendors use **AI-driven analytics and historical data** to anticipate demand fluctuations.

5. **Strengthens Supplier-Customer Collaboration:** VMI builds long-term partnerships, leading to **better pricing and service agreements.**

How It Works

1. **Establish a VMI Agreement:** Vendor and customer define roles, inventory thresholds, and data-sharing protocols.

2. **Integrate Data-Sharing Technology:** Businesses use **ERP (Enterprise Resource Planning) or cloud-based inventory management systems** to enable real-time visibility.

3. **Monitor Inventory & Sales Data:** The vendor tracks inventory usage and **predicts restocking needs** based on demand trends.

4. **Automate Inventory Replenishment:** The system automatically **places restocking orders** when stock levels fall below a predefined threshold.

5. **Continuously Optimize Supply Chain:** Businesses refine inventory policies based on **historical data, seasonal trends, and market fluctuations.**

Application

- **Retail & Consumer Goods:** Walmart and Target use VMI to ensure steady product supply from major brands.

- **Manufacturing & Automotive:** Toyota and Ford implement VMI to **streamline parts procurement for just-in-time (JIT) production.**

- **Pharmaceuticals & Healthcare:** Hospitals and pharmacies use VMI to **maintain critical medical supplies and reduce expiration-related waste.**

- **Electronics & Technology:** Companies like Dell and HP rely on VMI for **timely component replenishment without excess stock.**

- **Food & Beverage:** McDonald's uses VMI to **manage perishable inventory and prevent supply shortages.**

Key Insights

1. **VMI Enhances Supply Chain Efficiency:** Real-time monitoring and automated replenishment **reduce delays and disruptions.**

2. **Technology is a Key Enabler:** Cloud-based inventory management and **AI-driven forecasting** improve VMI accuracy.

3. **Not Suitable for Every Business:** VMI works best in industries with **predictable demand and strong vendor partnerships.**

4. **Requires Trust & Collaboration:** Both the customer and vendor must **align their goals, share data transparently, and commit to mutual success.**

5. **Can Be a Competitive Advantage:** Companies that implement VMI effectively gain **cost savings, improved service levels, and stronger supplier relationships.**

Conclusion

The **Vendor-Managed Inventory (VMI) Strategy** is a powerful tool for businesses looking to **optimize inventory management, reduce costs, and improve supply chain responsiveness.** By leveraging **real-time data, automated replenishment, and strategic partnerships,** companies can maintain **leaner, more efficient operations** while ensuring product availability. However, successful implementation requires **collaboration, trust, and investment in the right technology.** Businesses that adopt VMI effectively can achieve **greater efficiency, lower costs, and a stronger competitive edge in their industry.**

Financial & Investment Strategies, Managing money to maximize growth and profitability:

61. Bootstrapping Strategy

Bootstrapping Strategy: A Comprehensive Breakdown

Theory

The **Bootstrapping Strategy** is a business approach where entrepreneurs build and grow their company **without external funding** from investors or venture capitalists. Instead, they rely on **personal savings, revenue generation, reinvested profits, and cost-cutting measures** to sustain operations and scale the business.

Bootstrapping is based on the principles of **financial discipline, resource efficiency, and organic growth**. Businesses that adopt this strategy aim to **minimize debt, maintain control, and achieve self-sufficiency** without diluting ownership.

Key characteristics of bootstrapping include:

1. **Self-Funding:** Founders use their personal funds or reinvest early profits into the business.

2. **Lean Operations:** Companies prioritize **low-cost strategies, automation, and streamlined workflows** to maximize efficiency.

3. **Customer-Funded Growth:** Revenue from early customers sustains and expands the business.

4. **Profit Reinvestment:** Profits are reinvested instead of seeking external capital.

5. **Gradual Scaling:** Growth is **steady and sustainable**, avoiding rapid expansion that requires heavy investment.

By bootstrapping, businesses **maintain financial independence and flexibility** while proving their viability before seeking external funding (if needed).

Example

A well-known example of bootstrapping is **Mailchimp**. The email marketing platform was **fully self-funded** for years, relying on **customer revenue and reinvested profits** rather than venture capital. By maintaining financial independence, Mailchimp scaled organically and was eventually acquired by **Intuit for $12 billion in 2021**, proving the power of bootstrapping.

Another example is **Spanx**, founded by Sara Blakely with just $5,000 in personal savings. She grew the business without outside funding, and it later became a **billion-dollar company**, demonstrating how disciplined spending and customer-driven growth can lead to massive success.

Why It Works

1. **Full Ownership & Control:** Founders retain **100% equity**, avoiding dilution from investors or shareholders.

2. **Encourages Financial Discipline:** Companies learn to **operate lean, minimize waste, and prioritize efficiency** from the start.

3. **Customer-Focused Growth:** Businesses are driven by **customer needs and revenue**, rather than investor expectations.

4. **Less Risk of Debt & External Pressure:** Without loans or investor funding, businesses **avoid high-interest obligations and external influence.**

5. **Stronger Long-Term Sustainability:** Bootstrapped businesses tend to have **solid financial foundations, reducing dependency on external capital.**

How It Works

1. **Start with Personal Funds:** Entrepreneurs invest their **own money and resources** to launch the business.

2. **Generate Revenue Quickly:** The focus is on **early sales, cash flow management, and rapid customer acquisition.**

3. **Keep Costs Low:** Businesses **minimize expenses, leverage free tools, and outsource strategically** to save money.

4. **Reinvest Profits for Growth:** Instead of seeking external funding, **profits are reinvested into product development, marketing, and scaling.**

5. **Leverage Partnerships & Barter Systems:** Entrepreneurs collaborate with **other businesses, trade services, and use sweat equity** to minimize costs.

Application

- **Technology & SaaS:** Mailchimp, Basecamp, and Zoho scaled through customer-funded models without VC backing.

- **Retail & E-commerce:** Spanx and Gymshark bootstrapped through **low-cost marketing and direct-to-consumer (DTC) strategies.**

- **Consulting & Freelancing:** Independent agencies and personal brands grow organically by **offering services before scaling into products.**

- **Content Creation & Digital Businesses:** Bloggers, YouTubers, and online educators bootstrap by monetizing **ads, subscriptions, and sponsorships.**
- **Manufacturing & Physical Products:** Small brands use **pre-orders, crowdfunding, or minimal inventory models** to self-fund production.

Key Insights

1. **Bootstrapping is a Long-Term Strategy:** Growth is **slower but more sustainable** compared to VC-backed startups.
2. **Profitability is Prioritized Over Growth:** Bootstrapped companies focus on **cash flow and profitability**, rather than rapid expansion.
3. **Creativity & Resourcefulness Are Essential:** Founders must **find low-cost marketing strategies, partnerships, and automation tools** to scale efficiently.
4. **Bootstrapping Requires Financial Discipline:** Companies must **control spending, reinvest wisely, and optimize revenue streams.**
5. **Not Every Business Needs VC Funding:** Many successful companies prove that **self-funded businesses can achieve billion-dollar valuations.**

Conclusion

The **Bootstrapping Strategy** is an effective way to build a business **independently, efficiently, and sustainably** without relying on external investors. Companies that master **lean operations, customer-driven growth, and smart financial management** can achieve **long-term success while maintaining full ownership.** While bootstrapping requires patience and discipline, its rewards—**financial independence, control, and long-term profitability—**make it a powerful business strategy.

62. Venture Capital Strategy

Venture Capital Strategy: A Comprehensive Breakdown

Theory

The **Venture Capital (VC) Strategy** is a business approach where startups and high-growth companies secure funding from **venture capital firms, angel investors, or private equity groups** in exchange for equity (ownership stake). This strategy is commonly used by **technology startups, biotech firms, and innovative businesses** that require substantial capital to scale rapidly but may not yet be profitable.

Venture capital investment follows a structured process:

1. **Seed Stage:** Early-stage funding used for **product development and market research.**

2. **Series A & B Rounds:** Funding to **expand operations, acquire customers, and refine the business model.**

3. **Series C & Beyond:** Investment for **scaling, market expansion, and preparing for an IPO or acquisition.**

4. **Exit Strategy:** VC firms seek a return on investment (ROI) through an **initial public offering (IPO), acquisition, or buyout.**

The **VC model operates on high-risk, high-reward principles.** Investors fund multiple startups, expecting **only a few to succeed significantly** and generate massive returns. In exchange for capital, VC firms typically **influence strategic decisions, offer mentorship, and help businesses scale.**

Example

A famous example of venture capital success is **Uber**, which received early funding from **Benchmark Capital and Sequoia Capital.** These VC firms provided millions in funding during Uber's early growth stages, enabling the company to expand globally. Uber eventually went public in **2019 with a $75 billion valuation**, generating significant returns for its investors.

Another example is **Airbnb**, which secured venture capital funding from **Greylock Partners and Andreessen Horowitz.** This allowed the company to expand globally, enhance its platform, and dominate the short-term rental market before its **2020 IPO.**

Why It Works

1. **Provides Large-Scale Funding:** Startups access **substantial capital without immediate repayment obligations,** unlike traditional loans.

2. **Accelerates Growth:** VC-backed businesses **expand faster, hire top talent, and develop technology more efficiently.**

3. **Brings Strategic Expertise:** Investors offer **mentorship, industry connections, and operational guidance** to improve success chances.

4. **Increases Market Credibility:** Securing VC funding signals **strong growth potential, attracting more customers and partners.**

5. **Enables Innovation:** High-risk industries like **AI, biotech, and fintech** benefit from VC funding to develop cutting-edge solutions.

How It Works

1. **Identify & Pitch to Investors:** Startups create a compelling **business plan, pitch deck, and financial projections** to attract investors.

2. **Negotiate Terms & Equity Share:** Venture capital firms provide funding in exchange for **a percentage of ownership and decision-making influence.**

3. **Deploy Capital for Growth:** The startup uses funds for **product development, hiring, marketing, and global expansion.**

4. **Achieve Growth Milestones:** Companies must meet **key performance indicators (KPIs) and revenue targets** to secure additional funding rounds.

5. **Exit Strategy Execution:** Investors realize profits through an **IPO, acquisition, or secondary stock sale.**

Application

- **Technology & SaaS:** Companies like **Facebook, Google, and Zoom** were VC-backed before becoming industry giants.

- **Biotech & Healthcare:** Firms like **Moderna and BioNTech** received VC funding to develop breakthrough medical innovations.

- **E-commerce & Retail: Amazon and Shopify** leveraged venture capital to expand operations early on.

- **Fintech & AI:** Startups like **Stripe and OpenAI** secure venture capital to develop advanced financial and artificial intelligence solutions.

- **Consumer Goods: Warby Parker and Allbirds** used VC funding to scale their direct-to-consumer (DTC) brands.

Key Insights

1. **Venture Capital is for High-Growth Companies:** Only **scalable, innovative, and disruptive** startups attract VC funding.

2. **Equity Dilution is a Tradeoff:** Founders give up ownership, but in return, gain **capital, mentorship, and market access.**

3. **VC Funding Comes with Expectations:** Investors demand **rapid growth, profitability milestones, and an exit strategy.**

4. **Competition for Funding is Intense:** Only a **small percentage of startups** secure venture capital, requiring a strong pitch and business model.

5. **VC Firms Prioritize ROI:** Investors look for **10x+ returns**, meaning startups must prove **market demand and scalability potential.**

Conclusion

The **Venture Capital Strategy** is a powerful funding method for startups that need **large-scale capital, strategic guidance, and rapid market expansion.** While it enables **high growth, innovation, and industry dominance,** it also requires **founders to relinquish equity and meet aggressive performance targets.** Companies that successfully leverage VC funding can become **industry leaders, disrupt traditional markets, and achieve billion-dollar valuations.**

63. Private Equity Strategy

Private Equity Strategy: A Comprehensive Breakdown

Theory

The **Private Equity (PE) Strategy** is a business approach where investment firms acquire, restructure, and manage companies to **increase their value before selling them for a profit.** Private equity firms raise capital from **institutional investors, pension funds, high-net-worth individuals, and endowments** to fund these acquisitions.

Private equity investments typically focus on **mature businesses** with potential for **growth, operational improvements, or financial restructuring.** Unlike venture capital (which funds startups), private equity targets **established companies** in need of capital infusion, efficiency improvements, or strategic direction.

There are several types of **private equity investments**:

1. **Leveraged Buyouts (LBOs):** Using a mix of debt and equity to acquire a company, then restructuring it to improve profitability before selling it.
2. **Growth Equity:** Investing in fast-growing companies that need capital to expand without losing control.
3. **Distressed Investments:** Acquiring companies in financial trouble, restructuring them, and turning them profitable.
4. **Management Buyouts (MBOs):** Investing in companies where existing management takes ownership with PE funding.
5. **Secondary Buyouts:** One PE firm sells a company to another PE firm instead of taking it public.

Private equity firms typically **hold investments for 3-7 years**, implementing strategic changes before exiting through an **initial public offering (IPO), merger, or resale to another investor.**

Example

A notable example of private equity success is **Blackstone Group's acquisition of Hilton Hotels in 2007.** Blackstone acquired Hilton for **$26 billion in a leveraged buyout (LBO),** improved its operations, expanded its global footprint, and **took it public in 2013**, generating billions in profit.

Another example is **3G Capital and Berkshire Hathaway's acquisition of Kraft Heinz.** The firms restructured the company, cut operational costs, and optimized supply chain management to **maximize shareholder value.**

Why It Works

1. **Drives Business Efficiency:** PE firms restructure companies by **cutting costs, streamlining operations, and improving management.**

2. **Access to Large Capital Pools:** PE firms use **both investor funds and debt financing** to acquire businesses and maximize returns.

3. **Focus on Value Creation:** Unlike public companies focused on short-term earnings, PE firms take **long-term strategic actions** to enhance company value.

4. **Stronger Governance & Leadership:** PE-backed companies benefit from **experienced management teams and industry experts.**

5. **High Return Potential:** Successful PE deals generate **significant ROI for investors**, often far higher than traditional stock market investments.

How It Works

1. **Identify Target Companies:** PE firms look for businesses with **growth potential, operational inefficiencies, or undervalued assets.**

2. **Acquire the Company (LBO or Equity Investment):** The firm purchases the company, often using **debt financing.**

3. **Implement Value-Enhancing Strategies:** PE firms improve **efficiency, profitability, and competitive positioning.**

4. **Grow or Restructure the Business:** Depending on the investment type, companies **expand, optimize, or undergo financial restructuring.**

5. **Exit Strategy Execution:** The firm sells the company via an **IPO, merger, acquisition, or secondary buyout, realizing profits.**

Application

- **Retail & Consumer Goods: 3G Capital's buyout of Kraft Heinz** streamlined operations and enhanced profitability.

- **Technology & Software: Silver Lake Partners' investment in Dell Technologies** enabled expansion and digital transformation.

- **Healthcare & Pharmaceuticals: TPG Capital and KKR's investment in Biotech firms** accelerated growth and R&D.

- **Manufacturing & Industrial Firms: Carlyle Group's restructuring of manufacturing businesses** improved cost efficiency.

- **Real Estate & Hospitality: Blackstone's real estate acquisitions** transformed undervalued properties into high-value assets.

Key Insights

1. **PE Focuses on Transforming Businesses:** Unlike venture capital, private equity works with **established companies needing efficiency improvements or restructuring.**

2. **Debt Plays a Key Role in LBOs:** PE firms leverage **debt financing to maximize returns**, but this can increase financial risk.

3. **Exiting at the Right Time is Crucial:** Successful PE firms know **when to sell a business to maximize profits.**

4. **Strong Management is a Competitive Advantage:** The best PE deals **install experienced leadership teams** to drive transformation.

5. **Risk is High, but Rewards Are Higher:** PE firms take **calculated risks** and expect **high returns over a multi-year investment horizon.**

Conclusion

The **Private Equity Strategy** is a powerful investment model that **acquires, restructures, and enhances businesses** for long-term value creation. By leveraging **debt financing, operational improvements, and strategic leadership,** PE firms generate

significant returns for investors. While the strategy carries **financial risk, its potential for high growth, strong governance, and transformative impact** makes it a cornerstone of modern investment and corporate growth.

64. Crowdfunding Strategy

Crowdfunding Strategy: A Comprehensive Breakdown

Theory

The **Crowdfunding Strategy** is a business approach where entrepreneurs, startups, or creative projects raise capital from a large group of individuals, typically via online platforms. Instead of seeking funding from venture capitalists or banks, businesses **leverage public interest and small contributions** from a wide audience.

Crowdfunding is based on the principle of **democratized finance**, allowing businesses and individuals to secure funding by offering **rewards, equity, or early access to products/services.**

There are four main types of crowdfunding:

1. **Reward-Based Crowdfunding:** Backers receive a product, service, or exclusive perks (e.g., Kickstarter, Indiegogo).

2. **Equity Crowdfunding:** Investors receive **shares or ownership stakes** in the company (e.g., Crowdcube, Seedrs).

3. **Debt Crowdfunding (Peer-to-Peer Lending):** Individuals lend money to businesses **with an agreement for repayment** (e.g., Funding Circle, LendingClub).

4. **Donation-Based Crowdfunding:** Supporters contribute without expecting anything in return (e.g., GoFundMe for social causes).

Crowdfunding is particularly effective for **startups, creative projects, social enterprises, and early-stage product launches** that require capital but lack access to traditional funding sources.

Example

A notable example of crowdfunding success is **Oculus Rift** (a VR headset), which raised **$2.4 million on Kickstarter in 2012** before being acquired by Facebook for **$2 billion in 2014.** The campaign generated massive public interest, validated demand, and attracted larger investors.

Another example is **Pebble Smartwatch**, which raised over **$20 million on Kickstarter**, proving there was strong market demand before mass production.

Why It Works

1. **Provides Access to Capital Without Debt:** Businesses can secure funding **without taking loans or giving up control.**

2. **Validates Market Demand:** If people are willing to pre-order or invest, it confirms that **the product has market potential.**

3. **Creates Early Brand Advocates:** Backers often become **loyal customers and promoters** of the brand.

4. **Generates Publicity & Awareness:** Crowdfunding campaigns create **buzz, media coverage, and word-of-mouth marketing.**

5. **Engages the Community:** Businesses build a **direct relationship with customers and investors,** increasing trust and engagement.

How It Works

1. **Choose a Crowdfunding Platform:** Businesses select **Kickstarter, Indiegogo, GoFundMe, or equity-based platforms** based on their needs.

2. **Create a Compelling Campaign:** A successful campaign includes a **clear value proposition, engaging storytelling, a strong pitch video, and attractive rewards or investment terms.**

3. **Set a Funding Goal & Timeline:** Campaigns define how much money they need and set a deadline for contributions.

4. **Promote the Campaign:** Businesses use **social media, email marketing, PR, and influencer partnerships** to reach potential backers.

5. **Engage & Update Supporters:** Regular communication with backers **maintains trust, excitement, and credibility.**

6. **Deliver Promises & Scale:** Once funded, businesses must fulfil **rewards, manufacture products, or execute the funded project.**

Application

- **Tech Startups:** Pebble, Oculus Rift, and Coolest Cooler launched innovative products via crowdfunding.

- **Creative & Arts Projects:** Filmmakers, musicians, and artists use crowdfunding to **fund creative work (e.g., Veronica Mars movie, independent albums).**

- **Social Enterprises & Nonprofits:** Charities and impact-driven businesses raise funds for **social causes (e.g., TOMS Shoes, charity water).**

- **E-commerce & Consumer Products:** Brands use crowdfunding to test **new product demand before full-scale production.**

- **Gaming Industry:** Video game developers **pre-sell games via crowdfunding**, reducing financial risk.

Key Insights

1. **Crowdfunding is More Than Just Fundraising:** It helps validate ideas, build brand loyalty, and generate market buzz.

2. **Marketing & Storytelling Are Critical:** A successful campaign requires **a strong narrative, engaging visuals, and emotional appeal.**

3. **Not All Campaigns Succeed:** Many crowdfunding efforts **fail due to poor planning, weak promotion, or unrealistic funding goals.**

4. **Regulatory Considerations for Equity Crowdfunding:** Businesses must **comply with investment laws and financial regulations** when offering equity.

5. **Crowdfunding Can Attract Bigger Investors:** Successful campaigns often **catch the attention of venture capitalists, angel investors, and corporate buyers.**

Conclusion

The **Crowdfunding Strategy** is an innovative way for **startups, creators, and social enterprises to raise capital, validate ideas, and build a loyal customer base.** By leveraging online platforms, storytelling, and community engagement, businesses can **secure funding without traditional financial barriers.** However, success requires **careful planning, compelling marketing, and transparent execution** to deliver on promises and maintain credibility.

65. Leveraging Strategy

Leveraging Strategy: A Comprehensive Breakdown

Theory

The **Leveraging Strategy** is a business approach that involves using existing assets, resources, or external factors to amplify growth, increase profitability, or gain a competitive advantage. Companies apply leverage in various forms, such as **financial leverage, operational leverage, and strategic partnerships**, to maximize returns while minimizing investment.

There are three primary types of leverage:

1. **Financial Leverage:** Using debt (loans, bonds, or credit) to expand operations, acquire assets, or invest in growth opportunities.

2. **Operational Leverage:** Maximizing fixed costs to drive profitability; for example, investing in technology to increase efficiency and reduce variable costs.
3. **Strategic Leverage:** Utilizing partnerships, intellectual property, brand strength, or customer networks to scale without significant capital investment.

By applying leverage, businesses can **achieve exponential growth, improve efficiency, and enhance profitability** while **reducing the need for extensive upfront investment.** However, excessive leverage, particularly in financial contexts, can also lead to **higher risk, debt accumulation, and market vulnerability.**

Example

A classic example of leveraging strategy is **Tesla's use of financial leverage and strategic partnerships**. Tesla secured **government subsidies and loans** to fund R&D and expand production facilities. Additionally, Tesla leveraged **battery technology partnerships (e.g., Panasonic) and carbon credit sales** to increase profitability without traditional advertising costs.

Another example is **Amazon**, which leveraged its **logistics infrastructure and cloud computing capabilities (AWS)** to expand beyond e-commerce into **enterprise cloud services, AI, and logistics solutions** while using minimal external investment.

Why It Works

1. **Maximizes Growth Potential:** Businesses can **expand operations, invest in new markets, and scale faster** without using only their own capital.

2. **Enhances Competitive Advantage:** Leveraging **brand reputation, technology, or partnerships** allows businesses to stay ahead of competitors.

3. **Improves Efficiency & Profitability:** Companies use **fixed assets, automation, or operational enhancements** to drive long-term gains.

4. **Reduces Capital Requirements:** Instead of funding everything internally, firms **use external resources like investors, partners, or debt.**

5. **Creates Long-Term Sustainability:** Strategic leveraging helps businesses **achieve sustainable expansion with optimized risk management.**

How It Works

1. **Identify Leverage Opportunities:** Companies assess **which assets, relationships, or financial instruments** can drive growth.

2. **Develop a Leverage Plan:** A structured approach is created, balancing **risk vs. reward** while ensuring sustainability.

3. **Implement Financial, Operational, or Strategic Leverage:** Businesses use **debt, partnerships, technology, or brand power** to amplify impact.

4. **Monitor & Manage Risks:** Since leverage increases exposure to potential losses, businesses must **analyse financial stability, market trends, and competitive positioning.**

5. **Optimize & Scale:** Once leverage generates results, businesses refine strategies and **expand operations while managing associated risks.**

Application

- **Financial Sector:** Investment firms and real estate developers use **debt leverage to acquire properties and increase returns.**

- **Technology & Startups:** Companies like **Tesla, Uber, and Airbnb** leverage partnerships, funding, and technology to scale rapidly.

- **Retail & E-commerce: Amazon leverages logistics, AI, and cloud services** to expand beyond traditional e-commerce.

- **Manufacturing & Industrial:** Businesses **leverage automation and economies of scale** to optimize production and reduce costs.

- **Media & Branding:** Influencers, content creators, and brands leverage **social media, digital platforms, and collaborations** to expand their reach.

Key Insights

1. **Leverage is a Double-Edged Sword:** While it can accelerate growth, over-leveraging—especially financial—can lead to excessive risk and instability.

2. **Strategic Partnerships Enhance Leverage:** Collaborations with **suppliers, investors, or technology providers** amplify scalability with minimal investment.

3. **Technology & Automation Improve Operational Leverage:** Investing in AI, robotics, and cloud services **reduces long-term variable costs and boosts efficiency.**

4. **Leverage Must Be Managed Wisely:** Businesses must balance **debt vs. cash flow, expansion vs. stability, and risk vs. reward** to sustain long-term success.

5. **Leverage Can Drive Competitive Advantage:** Companies that successfully apply leverage **outperform competitors in efficiency, market reach, and innovation.**

Conclusion

The **Leveraging Strategy** is a powerful method for businesses to **expand, optimize profitability, and gain market dominance** without requiring excessive capital. Whether through **financial tools, strategic partnerships, or operational efficiencies,** leveraging enables companies to **scale efficiently while managing risks.** However, **careful execution and risk assessment** are crucial to ensure that leveraging leads to **sustainable, long-term success.**

66. Dividend Strategy

Dividend Strategy: A Comprehensive Breakdown

Theory

The **Dividend Strategy** is a business approach where companies regularly distribute a portion of their profits to shareholders as dividends. This strategy is commonly used by **established, financially stable companies** that generate consistent revenue and want to reward investors while maintaining long-term growth.

Dividends are typically issued in **cash or additional shares (stock dividends)** and can follow different payout structures:

1. **Regular Dividends:** Fixed payments made quarterly or annually (e.g., Coca-Cola, Johnson & Johnson).

2. **Special Dividends:** One-time payments issued when a company has excess cash.

3. **Dividend Growth Strategy:** Businesses gradually **increase dividends** over time to attract long-term investors.

4. **High Dividend Yield Strategy:** Companies offer **higher-than-average payouts** to appeal to income-focused investors.

Companies following a dividend strategy aim to balance **profit distribution with reinvestment** in operations, ensuring sustainable financial health while rewarding shareholders. This approach **attracts investors seeking steady income** and signals confidence in the company's long-term stability.

Example

A leading example of a dividend strategy is **Procter & Gamble (P&G)**, which has paid and increased dividends for over **65 consecutive years.** This consistent payout has **attracted long-term investors** and solidified P&G's reputation as a **reliable income-generating stock.**

Another example is **Apple**, which initially focused on growth but later introduced dividends in **2012** after becoming highly profitable. This move **attracted income-focused investors** while maintaining growth through innovation and acquisitions.

Why It Works

1. **Attracts Long-Term Investors:** Investors seeking **stable returns** prefer companies with strong dividend histories.

2. **Builds Shareholder Confidence:** Regular dividend payments indicate **financial strength and business stability.**

3. **Enhances Stock Value & Market Perception:** Companies with **reliable dividends** are often perceived as **less risky investments.**

4. **Provides Passive Income to Investors:** Retirees and conservative investors **rely on dividends** as a steady income source.

5. **Encourages Financial Discipline:** Companies that commit to dividends must maintain **strong cash flow management** and avoid unnecessary risks.

How It Works

1. **Determine Profit Allocation:** Companies decide how much profit to **distribute vs. reinvest** in growth.

2. **Set Dividend Payout Ratio:** The percentage of earnings paid as dividends is established (e.g., **50% payout means half of earnings go to shareholders**).

3. **Decide Payment Frequency:** Dividends can be **paid quarterly, annually, or as one-time special dividends.**

4. **Announce Dividend Policy:** Investors receive clear guidance on payout schedules and expected returns.

5. **Ensure Financial Sustainability:** Companies must **balance dividend commitments with operational reinvestment and debt management.**

Application

- **Blue-Chip Stocks:** Companies like **Coca-Cola, Johnson & Johnson, and McDonald's** consistently pay dividends to shareholders.

- **Utility & Energy Companies:** Businesses like **Duke Energy and ExxonMobil** offer **high-yield dividends** due to stable revenue.

- **Real Estate Investment Trusts (REITs):** REITs distribute **90%+ of income** as dividends, attracting **income-focused investors.**

- **Tech Giants Adopting Dividends:** Apple and Microsoft **introduced dividends** after achieving long-term profitability.

- **Dividend-Focused ETFs & Funds:** Mutual funds and ETFs focused on dividend-paying stocks provide diversified **income streams to investors.**

Key Insights

1. **Dividend Stocks Are Less Volatile:** Companies with **strong dividend histories** often experience **less market fluctuation.**

2. **Not All Companies Should Pay Dividends:** High-growth startups **(e.g., Amazon, Tesla)** reinvest profits into expansion instead of issuing dividends.

3. **Dividend Growth Matters More Than Yield:** A company that **gradually increases dividends** signals strong financial health and sustainability.

4. **Dividend Cuts Can Hurt Investor Trust:** Reducing or eliminating dividends **signals financial trouble,** often leading to stock price declines.

5. **Balancing Growth & Dividends is Key:** Companies must **reinvest enough in R&D and expansion** while maintaining **attractive dividends for investors.**

Conclusion

The **Dividend Strategy** is a proven approach for companies that generate **consistent profits** and aim to **reward investors while maintaining financial health.** Businesses like **P&G, Coca-Cola, and Apple** have successfully implemented this strategy to **build investor confidence, attract long-term shareholders, and enhance stock value.** However, companies must carefully **balance dividend payouts with reinvestment to sustain growth and avoid financial strain.**

67. Stock Buyback Strategy

Stock Buyback Strategy: A Comprehensive Breakdown

Theory

The **Stock Buyback Strategy**, also known as **share repurchase**, is a financial strategy where a company buys back its own shares from the open market. This reduces the number of outstanding shares, effectively increasing the ownership percentage of remaining shareholders. Companies typically use this strategy when they believe their stock is undervalued or when they have excess cash that is not needed for immediate investments.

The strategy is based on **capital structure optimization and shareholder value enhancement**. By repurchasing shares, companies can:

1. **Increase Earnings Per Share (EPS):** With fewer shares in circulation, the company's **EPS improves, making financial performance look stronger**.

2. **Return Excess Cash to Shareholders:** Instead of paying dividends, companies can **buy back shares, indirectly benefiting investors through stock price appreciation**.

3. **Signal Confidence in Growth:** A stock buyback often indicates that **management believes the company is financially strong and the stock is undervalued**.

4. **Reduce Dilution:** Buybacks counteract the effect of stock-based compensation for employees, ensuring that shareholders don't lose ownership value.

5. **Optimize Capital Structure:** Companies with excess cash can **reduce equity without increasing debt**, leading to a more efficient balance sheet.

Companies execute buybacks through two main methods:

- **Open Market Purchases:** Buying shares gradually from the stock exchange.
- **Tender Offers:** Offering shareholders the option to sell shares back at a premium price.

Example

A well-known example of a stock buyback strategy is **Apple**. Since 2012, Apple has aggressively repurchased shares, spending over **$500 billion** on stock buybacks. This has significantly boosted **earnings per share, increased stock value, and rewarded long-term investors** while maintaining financial flexibility.

Another example is **Berkshire Hathaway**, where Warren Buffett uses stock buybacks selectively when he believes the stock is **trading below intrinsic value**, ensuring that the remaining shareholders benefit from increased ownership.

Why It Works

1. **Increases Shareholder Value:** By reducing the supply of shares, demand increases, often leading to **higher stock prices.**

2. **Boosts Investor Confidence:** A buyback signals that **management believes in the company's future growth** and financial strength.

3. **Enhances Financial Ratios:** Lower share count improves key financial metrics like **EPS, return on equity (ROE), and price-to-earnings (P/E) ratio.**

4. **Provides an Alternative to Dividends:** Instead of dividends (which trigger taxes for investors), stock buybacks offer a **tax-efficient way to return cash to shareholders.**

5. **Maintains Flexibility:** Unlike dividends, buybacks are **optional and don't create long-term payout commitments.**

How It Works

1. **Assess Financial Position:** Companies evaluate **cash reserves, debt levels, and capital expenditure needs** before deciding on a buyback.

2. **Determine Buyback Method:** Decide between **open-market purchases or tender offers** based on pricing strategy and shareholder interest.

3. **Announce the Buyback Plan:** Companies publicly disclose their buyback program to ensure **transparency and investor awareness**.

4. **Execute the Buyback Over Time:** Stock repurchases are made **gradually or in bulk** depending on market conditions and price movements.

5. **Monitor Impact & Adjust Strategy:** Companies continuously assess how buybacks **affect stock price, EPS, and overall market perception**.

Application

- **Technology Companies:** Apple, Microsoft, and Alphabet use buybacks to **return capital without disrupting growth investments**.

- **Financial Sector:** JPMorgan Chase and Goldman Sachs conduct buybacks to **enhance stockholder returns and optimize capital structures**.

- **Consumer Goods & Retail:** McDonald's and Starbucks buy back shares to **boost stock prices while maintaining dividend payouts**.

- **Industrials & Energy:** ExxonMobil and General Electric use buybacks **to stabilize stock prices and reward long-term shareholders.**

Key Insights

1. **Buybacks Work Best When Stock is Undervalued:** Repurchasing overvalued stock **destroys shareholder value instead of enhancing it.**

2. **Not a Substitute for Growth Investment:** Companies must balance buybacks with **R&D, acquisitions, and business expansion.**

3. **Over-Leveraging Can Backfire:** If a company funds buybacks with excessive debt, it may **weaken financial stability.**

4. **Market Perception Matters:** Investors react differently to buybacks—some see them as **a sign of strength**, while others **question the lack of reinvestment in growth.**

5. **Buybacks Should Be Strategic, Not Routine:** Companies should use buybacks **opportunistically rather than habitually**, ensuring they provide real value.

Conclusion

The **Stock Buyback Strategy** is a powerful financial tool for **enhancing shareholder value, optimizing capital structure, and signalling market confidence**. When executed correctly—like in the cases of Apple and Berkshire Hathaway—it helps improve

EPS, stock prices, and investor sentiment**. However, businesses must carefully balance **buybacks with growth investments and financial stability** to ensure **long-term success and sustainability**.

68. IPO Strategy

IPO Strategy: A Comprehensive Breakdown

Theory

The **Initial Public Offering (IPO) Strategy** is a business approach where a privately held company transitions into a **publicly traded company** by offering shares to institutional and retail investors through the stock market. This move allows businesses to **raise capital, increase market visibility, and provide liquidity for early investors and employees.**

The IPO process is structured into key stages:

1. **Pre-IPO Preparation:** The company evaluates **financial performance, market conditions, and business scalability** to determine readiness.
2. **Hiring Underwriters & Legal Advisors:** Investment banks (e.g., Goldman Sachs, Morgan Stanley) guide the process,

helping determine the **company's valuation, pricing strategy, and share structure.**

3. **Regulatory Filings & Roadshows:** The company submits documents like the **S-1 filing (in the U.S.)** to financial regulators (e.g., SEC), followed by roadshows where executives present the investment case to institutional investors.

4. **Setting the IPO Price & Launch:** The underwriters finalize the **offer price per share, allocate shares to investors, and execute the stock market debut.**

5. **Post-IPO Performance & Compliance:** Once public, the company must **adhere to financial reporting regulations, manage shareholder expectations, and drive sustainable growth.**

An IPO strategy allows companies to **expand operations, pay off debt, and increase brand credibility**, but it also comes with challenges such as **increased scrutiny, compliance costs, and market volatility.**

Example

A notable IPO example is **Facebook's (now Meta) 2012 IPO**. The company raised **$16 billion** at a valuation of **$104 billion**, making it one of the largest tech IPOs in history. Despite initial stock price fluctuations, Facebook leveraged IPO proceeds to **expand its platform, acquire Instagram and WhatsApp, and invest in AI and the metaverse.**

Another example is **Alibaba's 2014 IPO**, which raised **$25 billion**, making it the largest IPO globally. Alibaba used the capital to **expand its e-commerce business, strengthen cloud computing services, and enter new markets.**

Why It Works

1. **Raises Substantial Capital:** IPOs provide companies with **large-scale funding** to fuel **expansion, acquisitions, and innovation.**

2. **Enhances Market Credibility:** A public listing **boosts brand recognition and trust** among investors, customers, and partners.

3. **Provides Liquidity to Early Investors & Employees:** Venture capitalists, private equity firms, and employees with stock options **can cash out at market value.**

4. **Enables Future Fundraising:** Public companies can issue additional shares via **secondary offerings** to raise more capital.

5. **Increases Growth Opportunities:** The **higher valuation and stock liquidity** allow companies to **attract top talent, improve financial flexibility, and negotiate better deals.**

How It Works

1. **Assess Readiness:** Companies ensure they have **strong financials, predictable revenue, and market growth potential.**
2. **Hire Investment Banks:** Underwriters help structure the IPO, including **valuation, share pricing, and investor outreach.**
3. **File Regulatory Documents:** Companies submit **financial disclosures (e.g., S-1 form) to regulatory bodies** like the SEC.
4. **Conduct Roadshows:** Executives meet with institutional investors to **generate demand and ensure a successful listing.**
5. **Launch IPO & Monitor Performance:** Shares begin trading on the stock exchange, with the company **managing investor relations and compliance.**

Application

- **Technology & Startups:** Companies like **Facebook, Uber, and Airbnb** use IPOs to raise capital for expansion.

- **Retail & E-commerce: Alibaba and Shopify** leveraged IPO proceeds to scale operations globally.

- **Healthcare & Biotech: Moderna** used IPO funding to accelerate mRNA vaccine development.

- **Financial & Banking Sector: Visa and Goldman Sachs** went public to strengthen capital reserves and enhance global reach.

- **Energy & Industrials: Tesla and ExxonMobil** used public markets to finance infrastructure and R&D.

Key Insights

1. **Timing is Critical:** Market conditions, economic stability, and industry trends **impact IPO success and stock performance.**

2. **Not All IPOs Succeed:** Some IPOs (e.g., WeWork) **fail due to overvaluation, lack of profitability, or investor scepticism.**

3. **Regulatory Compliance is Ongoing:** Public companies face **higher scrutiny, quarterly reporting requirements, and governance standards.**

4. **Valuation Can Be Volatile:** Stock prices may **fluctuate post-IPO** based on market sentiment, financial performance, and external factors.

5. **Alternatives to IPOs Exist:** Companies can explore **SPACs (Special Purpose Acquisition Companies) or Direct Listings** as alternative public market entry methods.

Conclusion

The **IPO Strategy** is a high-impact method for companies to **raise capital, increase market visibility, and expand operations.** While it provides numerous benefits, including **financial liquidity and credibility,** it also introduces **regulatory challenges, public scrutiny, and stock price volatility.** Businesses that **strategically time their IPO, ensure financial stability, and execute a strong post-IPO growth plan** can maximize success and long-term shareholder value.

69. Tax Optimization Strategy

Tax Optimization Strategy: A Comprehensive Breakdown

Theory

The **Tax Optimization Strategy** is a financial approach where businesses structure their operations, investments, and expenses in a way that legally minimizes tax liabilities while remaining compliant with tax regulations. The goal is to **reduce tax burdens, maximize after-tax profits, and enhance cash flow** without engaging in illegal tax evasion.

This strategy is based on principles of **tax efficiency, strategic planning, and regulatory compliance.** Businesses use various tactics such as:

1. **Tax Deductions & Credits:** Leveraging allowable expenses, R&D credits, and depreciation to reduce taxable income.

2. **Legal Entity Structuring:** Establishing **subsidiaries, holding companies, or offshore entities** to take advantage of lower tax rates.

3. **Income Deferral & Accelerated Depreciation:** Managing revenue recognition and asset depreciation to **optimize tax timing.**

4. **Transfer Pricing & International Tax Planning:** Multinational companies allocate profits across **low-tax jurisdictions** to reduce overall tax liabilities.

5. **Tax-Advantaged Investments:** Using **municipal bonds, retirement plans, or tax-exempt funds** to shelter income from taxation.

Tax optimization helps businesses **improve profitability, reinvest more capital, and maintain a competitive edge** while ensuring compliance with tax laws in different jurisdictions.

Example

A well-known example of tax optimization is **Apple's use of international tax structuring.** Apple strategically routes international profits through **subsidiaries in Ireland**, where corporate tax rates are lower, significantly reducing its global tax bill. This approach has saved Apple **billions in taxes** while remaining compliant with legal frameworks.

Another example is **Amazon**, which minimizes taxable income by reinvesting profits into **R&D, infrastructure, and acquisitions**, taking advantage of **tax credits and deductions** to reduce corporate taxes.

Why It Works

1. **Maximizes After-Tax Profits:** Businesses retain more earnings by **reducing unnecessary tax expenses** through legal deductions.

2. **Enhances Cash Flow for Growth:** Companies can **reinvest savings into expansion, innovation, and acquisitions** instead of paying excessive taxes.

3. **Competitive Advantage:** Lower tax burdens **improve financial flexibility**, allowing businesses to **offer better pricing, increase market share, or boost investor returns.**

4. **Leverages Legal Tax Incentives:** Governments offer **tax credits, deductions, and exemptions** to encourage business investments in certain industries or regions.

5. **Protects Shareholder Value:** By minimizing tax expenses, companies **increase net earnings per share (EPS)** and enhance investor confidence.

How It Works

1. **Analyse Business Structure & Tax Exposure:** Companies assess their **revenue sources, expenses, and taxable income** to identify optimization opportunities.

2. **Utilize Tax-Efficient Entities:** Businesses choose the right **corporate structure (LLC, S-Corp, C-Corp, offshore entity)** to minimize tax liabilities.

3. **Optimize Expenses & Deductions:** Companies leverage **tax-deductible expenses**, such as salaries, benefits, and operational costs, to lower taxable income.

4. **Strategic Income Shifting & Deferral:** Revenue is structured to **optimize tax timing**, such as delaying income recognition or accelerating deductible expenses.

5. **Leverage International Tax Planning:** Multinational firms allocate profits strategically in **low-tax jurisdictions** while complying with **transfer pricing regulations**.

6. **Ensure Compliance & Audit Readiness:** Businesses regularly update tax strategies based on **legal changes, financial performance, and tax audits.**

Application

- **Technology Companies:** Apple, Google, and Microsoft use **offshore tax structures and R&D credits** to optimize global tax burdens.

- **Retail & E-commerce:** Amazon reinvests heavily in **logistics, AI, and cloud computing** to reduce taxable profits.

- **Manufacturing & Energy:** Tesla and ExxonMobil use **depreciation and energy tax credits** to lower tax liabilities.

- **Healthcare & Pharmaceuticals:** Pfizer and Johnson & Johnson structure **patents and IP licensing** to manage global taxes.

- **Financial Services:** Hedge funds and banks use **tax-efficient investment vehicles and capital gains tax strategies** to reduce liabilities.

Key Insights

1. **Tax Optimization is Legal, Tax Evasion is Not:** Businesses must operate **within tax regulations** to avoid legal penalties.

2. **Government Incentives Should Be Utilized:** Tax credits and deductions exist to **encourage investment, R&D, and job creation**—businesses should take full advantage.

3. **International Tax Planning Must Be Transparent:** OECD regulations, BEPS (Base Erosion and Profit Shifting) frameworks, and country-specific tax laws require careful compliance.

4. **Tax Efficiency Benefits Long-Term Growth:** Lower tax burdens provide **more resources for innovation, expansion, and competitive pricing.**

5. **Regular Review is Essential:** Tax laws change frequently; companies must **continuously refine their tax strategies** to stay compliant and optimize benefits.

Conclusion

The **Tax Optimization Strategy** is a critical financial tool that allows businesses to **reduce tax liabilities, improve cash flow, and enhance profitability** while staying compliant with local and international tax laws. By **leveraging deductions, international structuring, and government incentives**, companies can **maximize shareholder value, reinvest savings, and maintain a competitive advantage.** However, **transparent reporting and ethical tax planning** are essential to ensure long-term success and regulatory compliance.

70. Cash Flow Management Strategy

Cash Flow Management Strategy: A Comprehensive Breakdown

Theory

The **Cash Flow Management Strategy** is a financial approach where businesses optimize **incoming and outgoing cash** to ensure liquidity, stability, and long-term financial health. Cash flow represents the **movement of money in and out of a business**, and effective management ensures that a company can **pay expenses, invest in growth, and avoid financial distress.**

Cash flow is categorized into three main types:

1. **Operating Cash Flow:** Money generated from core business activities (e.g., sales revenue, payments from customers).

2. **Investing Cash Flow:** Cash spent on or earned from **investments, acquisitions, or asset sales.**

3. **Financing Cash Flow:** Funds from **loans, equity issuance, dividends, and debt repayment.**

A strong cash flow management strategy involves:

- **Optimizing receivables (getting paid faster).**
- **Controlling payables (managing expenses and extending payment terms).**
- **Maintaining an emergency cash reserve.**
- **Reducing unnecessary expenditures.**
- **Leveraging short-term financing when needed.**

Cash flow is crucial because **even profitable businesses can fail due to liquidity issues** if they cannot meet short-term obligations like payroll, rent, or supplier payments.

Example

A prime example of cash flow management is **Amazon's negative working capital cycle.** Amazon collects payments from customers **immediately** but negotiates **extended payment terms** with suppliers. This means Amazon holds cash for **longer periods before paying suppliers**, improving liquidity and allowing reinvestment in expansion and innovation.

Another example is **Apple**, which strategically manages cash flow by **holding large reserves** and using **share buybacks and dividends** to optimize capital allocation while maintaining operational flexibility.

Why It Works

1. **Ensures Liquidity & Business Stability:** Proper cash flow management prevents **cash shortages that can lead to missed payments or business failure.**

2. **Improves Financial Flexibility:** A company with strong cash flow can **invest in growth opportunities, acquisitions, or market expansion.**

3. **Reduces Dependency on Debt:** Businesses with positive cash flow can operate without excessive **borrowings and interest expenses.**

4. **Enhances Supplier & Investor Confidence:** A well-managed cash flow ensures **timely payments to suppliers and dividends to investors, building trust.**

5. **Prevents Financial Crises:** Companies can navigate **economic downturns or unexpected expenses** by maintaining strong cash flow control.

How It Works

1. **Monitor & Forecast Cash Flow:** Businesses track **daily, weekly, and monthly cash flow trends** to anticipate shortages or surpluses.

2. **Optimize Accounts Receivable:** Encourage **faster payments** by offering early-payment discounts or automating invoicing systems.

3. **Manage Accounts Payable Strategically:** Negotiate **longer payment terms** with suppliers to keep more cash on hand.

4. **Control Expenses & Avoid Overspending:** Businesses identify **non-essential costs and reduce unnecessary expenditures.**

5. **Use Short-Term Financing If Necessary:** Lines of credit, business loans, or factoring services help bridge temporary cash gaps.

6. **Build a Cash Reserve:** Setting aside emergency funds ensures the company can **handle unexpected financial challenges.**

Application

- **Retail & E-commerce:** Amazon uses efficient **inventory and payment cycles** to maximize liquidity.

- **Manufacturing:** Tesla carefully manages **production costs and supplier payments** to maintain cash reserves.

- **Technology & Startups:** Google and Apple reinvest **cash surpluses into R&D and acquisitions.**

- **Small Businesses & Service Providers:** Restaurants and consulting firms track **seasonal cash flow patterns** to adjust spending accordingly.

- **Healthcare & Pharmaceuticals:** Hospitals and biotech firms optimize **insurance reimbursements and supplier payment terms.**

Key Insights

1. **Cash Flow is More Important Than Profitability:** A profitable business can still fail if it lacks cash to meet short-term expenses.

2. **Forecasting Prevents Cash Shortages:** Companies must anticipate **future cash needs and plan accordingly.**

3. **Optimizing Payment Cycles is Crucial:** Collecting revenue faster while delaying expenses improves cash flow balance.

4. **Emergency Cash Reserves Are Essential:** Businesses should maintain **a financial cushion** to handle **economic downturns or unexpected costs.**

5. **Technology Improves Cash Flow Efficiency:** Automated **invoicing, expense tracking, and digital payment systems** enhance cash flow management.

Conclusion

A strong **Cash Flow Management Strategy** ensures businesses maintain **financial stability, reduce risk, and seize growth opportunities.** Companies like **Amazon and Apple** demonstrate the power of optimizing **receivables, payables, and reserves** to maintain liquidity. By implementing **strategic forecasting, cost control, and payment cycle optimization**, businesses can enhance **long-term financial health and resilience.**

Customer Experience & Retention Strategies, Building long-term customer relationships:

71. Customer-Centric Strategy

Customer-Centric Strategy: A Comprehensive Breakdown

Theory

The **Customer-Centric Strategy** is a business approach that prioritizes the needs, preferences, and experiences of customers at every stage of the company's operations. Instead of focusing solely on **products, services, or sales**, businesses with a customer-centric mindset **design their strategies around delivering value and long-term satisfaction** to their customers.

This strategy is rooted in **customer experience (CX), personalization, and data-driven decision-making**. Key principles include:

1. **Deep Customer Understanding:** Businesses gather insights from **customer feedback, behaviour analysis, and market research** to align with expectations.

2. **Personalization & Customization:** Using **AI, CRM systems, and customer segmentation**, businesses tailor products and services to individual preferences.

3. **Omnichannel Engagement:** Providing a **seamless experience across all touchpoints**—physical stores, websites, social media, and mobile apps.

4. **Customer-First Culture:** Employees at all levels prioritize **customer satisfaction and problem-solving.**

5. **Long-Term Relationship Building:** Instead of focusing only on one-time sales, businesses nurture **loyalty through consistent engagement and value delivery.**

A successful **customer-centric company aligns all business functions—marketing, sales, product development, and customer service—toward exceeding customer expectations.**

Example

A leading example of customer-centricity is **Amazon**. The company's entire business model revolves around **customer convenience, fast delivery, personalized recommendations, and seamless user experience**. Features like **one-click purchasing, AI-driven product suggestions, and a hassle-free return policy** demonstrate Amazon's dedication to putting customers first.

Another example is **Apple**, which prioritizes **customer satisfaction through high-quality design, user-friendly interfaces, and superior customer service**. Apple's in-store Genius Bar provides expert support, reinforcing customer trust and long-term loyalty.

Why It Works

1. **Enhances Customer Loyalty & Retention:** Happy customers are more likely to become **repeat buyers and brand advocates.**

2. **Increases Customer Lifetime Value (CLV):** Businesses focusing on customer relationships generate **higher long-term revenue.**

3. **Strengthens Brand Reputation:** Companies known for **excellent customer service and engagement** gain a competitive advantage.

4. **Improves Business Agility:** A customer-centric approach helps companies **quickly adapt to changing market needs.**

5. **Boosts Revenue & Profitability:** Businesses that prioritize customer experience outperform competitors in **sales and market share.**

How It Works

1. **Gather & Analyse Customer Data:** Use surveys, feedback, and analytics to **understand customer preferences, pain points, and expectations.**

2. **Personalize Customer Interactions:** Implement AI-driven **recommendations, targeted promotions, and tailored communication** to improve engagement.

3. **Ensure Seamless Omnichannel Support:** Provide a **consistent experience across online, mobile, social media, and in-store interactions.**

4. **Empower Employees to Prioritize Customers:** Train staff to **solve problems proactively and go the extra mile** in customer service.

5. **Measure & Optimize Customer Experience (CX):** Track **Net Promoter Score (NPS), Customer Satisfaction (CSAT), and retention rates** to refine strategies.

Application

- **E-commerce & Retail:** Amazon and Zappos focus on **fast shipping, personalized recommendations, and customer-friendly policies.**

- **Technology & Consumer Electronics:** Apple and Samsung prioritize **user-friendly designs and superior after-sales support.**

- **Financial Services:** Banks like Chase and American Express enhance **digital banking experiences and proactive customer service.**

- **Hospitality & Travel:** Hotels like Ritz-Carlton and airlines like Delta provide **personalized service and loyalty programs.**

- **Healthcare & Wellness:** Companies like Mayo Clinic focus on **patient-centric care, digital health solutions, and personalized treatment plans.**

Key Insights

1. **Customer-Centricity is More Than Just Service:** It involves every touchpoint—from product design to post-purchase engagement.

2. **Technology Enhances Personalization:** AI, CRM systems, and data analytics help companies **tailor experiences for individual customers.**

3. **Employee Training is Essential:** A customer-first culture starts with **empowering employees to prioritize customer satisfaction.**

4. **Customer Feedback Drives Innovation:** Businesses that **actively listen to customers** can adapt products and services **to meet evolving needs.**

5. **Retention is More Profitable Than Acquisition:** Loyal customers generate more revenue than new customers, **reducing acquisition costs** and increasing CLV.

Conclusion

The **Customer-Centric Strategy** is a powerful business approach that **drives loyalty, improves brand reputation, and enhances profitability** by putting customer needs at the core of decision-making. Companies like **Amazon, Apple, and Ritz-Carlton** demonstrate how **personalization, omnichannel experiences, and long-term engagement** create sustainable success. Businesses that adopt **a customer-first mindset, leverage technology, and continuously optimize customer experience** will remain **competitive and profitable in an increasingly customer-driven market.**

72. Customer Feedback Loop Strategy

Customer Feedback Loop Strategy: A Comprehensive Breakdown

Theory

The **Customer Feedback Loop Strategy** is a business approach where companies actively collect, analyse, and implement customer feedback to improve products, services, and customer experiences. The goal is to create a **continuous cycle of listening, learning, and improving** based on real customer insights.

This strategy is built on the principles of **customer-centricity, iterative improvement, and data-driven decision-making**. The feedback loop consists of three key stages:

1. **Collect Feedback:** Businesses gather customer insights through **surveys, reviews, social media, and direct interactions.**

2. **Analyse & Prioritize Insights:** Identifying recurring themes and pain points to determine **which improvements will have the biggest impact.**

3. **Implement & Iterate:** Making necessary changes based on feedback, then **measuring the impact** to refine further improvements.

By continuously refining products and services based on customer input, businesses can improve **customer satisfaction, loyalty, and competitive advantage** while minimizing costly mistakes.

Example

A great example of the customer feedback loop in action is **Slack**. Slack collects feedback through **in-app surveys, customer support tickets, and social media**, then prioritizes improvements based on user pain points. Features like **dark mode, workflow automation, and improved search functionality** were developed based on direct customer requests, making Slack more intuitive and user-friendly.

Another example is **Starbucks**, which launched **My Starbucks Idea**, an online platform where customers could submit suggestions. This initiative led to new offerings like **mobile**

ordering, oat milk options, and Wi-Fi availability in stores, enhancing customer experience and driving loyalty.

Why It Works

1. **Enhances Customer Satisfaction & Retention:** Customers feel valued when their feedback leads to real improvements, increasing **brand loyalty.**

2. **Reduces Product Development Risks:** Businesses make **data-backed decisions**, reducing the likelihood of launching unpopular features.

3. **Encourages Innovation & Competitive Edge:** Continuous feedback leads to **better products, services, and user experiences** that keep companies ahead of competitors.

4. **Boosts Engagement & Brand Advocacy:** Customers who see their input implemented become **brand advocates and promoters.**

5. **Improves Operational Efficiency:** Companies can streamline **processes, reduce churn, and enhance customer support** by addressing common pain points.

How It Works

1. **Collect Customer Feedback:** Use **surveys, reviews, live chat, support tickets, social media, and focus groups** to gather insights.

2. **Analyse & Categorize Insights:** Identify trends in customer complaints, feature requests, and satisfaction scores.

3. **Prioritize Actionable Changes:** Focus on improvements that will have the **biggest impact on user experience and business success.**

4. **Implement Changes & Communicate Updates:** Roll out updates and let customers know their feedback was valued and implemented.

5. **Measure Impact & Refine Further:** Track **customer satisfaction (CSAT), Net Promoter Score (NPS), and retention rates** to ensure continuous improvement.

Application

- **Tech & SaaS: Slack, Zoom, and Google** improve software usability based on customer requests.

- **Retail & E-commerce: Amazon and Nike** optimize product recommendations and customer service using feedback loops.

- **Hospitality & Food Industry: Starbucks and McDonald's** introduce menu changes and mobile ordering based on customer insights.

- **Financial Services: Banks like Chase and fintech companies like PayPal** refine user interfaces and security features through feedback loops.

- **Healthcare & Wellness: Telehealth companies and fitness apps** update features based on patient and user feedback.

Key Insights

1. **Listening to Customers Drives Growth:** Companies that actively implement feedback **outperform competitors by aligning with user needs.**

2. **Feedback Should Be Continuous & Multichannel:** Businesses must collect insights across **various touchpoints** to get a holistic view.

3. **Not All Feedback is Equal:** Prioritizing the **most impactful suggestions** ensures resources are used efficiently.

4. **Transparency Builds Trust:** When companies acknowledge and act on feedback, **customers feel valued and are more likely to stay loyal.**

5. **Technology Enhances Feedback Loops:** AI, CRM tools, and analytics help **automate feedback collection, analysis, and execution.**

Conclusion

The **Customer Feedback Loop Strategy** is essential for businesses that prioritize **continuous improvement, customer satisfaction, and long-term success.** Companies like **Slack, Starbucks, and Amazon** have mastered this approach by actively listening, implementing, and iterating based on user insights. Businesses that integrate **systematic feedback collection, analysis, and action** into their operations will foster **customer loyalty, drive innovation, and maintain a strong competitive edge.**

73. Hyper-Personalization Strategy

Hyper-Personalization Strategy: A Comprehensive Breakdown

Theory

The **Hyper-Personalization Strategy** is an advanced marketing and customer experience approach that leverages **artificial intelligence (AI), big data, and real-time analytics** to deliver highly tailored experiences for individual customers. Unlike traditional personalization, which segments customers into broad categories, **hyper-personalization customizes interactions at an individual level** based on real-time behaviour, preferences, and past interactions.

This strategy is built on the principles of **data-driven decision-making, AI automation, and behavioural analysis**. Businesses implementing hyper-personalization focus on:

1. **Real-Time Customer Insights:** Using AI and machine learning to track **browsing behaviour, purchase history, and preferences.**

2. **Dynamic Content & Product Recommendations:** Delivering **customized emails, ads, website content, and offers** tailored to each customer.

3. **Omnichannel Personalization:** Creating **seamless experiences across multiple touchpoints**—websites, apps, emails, chatbots, and in-store interactions.

4. **Predictive Analytics & AI Automation:** Forecasting customer needs and automating personalized engagement **before customers express them.**

5. **Customized Pricing & Offers:** Adjusting prices, discounts, or recommendations **based on user-specific data and engagement levels.**

Hyper-personalization helps businesses **increase engagement, enhance customer loyalty, and maximize conversions** by making every interaction feel unique and relevant.

Example

A powerful example of hyper-personalization is **Netflix's recommendation engine.** Netflix collects and analyses user data, including **watch history, time spent on content, device usage, and search behaviour,** to **dynamically curate a personalized homepage** for each user. Even movie thumbnails are tailored based on **individual viewing habits.**

Another example is **Amazon's AI-driven product recommendations**. By analysing purchase history, browsing behaviour, and real-time interactions, Amazon **suggests highly relevant products, bundles, and discounts** to each user, increasing conversion rates and average order value.

Why It Works

1. **Increases Engagement & Retention:** Customers respond positively to brands that understand and anticipate their needs.

2. **Boosts Conversions & Sales:** Tailored recommendations result in **higher click-through rates and purchase intent.**

3. **Enhances Customer Satisfaction:** Personalized interactions create a **seamless and enjoyable experience, increasing brand loyalty.**

4. **Optimizes Marketing ROI:** Hyper-personalized marketing **reduces ad spend waste** by targeting the right audience with precise messaging.

5. **Differentiates Brands in Competitive Markets:** Businesses that implement hyper-personalization **stand out by offering superior experiences.**

How It Works

1. **Collect & Integrate Customer Data:** Gather data from **browsing activity, purchase history, social media, CRM, and IoT devices.**

2. **Leverage AI & Machine Learning:** Use **predictive analytics, AI algorithms, and automation** to process and analyse real-time customer behaviour.

3. **Deliver Dynamic & Contextual Content:** Personalize **emails, website experiences, chat interactions, and push notifications** in real-time.

4. **Refine & Optimize Continuously:** Measure **engagement rates, conversions, and customer satisfaction** to improve the strategy over time.

5. **Ensure Privacy & Compliance:** Follow **data protection regulations (GDPR, CCPA)** while maintaining customer trust with transparent data policies.

Application

- **E-commerce & Retail: Amazon, Nike, and Sephora** use AI to offer real-time product recommendations and custom pricing.

- **Streaming & Entertainment: Netflix, Spotify, and YouTube** personalize content recommendations based on user preferences.

- **Finance & Banking: Chase and American Express** tailor financial advice, credit card offers, and fraud detection based on user behaviour.

- **Healthcare & Wellness: Fitbit and telehealth platforms** personalize health insights, workout plans, and medication reminders.

- **Hospitality & Travel: Marriott and Expedia** offer custom travel suggestions, hotel upgrades, and location-based deals.

Key Insights

1. **Hyper-Personalization Requires AI & Big Data:** Traditional segmentation isn't enough—**real-time analytics and predictive AI** are essential.

2. **Real-Time Engagement is Critical:** Businesses must personalize interactions **as they happen**, not just based on past data.

3. **Data Privacy & Trust Must Be Managed:** Customers expect transparency in **how their data is used for personalization.**

4. **Personalization Should Feel Natural, Not Intrusive:** Over-personalization can be seen as **creepy** if not implemented thoughtfully.

5. **Customer Expectations Are Evolving:** Businesses that fail to personalize will **lose engagement and loyalty** to competitors offering tailored experiences.

Conclusion

The **Hyper-Personalization Strategy** transforms customer engagement by leveraging **AI, real-time analytics, and predictive insights** to create **tailored, context-aware experiences.** Companies like **Netflix, Amazon, and Spotify** demonstrate how hyper-personalization **drives loyalty, maximizes conversions, and enhances satisfaction.** Businesses that adopt this strategy while maintaining **data transparency and ethical AI use** will gain a **significant competitive advantage in an increasingly digital and customer-driven marketplace.**

74. Surprise & Delight Strategy

Surprise & Delight Strategy: A Comprehensive Breakdown

Theory

The **Surprise & Delight Strategy** is a business approach that enhances customer experience by providing unexpected rewards, gifts, or experiences that exceed customer expectations. Unlike traditional loyalty programs, which offer predictable rewards, **this strategy creates emotional connections by delivering pleasant surprises that leave lasting impressions.**

This approach is based on **behavioural psychology, emotional marketing, and customer-centric engagement.** Key principles include:

1. **Personalization & Thoughtfulness:** Tailoring surprises based on customer preferences or behaviours enhances their impact.

2. **Emotional Connection:** Unexpected delights evoke positive emotions, strengthening **brand affinity and customer loyalty.**

3. **Memorability & Word-of-Mouth Marketing:** Customers who receive pleasant surprises are more likely to **share their experiences on social media, boosting brand reputation.**

4. **Spontaneity & Authenticity:** The element of surprise makes interactions feel **genuine rather than transactional.**

5. **Enhancing Customer Loyalty Beyond Transactions:** Customers appreciate brands that recognize them beyond purchases, fostering **deeper engagement.**

When effectively implemented, **Surprise & Delight fosters brand advocacy, strengthens relationships, and differentiates businesses in competitive markets.**

Example

A well-known example of this strategy is **Zappos' customer service approach.** The company is famous for upgrading shipping to **free overnight delivery unexpectedly** and occasionally **sending flowers or handwritten thank-you notes** to customers. These gestures create **positive emotional experiences, turning one-time buyers into lifelong fans.**

Another great example is **Starbucks' occasional free drink giveaways.** Randomly surprising customers with a complimentary coffee strengthens **loyalty and brand love, leading to repeat visits and word-of-mouth promotion.**

Why It Works

1. **Triggers Positive Emotions & Customer Happiness:** People remember **how brands make them feel,** and unexpected rewards boost emotional engagement.

2. **Encourages Word-of-Mouth & Social Sharing:** Customers often share their experiences on **social media, driving organic brand exposure.**

3. **Increases Customer Retention & Lifetime Value:** Customers who feel valued are more likely to **return and engage with the brand long-term.**

4. **Differentiates Brands from Competitors:** Many businesses focus solely on transactions; **this strategy builds emotional loyalty beyond price and products.**

5. **Enhances Brand Reputation & Trust:** Thoughtful surprises create a **humanized brand image, making companies more relatable and customer-friendly.**

How It Works

1. **Identify Moments to Surprise Customers:** Pinpoint key touchpoints—**first purchase, birthdays, anniversaries, or milestones**—where surprises have the most impact.

2. **Deliver Personalized & Meaningful Gestures:** Send **unexpected gifts, exclusive discounts, handwritten notes, or service upgrades** tailored to each customer.

3. **Empower Employees to Create Memorable Moments:** Train staff to go beyond standard service, allowing **spontaneous acts of kindness** to delight customers.

4. **Leverage Data & AI to Personalize Experiences:** Use customer data to identify **loyal customers, frequent buyers, and special occasions** for targeted surprises.

5. **Encourage Sharing & Community Engagement:** Make the experience **shareable** by adding a fun or social element, such as **branded packaging or social media challenges.**

Application

- **E-commerce & Retail: Amazon and Sephora** surprise loyal customers with exclusive discounts or free samples.

- **Hospitality & Travel: Ritz-Carlton and Delta Airlines** offer unexpected **upgrades, personalized service, and handwritten thank-you notes.**

- **Food & Beverage: Starbucks and Domino's** provide random **free drinks or meal upgrades to surprise customers.**

- **Subscription Services: Spotify and Netflix** curate personalized playlists or recommend exclusive content based on user behaviour.

- **Banking & Finance: American Express and Chase** reward customers with **exclusive perks, early access to offers, and surprise cashback bonuses.**

Key Insights

1. **Surprise & Delight is About Emotional Impact:** The key is making customers feel **appreciated, valued, and excited about engaging with the brand.**

2. **It's Not About Expensive Gifts:** Small, meaningful gestures—like a **personalized thank-you email or free shipping upgrade**—can have a big impact.

3. **Personalization Enhances the Effect:** A surprise is more powerful when **it's tailored to the customer's preferences and behaviours.**

4. **Encouraging Sharing Amplifies Reach:** Brands can create **viral moments** by encouraging customers to share their surprises online.

5. **Authenticity is Crucial:** Customers can tell when surprises are **gimmicky or forced**—the best surprises feel **genuine and thoughtful.**

Conclusion

The **Surprise & Delight Strategy** is a powerful tool for building **customer loyalty, enhancing brand reputation, and creating emotional connections** with consumers. Companies like **Zappos, Starbucks, and Ritz-Carlton** have successfully used this approach to turn **casual customers into brand advocates.** By focusing on **unexpected, meaningful, and personalized gestures**, businesses can differentiate themselves and create **lasting, positive brand experiences.**

75. Social Proof Strategy

Social Proof Strategy: A Comprehensive Breakdown

Theory

The **Social Proof Strategy** is a business approach that leverages **the influence of others' actions, opinions, and experiences** to build trust, credibility, and drive conversions. It is based on the psychological principle that **people tend to follow the behaviours of others, especially in uncertain situations.**

Social proof can take various forms, including:

1. **Customer Reviews & Testimonials:** Positive feedback from real users builds credibility.
2. **Influencer & Celebrity Endorsements:** High-profile figures validate a brand's reputation.

3. **User-Generated Content (UGC):** Customers sharing their experiences via photos, videos, or social media posts increase authenticity.

4. **Expert & Industry Endorsements:** Recognized professionals or media coverage enhance brand authority.

5. **Social Media Engagement & Metrics:** High numbers of followers, likes, and shares indicate popularity and trustworthiness.

6. **Case Studies & Success Stories:** Demonstrating real-world effectiveness reassures potential customers.

7. **"Best-Seller" & "Most Popular" Labels:** Highlighting what others are choosing influences purchasing decisions.

By strategically integrating social proof, businesses **reduce buyer hesitation, establish trust, and create a powerful influence loop** that drives engagement and conversions.

Example

A well-known example of social proof in action is **Amazon's customer reviews and ratings system**. Before purchasing, shoppers **rely on user-generated ratings, testimonials, and verified purchase reviews** to validate product quality. Products with higher ratings and more reviews tend to sell better.

Another example is **Nike's influencer marketing strategy**. By partnering with celebrities like **Michael Jordan, Cristiano Ronaldo, and Serena Williams**, Nike strengthens its brand authority and appeal. Seeing elite athletes endorse the brand **creates aspirational value and trust** among consumers.

Why It Works

1. **Builds Trust & Credibility:** Consumers trust **peer recommendations and authentic experiences** more than traditional advertising.

2. **Reduces Decision-Making Anxiety:** Seeing others validate a product/service **removes uncertainty and risk for new buyers.**

3. **Boosts Conversions & Sales:** Social proof **creates urgency and desire**, leading to increased sales and engagement.

4. **Strengthens Brand Authority:** Expert endorsements and high engagement **position a brand as an industry leader.**

5. **Encourages User-Generated Content (UGC):** Customers naturally share experiences, amplifying **word-of-mouth marketing.**

How It Works

1. **Collect & Display Customer Reviews:** Showcase testimonials, ratings, and user feedback **on websites, social media, and marketing materials.**

2. **Leverage Influencers & Brand Advocates:** Partner with influencers or satisfied customers who can **authentically promote products.**

3. **Highlight Social Media Engagement:** Display follower counts, likes, and trending hashtags to **demonstrate brand popularity.**

4. **Use "Best-Seller" & Popularity Indicators:** Labels like "Top Rated," "Most Sold," or "Trending Now" create a bandwagon effect.

5. **Create Case Studies & Success Stories:** Share **before-and-after transformations, testimonials, or client achievements** to provide tangible proof of value.

6. **Encourage UGC & Community Engagement:** Run campaigns that **incentivize customers to share experiences through photos, videos, or testimonials.**

Application

- **E-commerce & Retail:** Amazon, Sephora, and Etsy use **customer reviews, ratings, and UGC** to influence purchase decisions.

- **Technology & SaaS:** Companies like HubSpot and Salesforce highlight **case studies and industry awards** to showcase credibility.

- **Food & Beverage:** Starbucks and McDonald's promote **social media check-ins, UGC, and influencer partnerships** to increase engagement.

- **Fashion & Lifestyle Brands:** Zara and Gymshark use **social media influencers and community-driven UGC** to drive brand visibility.

- **Finance & Services:** Financial platforms like Robinhood and PayPal showcase **user success stories and referral incentives** to attract new users.

Key Insights

1. **Authenticity is Crucial:** Customers trust **real experiences more than staged promotions**—genuine social proof drives higher engagement.

2. **Quantity Matters, But Quality is Key:** A few detailed, high-quality testimonials can be **more persuasive than hundreds of generic reviews.**

3. **Encourage Customers to Share Experiences:** Businesses should actively request reviews, testimonials, and UGC to **amplify social proof efforts.**

4. **Leverage Multiple Social Proof Types:** Combining **reviews, influencer endorsements, case studies, and social engagement** enhances credibility.

5. **Social Proof is Self-Reinforcing:** The more people engage with a product or service, the stronger the **trust and influence effect becomes.**

Conclusion

The **Social Proof Strategy** is a powerful marketing approach that leverages **customer behaviour, reviews, and influencer validation** to build credibility and drive sales. Brands like **Amazon, Nike, and Starbucks** effectively use **testimonials, UGC, and expert endorsements** to influence purchasing decisions. By integrating social proof across multiple channels, businesses can **enhance trust, increase conversions, and establish long-term brand loyalty.**

76. Community Building Strategy

Community Building Strategy: A Comprehensive Breakdown

Theory

The **Community Building Strategy** is a business approach that focuses on creating and nurturing a **loyal, engaged group of customers, users, or supporters** around a brand, product, or cause. Instead of just selling to customers, businesses **foster**

relationships, encourage interactions, and build a shared sense of belonging within a community.

This strategy is based on key psychological and social principles:

1. **Sense of Belonging:** People are more likely to remain loyal to brands that provide a **community where they feel valued and connected.**
2. **Social Identity & Shared Values:** Customers align with brands that reflect their **lifestyle, beliefs, and aspirations.**
3. **Peer-to-Peer Influence:** Community members **influence each other's decisions, creating organic word-of-mouth marketing.**
4. **Engagement & Retention:** Customers involved in a brand community **stay longer, buy more, and engage more frequently.**
5. **User-Generated Content & Advocacy:** A strong community generates **valuable content, feedback, and brand ambassadors** who promote the business naturally.

By **nurturing relationships instead of just transactions**, businesses gain long-term loyalty, increased brand trust, and a built-in network of engaged supporters.

Example

A powerful example is **LEGO Ideas**, a platform where LEGO fans submit and vote on new set ideas. Winning designs get produced as official LEGO sets, with creators receiving recognition and a share of the profits. This **engages the community, fosters creativity, and strengthens brand loyalty** by making customers feel like active contributors.

Another example is **Nike Run Club (NRC)**, which offers running challenges, community meetups, and personalized achievements. Runners **connect with each other, track progress, and feel part of a global fitness movement**, strengthening Nike's brand presence and emotional connection with its users.

Why It Works

1. **Fosters Deep Brand Loyalty:** People who feel connected to a brand community are **less likely to switch to competitors.**

2. **Encourages Word-of-Mouth Marketing:** Engaged members **naturally share their experiences** with friends and social networks.

3. **Creates Sustainable Engagement:** Unlike paid marketing campaigns, communities **generate ongoing engagement at a lower cost.**

4. **Drives Customer-Led Innovation:** Communities provide **real-time feedback, ideas, and inspiration** for product improvements.

5. **Enhances Brand Authority & Credibility:** A thriving community strengthens **brand trust, making it more influential in the industry.**

How It Works

1. **Define the Community's Purpose & Identity:** Establish the **core mission, values, and objectives** of the community (e.g., innovation, fitness, professional growth).

2. **Create a Dedicated Space for Interaction:** Use **social media groups, forums, apps, or physical events** to connect members.

3. **Encourage Member Participation & Contribution:** Gamify engagement through **challenges, exclusive content, Q&As, and discussions.**

4. **Highlight & Reward Loyal Members:** Recognize active members through **badges, special perks, ambassador programs, or featured content.**

5. **Foster Peer-to-Peer Interaction:** Let members support, mentor, and inspire each other, **reducing the need for direct brand involvement.**

Application

- **Retail & E-commerce:** Sephora's **Beauty Insider Community** allows customers to discuss makeup trends, review products, and get expert advice.

- **Technology & SaaS:** Salesforce's **Trailblazer Community** connects users to help each other solve problems and share best practices.

- **Fitness & Health:** Peloton's **interactive social features, leaderboards, and live classes** keep users engaged and motivated.

- **Education & Learning:** Duolingo's **language-learning community forums and social challenges** encourage users to stay consistent.

- **Gaming & Entertainment:** Twitch's **interactive live streaming community** enables direct engagement between streamers and fans.

Key Insights

1. **Communities Must Offer Value:** Members stay engaged when they **gain knowledge, connections, or exclusive access** from being part of the group.

2. **Authenticity is Critical:** A brand-led community should feel **genuine, not just a marketing tactic.**

3. **Consistency Builds Trust:** Regular engagement through **events, content, and discussions** maintains long-term participation.

4. **Community Growth Should Be Organic:** Encourage natural expansion **through invitations, word-of-mouth, and quality interactions.**

5. **User-Generated Content is a Powerful Asset:** Businesses can **leverage community-driven content for marketing, testimonials, and social proof.**

Conclusion

The **Community Building Strategy** is a long-term, high-impact approach that **turns customers into engaged, loyal brand advocates.** Companies like **LEGO, Nike, and Sephora** demonstrate how fostering **connection, shared purpose, and ongoing engagement** leads to **stronger relationships, higher retention, and increased brand influence.** Businesses that create **authentic, value-driven communities** will enjoy **sustainable growth and deeper customer loyalty in an increasingly competitive marketplace.**

77. Gamification Strategy

Gamification Strategy: A Comprehensive Breakdown

Theory

The **Gamification Strategy** is a business approach that incorporates **game-like elements** into non-gaming environments, such as marketing, customer engagement, employee motivation, and product design. The goal is to **enhance engagement,** encourage desired behaviours, and create enjoyable user experiences** by tapping into the psychology of competition, rewards, and achievement.

Gamification works by leveraging key behavioural psychology principles:

1. **Intrinsic Motivation:** People naturally enjoy challenges, achievements, and recognition.
2. **Extrinsic Rewards:** Users are incentivized through **badges, points, discounts, or exclusive benefits.**
3. **Social Influence & Competition:** Leaderboards, rankings, and social sharing encourage **community interaction and status-seeking behaviour.**
4. **Progression & Mastery:** Users stay engaged when they see **measurable progress and rewards for continued participation.**
5. **Personalization & Challenges:** Adaptive difficulty levels and personalized incentives **keep users motivated and invested.**

When applied effectively, gamification increases **customer retention, employee productivity, and user engagement,** creating stronger brand loyalty and participation.

Example

A well-known example is **Nike Run Club and Nike+**, which gamifies fitness by **tracking progress, awarding badges, and**

offering social challenges where users compete with friends. This **motivates users to run more, stay engaged, and build long-term loyalty to Nike products.**

Another example is **Duolingo**, the language-learning app. Duolingo uses **streaks, XP points, leaderboards, and rewards** to encourage daily learning. This gamified approach has significantly **increased user retention and engagement.**

Why It Works

1. **Increases Engagement & Participation:** Users are more likely to stay involved when activities feel **fun and rewarding.**

2. **Encourages Consistent Behaviour:** Daily challenges, streaks, and progress tracking **reinforce habits and long-term commitment.**

3. **Enhances Customer & Employee Loyalty:** Gamification fosters **brand interaction and motivation**, leading to higher retention.

4. **Creates a Competitive Advantage:** Businesses that gamify experiences stand out in **crowded markets by making interactions more enjoyable.**

5. **Boosts Productivity & Learning:** Employees and learners become more invested when progress is rewarded, **improving efficiency and knowledge retention.**

How It Works

1. **Define Business Goals:** Identify what behaviours the company wants to **incentivize—customer engagement, employee productivity, or social sharing.**

2. **Choose the Right Gamification Elements:** Use **points, leaderboards, levels, badges, challenges, and rewards** tailored to the audience.

3. **Integrate Gamification Across Platforms:** Apply game mechanics to **apps, websites, social media, or internal workplace systems.**

4. **Encourage Social Interaction & Competition:** Allow users to **compete, compare scores, and share achievements** with their peers.

5. **Measure & Optimize:** Track user participation and adjust **game mechanics** to improve effectiveness and engagement.

Application

- **Retail & E-commerce: Starbucks Rewards** offers points, levels, and free drinks for frequent purchases.

- **Education & Learning: Duolingo and Khan Academy** use streaks and badges to keep learners engaged.

- **Health & Fitness: Nike Run Club and Fitbit** encourage users to achieve fitness goals through badges and challenges.

- **Workplace Productivity: Salesforce's gamified CRM system** rewards employees for completing sales tasks.

- **Financial Services: Banking apps offer cashback, milestones, and challenges** for savings and spending habits.

Key Insights

1. **Gamification Must Align with Business Goals:** Simply adding points isn't enough—it must drive **meaningful engagement and customer actions.**

2. **Rewards Should Be Valuable but Sustainable:** Offering **non-monetary incentives** like status, recognition, or exclusive perks can be just as effective.

3. **Simplicity & Ease of Use Are Crucial:** Overcomplicated gamification can **discourage participation.** Keep the system intuitive.

4. **Social Features Amplify Engagement:** Leaderboards, challenges, and social sharing **enhance motivation and organic reach.**

5. **Gamification Should Evolve Over Time:** Constantly update challenges, rewards, and features to **prevent user fatigue and disengagement.**

Conclusion

The **Gamification Strategy** is a powerful way to **enhance engagement, build loyalty, and encourage desired behaviours** in customers, employees, and users. Companies like **Nike, Duolingo, and Starbucks** demonstrate how gamification **creates enjoyable experiences that drive long-term participation.** By strategically integrating **game mechanics, rewards, and social interaction,** businesses can differentiate themselves and foster **stronger customer and employee relationships.**

78. Self-Service Strategy

Self-Service Strategy: A Comprehensive Breakdown

Theory

The **Self-Service Strategy** is a business approach that allows customers to **access services, find information, and complete transactions independently, without direct human assistance.** This strategy improves efficiency, reduces costs, and enhances customer experience by enabling users to get what they need quickly and conveniently.

Self-service is based on **automation, digital transformation, and user empowerment**. Businesses implement this strategy to:

1. **Enhance Convenience:** Customers prefer solutions that let them **resolve issues or complete transactions on their own time.**

2. **Reduce Operational Costs:** Automating processes **lowers labour costs and increases efficiency.**

3. **Scale Customer Support Effortlessly:** Businesses can serve more customers without adding more staff.

4. **Improve Speed & Efficiency:** Self-service eliminates wait times, **reducing frustration and improving satisfaction.**

5. **Enable 24/7 Availability:** Unlike human-assisted services, self-service platforms operate **around the clock.**

Common self-service tools include:

- **Chatbots & AI Assistants** (e.g., automated customer support).

- **Self-Checkout Kiosks** (e.g., retail and grocery stores).

- **Online Knowledge Bases & FAQs** (e.g., customer help centres).

- **Mobile Apps & Self-Service Portals** (e.g., banking, insurance, and utility services).

- **Automated Order & Reservation Systems** (e.g., food ordering, airline check-ins).

By enabling customers to help themselves, businesses improve efficiency while maintaining **customer autonomy and satisfaction.**

Example

A well-known example of the self-service strategy is **McDonald's self-order kiosks.** These touchscreens allow customers to **customize orders, pay digitally, and reduce wait times,** leading to increased order accuracy and faster service. The result? **Higher customer satisfaction and increased sales.**

Another example is **Netflix**, which uses **self-service content discovery and personalized recommendations** to let users find movies and shows independently. By removing the need for human interaction, Netflix **streamlines user engagement while enhancing experience.**

Why It Works

1. **Empowers Customers:** Giving users control over their interactions increases **satisfaction and brand loyalty.**

2. **Reduces Customer Service Bottlenecks:** Businesses minimize **long queues, wait times, and call centre congestion.**

3. **Enhances Speed & Efficiency:** Customers complete tasks **faster than traditional service methods.**

4. **Decreases Business Costs:** Fewer support requests mean **lower labour expenses and operational costs.**

5. **Meets Customer Expectations:** Modern consumers prefer **digital, on-demand solutions** over waiting for human assistance.

How It Works

1. **Identify High-Demand Self-Service Areas:** Find processes that customers prefer to handle independently (e.g., payments, troubleshooting).

2. **Develop User-Friendly Self-Service Tools:** Create **intuitive, easy-to-use digital platforms** that require minimal guidance.

3. **Integrate AI & Automation:** Use chatbots, voice assistants, and machine learning to **answer questions and guide users.**

4. **Ensure 24/7 Availability:** Self-service tools should function **anytime, anywhere** to meet customer needs.

5. **Continuously Improve & Update:** Use customer feedback and analytics to **refine the self-service experience.**

Application

- **Retail & Fast Food: Amazon Go & McDonald's** use self-checkout and digital ordering kiosks.

- **Banking & Finance: Chase & PayPal** provide self-service online banking, mobile deposits, and automated financial tools.

- **Healthcare & Insurance: Kaiser Permanente & Aetna** offer **patient portals for scheduling, billing, and prescription management.**

- **Technology & SaaS: Netflix & Microsoft** provide **self-help troubleshooting guides and AI-powered chat support.**

- **Travel & Hospitality: Airlines and hotels** use **self-check-in kiosks and online booking systems.**

Key Insights

1. **User Experience is Critical:** If self-service tools are confusing, customers will revert to human support, defeating the purpose.

2. **Automation & AI Enhance Effectiveness:** Chatbots and machine learning improve **problem resolution without human intervention.**

3. **Self-Service Should Complement, Not Replace, Human Support:** Some customers still prefer speaking to a person, so a **hybrid model is ideal.**

4. **Security & Privacy Must Be Prioritized:** Digital self-service solutions require **robust cybersecurity to protect customer data.**

5. **Businesses Must Continuously Optimize Self-Service:** Regular updates, user feedback, and analytics help improve efficiency.

Conclusion

The **Self-Service Strategy** is a powerful tool for **enhancing customer convenience, reducing operational costs, and improving efficiency.** Companies like **McDonald's, Netflix, and Amazon** successfully implement self-service solutions that **empower users, streamline operations, and increase engagement.** However, businesses must ensure that self-service options are **intuitive, secure, and continuously optimized** to meet evolving customer expectations.

79. Referral Program Strategy

Referral Program Strategy: A Comprehensive Breakdown

Theory

The **Referral Program Strategy** is a business approach that incentivizes existing customers to **refer new customers** in exchange for rewards. This strategy leverages the power of **word-of-mouth marketing, trust, and social influence** to drive customer acquisition at a lower cost compared to traditional advertising.

Referral programs work based on **social proof and trust**, as people are more likely to try a product or service when it is recommended by **friends, family, or colleagues** rather than advertisements. Key principles of a successful referral strategy include:

1. **Trust & Credibility:** People trust recommendations from those they know, increasing **conversion rates** compared to other marketing channels.

2. **Incentivization:** Rewards (e.g., discounts, cash, free products) motivate customers to **actively promote the brand.**

3. **Win-Win Model:** Both the referrer and the referred customer often receive benefits, increasing engagement.

4. **Viral Potential:** A well-structured referral system can lead to **exponential growth** as new customers bring in additional referrals.

5. **Cost-Effective Customer Acquisition:** Referral programs often have a **lower cost per acquisition (CPA)** than paid advertising, making them **highly scalable.**

By creating an easy and rewarding referral process, businesses **turn their existing customers into brand advocates**, leading to sustainable and organic growth.

Example

A famous example of a successful referral program is **Dropbox's referral strategy**. Dropbox offered **500MB of free cloud storage** to both the referrer and the referred user. This incentive led to a **60% increase in sign-ups** and helped Dropbox grow from **100,000 users to 4 million in just 15 months**—all without excessive marketing costs.

Another example is **Tesla's referral program**, where Tesla owners could refer friends to buy a Tesla and earn rewards such as **free Supercharging miles, priority vehicle delivery, and even the chance to win a free Tesla Roadster**. This led to **massive word-of-mouth marketing and increased brand loyalty**.

Why It Works

1. **Leverages Social Proof:** People trust recommendations from personal connections more than traditional ads.

2. **Encourages Organic Growth:** Referral programs create a **self-sustaining acquisition loop** with minimal marketing spend.

3. **Increases Customer Retention:** Referred customers tend to be **more loyal and engaged** compared to customers from paid ads.

4. **Creates a Sense of Exclusivity & Urgency:** Offering **limited-time referral bonuses** boosts participation.

5. **Boosts Brand Advocacy:** Happy customers become **brand ambassadors**, continuously promoting the business.

How It Works

1. **Design an Appealing Incentive System:** Offer a **mutually beneficial reward** (e.g., discounts, store credit, free trials).
2. **Simplify the Referral Process:** Make sharing easy with **unique referral links, social media sharing, or in-app invites.**
3. **Promote the Referral Program:** Actively market the program through **emails, push notifications, website banners, and social media.**
4. **Track and Optimize Performance:** Use **analytics to measure referral rates, conversions, and customer retention.**
5. **Continuously Improve the Program:** Adjust rewards, referral limits, or bonus structures to **maximize engagement.**

Application

- **SaaS & Technology:** Dropbox, Uber, and Airbnb offer **discounts or credits** for referrals.

- **E-commerce & Retail:** Amazon and Sephora provide **store credits or loyalty points** for referring friends.

- **Finance & Banking:** PayPal and Robinhood give **cash bonuses** for referring new users.

- **Fitness & Wellness:** ClassPass and Peloton encourage referrals by offering **free classes or extended memberships.**

- **Subscription Services:** Netflix and Spotify use referral incentives to **grow their user base and engagement.**

Key Insights

1. **The Reward Must Be Valuable & Relevant:** The incentive should align with **what customers truly want (e.g., discounts, free perks, VIP access).**

2. **Ease of Sharing is Critical:** A complicated referral process **reduces participation rates.**

3. **Referred Customers Are High-Quality Leads:** Referred users **convert at higher rates and have a longer lifetime value.**

4. **Multi-Tier Referral Programs Work Well:** Offering **additional rewards for multiple referrals** encourages viral growth.

5. **Ongoing Optimization is Necessary:** Analyzing referral data helps businesses **adjust rewards and messaging** for maximum impact.

Conclusion

The **Referral Program Strategy** is a powerful and cost-effective way to **acquire new customers, boost retention, and strengthen brand advocacy.** Companies like **Dropbox, Tesla, and PayPal** have successfully scaled their businesses by leveraging the **trust and influence of their existing users.** By **offering valuable rewards, making referrals easy, and continuously optimizing the program**, businesses can create **a sustainable growth engine that turns customers into brand ambassadors.**

80. Subscription Retention Strategy

Subscription Retention Strategy: A Comprehensive Breakdown

Theory

The **Subscription Retention Strategy** is a business approach focused on keeping existing subscribers engaged, satisfied, and continuously renewing their subscriptions. Since acquiring new customers is far more expensive than retaining existing ones, businesses invest in **long-term customer relationships,**

personalized experiences, and ongoing value delivery to reduce churn and maximize customer lifetime value (CLV).

Retention strategies rely on **habit formation, engagement triggers, and loyalty-building techniques** to ensure that subscribers remain active and satisfied. Key principles include:

1. **Consistent Value Delivery:** Subscribers must feel they are continuously getting value from the service.

2. **Personalization & Engagement:** Tailoring content, offers, and communication to each user's preferences improves retention.

3. **Seamless User Experience:** An intuitive and frictionless experience reduces frustration and increases stickiness.

4. **Proactive Customer Support:** Addressing issues before they lead to cancellations prevents churn.

5. **Loyalty & Reward Systems:** Incentives, exclusive perks, and loyalty rewards encourage long-term commitment.

By keeping subscribers engaged and reducing churn, businesses create **sustainable revenue streams and stronger brand loyalty.**

Example

A great example of a strong subscription retention strategy is **Netflix**. Netflix **uses AI-driven personalized recommendations** to keep users engaged with relevant content. It also implements **seamless auto-renewals, flexible pricing plans, and original exclusive content**, ensuring customers remain subscribed.

Another example is **Amazon Prime**, which increases retention through **bundled benefits like free shipping, Prime Video, Prime Music, and exclusive deals**. By offering **multiple value propositions**, Amazon ensures subscribers see ongoing reasons to stay.

Why It Works

1. **Increases Customer Lifetime Value (CLV):** Long-term subscribers generate **consistent revenue**, maximizing business profitability.

2. **Reduces Churn & Improves Stability:** Fewer cancellations mean **predictable, steady revenue** and better forecasting.

3. **Enhances Brand Loyalty & Engagement:** Engaged subscribers **form habits around the service, making it harder to leave.**

4. **Encourages Word-of-Mouth Marketing:** Satisfied subscribers often **refer friends and promote the service organically.**

5. **Optimizes Customer Acquisition Costs (CAC):** Retaining customers costs significantly **less than acquiring new ones**, improving ROI.

How It Works

1. **Personalize Subscriber Experiences:** Use **AI, behavioural analytics, and feedback loops** to tailor content, offers, and engagement.

2. **Deliver Continuous Value:** Keep subscribers engaged by introducing **new features, exclusive content, and special perks.**

3. **Reduce Subscription Friction:** Ensure **easy onboarding, flexible billing options, and hassle-free renewals.**

4. **Implement Proactive Customer Support:** Use **live chat, automated support bots, and proactive problem resolution** to keep customers satisfied.

5. **Offer Loyalty & Reward Incentives:** Provide **discounts, free trials, VIP perks, and referral bonuses** for long-term subscribers.

6. **Analyse & Address Churn Risks:** Identify **inactive users, offer retention discounts, and re-engage at-risk subscribers.**

Application

- **Streaming Services: Netflix, Disney+, and Spotify** use personalized recommendations, original content, and exclusive perks to retain subscribers.

- **E-commerce & Memberships: Amazon Prime** keeps users subscribed by bundling **multiple benefits across shopping, entertainment, and services.**

- **SaaS & Cloud Services: Dropbox and Adobe Creative Cloud** implement tiered pricing, loyalty rewards, and seamless integrations.

- **Health & Fitness Apps: Peloton and Fitbit Premium** provide personalized workout plans, streak rewards, and community engagement.

- **Financial Services & Subscription Boxes: HelloFresh, Birchbox, and Dollar Shave Club** offer exclusive savings, early access, and premium features.

Key Insights

1. **Retention Starts at Onboarding:** A **strong first experience** increases the likelihood of long-term engagement.

2. **Data-Driven Personalization is Essential:** AI-driven recommendations and **tailored content** improve stickiness.

3. **Churn Prevention Requires Proactive Action:** Businesses should **monitor engagement levels and re-engage inactive users** before cancellations.

4. **Seamless Billing & Subscription Flexibility Reduce Drop-offs:** Offering **pause options, flexible pricing, and easy cancellations** prevents frustration.

5. **Loyalty Rewards & Exclusive Perks Strengthen Retention:** The more **value-added benefits subscribers receive, the harder it is to leave.**

Conclusion

The **Subscription Retention Strategy** is crucial for businesses that **depend on recurring revenue models**. Companies like **Netflix, Amazon Prime, and Spotify** have mastered **personalized engagement, exclusive content, and seamless experiences** to maximize retention. By implementing **proactive customer support, personalized offerings, and value-driven incentives**, businesses can **reduce churn, increase lifetime value, and build lasting customer relationships**.

Disruption & Future-Focused Strategies, Innovating for long-term dominance:

81. AI & Data-Driven Strategy

AI & Data-Driven Strategy: A Comprehensive Breakdown

Theory

The **AI & Data-Driven Strategy** is a business approach that leverages **artificial intelligence (AI), machine learning (ML), and**

big data analytics to enhance decision-making, optimize operations, and personalize customer experiences. Companies that implement this strategy use **real-time insights, predictive analytics, and automation** to gain a competitive edge, improve efficiency, and drive revenue growth.

The core principles of this strategy include:

1. **Data Collection & Integration:** Businesses aggregate structured and unstructured data from multiple sources (e.g., customer behaviour, sales trends, social media, IoT devices).

2. **Predictive & Prescriptive Analytics:** AI algorithms forecast trends, automate responses, and recommend actions.

3. **Personalization & Customer Insights:** AI enhances customer interactions through **personalized recommendations, dynamic pricing, and chatbots.**

4. **Operational Efficiency & Automation:** AI-driven tools optimize **inventory management, fraud detection, supply chain logistics, and workforce productivity.**

5. **Continuous Learning & Adaptability:** AI systems improve over time through **self-learning models that adapt to new patterns.**

By embedding AI and data-driven insights into business processes, companies **increase efficiency, enhance customer engagement, and unlock new revenue streams.**

Example

A great example of AI-driven strategy is **Amazon**, which utilizes AI for **personalized product recommendations, demand forecasting, warehouse automation, and customer service chatbots.** Its recommendation engine, powered by AI, **drives 35% of total sales**, showing how predictive analytics significantly enhances revenue.

Another example is **Tesla**, which collects real-time data from its vehicles to **improve self-driving capabilities and optimize vehicle performance.** Tesla's AI-driven software updates allow continuous improvement without requiring customers to buy new cars.

Why It Works

1. **Enhances Decision-Making:** AI processes vast amounts of data quickly, providing **data-driven insights for better strategic decisions.**

2. **Drives Efficiency & Cost Savings:** Automation reduces manual work, minimizes errors, and optimizes workflows.

3. **Increases Revenue & Market Competitiveness:** Businesses that leverage AI-driven insights improve **sales, pricing strategies, and customer retention.**

4. **Improves Customer Experience:** AI enables **hyper-personalization, real-time support, and seamless customer interactions.**

5. **Detects Patterns & Prevents Risks:** AI helps **identify fraud, cybersecurity threats, and operational inefficiencies before they escalate.**

How It Works

1. **Collect & Organize Data:** Gather **customer, market, and operational data** from multiple touchpoints.

2. **Implement AI & Analytics Tools:** Use **AI-powered CRM systems, predictive models, and automation platforms** to analyse data.

3. **Personalize & Automate Processes:** Deploy AI for **dynamic pricing, chatbots, recommendation engines, and workflow automation.**

4. **Optimize & Continuously Improve:** AI algorithms refine themselves using **machine learning feedback loops.**

5. **Monitor & Ensure Data Governance:** Implement **data privacy, compliance regulations, and ethical AI use** to maintain trust.

Application

- **E-commerce & Retail: Amazon and Walmart** use AI for personalized shopping experiences and inventory optimization.

- **Financial Services: JPMorgan and PayPal** apply AI for **fraud detection, credit risk analysis, and chatbot-driven customer support.**

- **Healthcare & Biotech: IBM Watson and Moderna** leverage AI for **diagnostics, drug discovery, and personalized treatments.**

- **Automotive & Manufacturing: Tesla and BMW** utilize AI in **autonomous driving and predictive maintenance.**

- **Media & Entertainment: Netflix and Spotify** use AI for content recommendations and user engagement.

Key Insights

1. **AI & Data Should Drive Business Strategy, Not Just Support It:** Businesses must integrate AI at a **strategic level, not just for operational efficiency.**

2. **Ethical AI Use & Data Privacy Are Critical:** Companies must ensure **transparent AI models and compliance with GDPR, CCPA, and other regulations.**

3. **Personalization & Automation Improve Customer Loyalty:** AI-driven **recommendations, chatbots, and predictive marketing** enhance engagement.

4. **AI Must Continuously Learn & Adapt:** The best AI systems **improve over time through machine learning and real-time feedback.**

5. **Competitive Advantage Lies in Data Quality:** AI is only as good as the data it analyses—**clean, relevant, and diverse datasets are essential.**

Conclusion

The **AI & Data-Driven Strategy** is transforming industries by enabling **smarter decision-making, automation, and personalization at scale.** Companies like **Amazon, Tesla, and Netflix** demonstrate how leveraging AI enhances **efficiency, customer experience, and revenue growth.** Businesses that invest in **AI-driven analytics, automation, and continuous learning** will remain competitive and future-proof in a rapidly evolving digital economy.

82. Blockchain Strategy

Blockchain Strategy: A Comprehensive Breakdown

Theory

The **Blockchain Strategy** is a business approach that leverages **decentralized, transparent, and secure blockchain technology** to enhance operations, security, and trust. Blockchain is a **distributed ledger system** that records transactions in a **secure, immutable, and decentralized** manner, eliminating the need for intermediaries and enhancing efficiency.

Key principles of blockchain strategy include:

1. **Decentralization:** Transactions are recorded across a distributed network, reducing reliance on central authorities (e.g., banks, regulators).

2. **Transparency & Trust:** Transactions are **publicly verifiable**, ensuring greater accountability and reducing fraud.

3. **Security & Immutability:** Data on the blockchain **cannot be altered or tampered with**, increasing data integrity.

4. **Smart Contracts:** Self-executing contracts automate processes **without human intervention, reducing operational costs.**

5. **Tokenization & Digital Assets:** Blockchain enables **tokenization of assets** (e.g., cryptocurrencies, NFTs, real estate, supply chain goods).

Businesses adopting blockchain **enhance security, reduce transaction costs, and streamline operations**, leading to increased trust and efficiency.

Example

A leading example of blockchain strategy is **IBM Food Trust**, which uses blockchain to track food supply chains. By recording transactions securely, IBM enables **farmers, suppliers, and retailers to trace food origins**, reducing fraud and improving food safety.

Another example is **Bitcoin**, the first successful decentralized cryptocurrency. It removes the need for traditional banking systems, allowing **peer-to-peer financial transactions without intermediaries**, demonstrating the power of blockchain in finance.

Why It Works

1. **Eliminates Middlemen & Reduces Costs:** Transactions occur directly between parties, reducing the need for **banks, brokers, and intermediaries.**

2. **Enhances Security & Fraud Prevention:** Blockchain's cryptographic security ensures **data integrity and prevents hacking.**

3. **Increases Transparency & Traceability:** Every transaction is recorded permanently, allowing businesses to **track supply chains, financial transactions, and digital ownership.**

4. **Automates & Speeds Up Transactions:** Smart contracts reduce **paperwork, delays, and administrative inefficiencies.**

5. **Boosts Consumer & Stakeholder Trust:** Decentralized and publicly verifiable records **increase confidence in transactions and data authenticity.**

How It Works

1. **Define Business Objectives:** Identify areas where blockchain can improve **efficiency, security, or transparency.**

2. **Select the Right Blockchain Type:**
    - **Public Blockchain** (e.g., Bitcoin, Ethereum) for open, decentralized applications.
    - **Private Blockchain** (e.g., Hyperledger) for business-specific applications with controlled access.

3. **Implement Smart Contracts & Automation:** Use **self-executing contracts** to **automate payments, agreements, and workflows.**

4. **Integrate with Existing Systems:** Ensure **seamless interoperability** with financial, supply chain, or customer management systems.

5. **Monitor, Scale & Secure the Network:** Continuously **optimize security, scalability, and compliance** to ensure long-term efficiency.

Application

- **Finance & Banking: JPMorgan and DeFi platforms** use blockchain for **cross-border payments, fraud prevention, and smart contracts.**

- **Supply Chain & Logistics: Walmart and Maersk** use blockchain for **real-time tracking of goods and reducing counterfeit risks.**

- **Healthcare & Pharmaceuticals: Pfizer and IBM Watson Health** leverage blockchain for **secure patient records and drug authentication.**

- **Real Estate & Legal: Propy and Smart Contracts** allow blockchain-based **property transactions without intermediaries.**

- **Digital Identity & Cybersecurity: Microsoft and Civic** use blockchain for **secure identity verification and fraud prevention.**

Key Insights

1. **Blockchain Adoption Requires Infrastructure & Integration:** Companies must ensure **existing systems can support blockchain integration.**

2. **Not Every Business Needs Blockchain:** Blockchain is most valuable for **industries requiring security, transparency, and decentralization.**

3. **Regulations & Compliance Are Evolving:** Governments are still defining **legal frameworks for blockchain applications.**

4. **Scalability & Energy Consumption Are Challenges:** Some blockchain networks require **high computing power, impacting efficiency.**

5. **Blockchain's Impact is Expanding Beyond Cryptocurrency:** It is now widely used in **finance, healthcare, supply chain, and digital identity management.**

Conclusion

The **Blockchain Strategy** transforms business operations by providing **decentralized security, transparency, and automation** through smart contracts and cryptographic verification. Companies like **IBM, Walmart, and JPMorgan** showcase blockchain's potential to **enhance trust, streamline transactions, and reduce fraud.** Businesses that strategically integrate blockchain will **future-proof operations, increase efficiency, and gain a competitive edge in the digital economy.**

83. Metaverse Strategy

Metaverse Strategy: A Comprehensive Breakdown

Theory

The **Metaverse Strategy** is a business approach that leverages **virtual, augmented, and mixed reality environments** to engage customers, create digital economies, and enhance brand experiences. The metaverse is a **shared, immersive digital space** where users can interact with brands, socialize, conduct business, and even own virtual assets through blockchain technology.

The strategy is built on key technological and business principles:

1. **Immersive Virtual Experiences:** Businesses create **3D environments, virtual storefronts, and interactive brand spaces** to enhance user engagement.

2. **Decentralization & Digital Ownership:** Blockchain enables **virtual real estate, digital goods, and NFTs (non-fungible tokens)** for secure ownership.

3. **Real-Time Social & Economic Interactions:** The metaverse allows for **real-time communication, events, and transactions** without physical limitations.

4. **Gamification & Engagement:** Brands integrate **game-like elements** to keep users active and immersed.

5. **Interoperability & Digital Identity:** Users have **persistent avatars and digital assets** that function across multiple platforms.

By adopting a **Metaverse Strategy**, businesses can **reach global audiences, create new revenue streams, and pioneer the future of digital interaction.**

Example

A notable example of a metaverse business strategy is **Nike's "Nikeland" in Roblox**, where users can explore a virtual world, participate in interactive games, and purchase **digital Nike gear for their avatars**. This has allowed Nike to engage with younger audiences and **monetize digital fashion.**

Another example is **Decentraland**, a blockchain-based virtual world where users and businesses can **buy virtual real estate, open virtual stores, and host events.** Major brands like **Samsung and JPMorgan** have established a presence there to attract digital consumers.

Why It Works

1. **Expands Brand Reach & Engagement:** The metaverse allows businesses to **interact with a global audience in immersive ways.**

2. **Creates New Revenue Streams:** Virtual goods, NFTs, and experiences can **generate additional profits** beyond physical products.

3. **Enhances Customer Experience & Loyalty:** Immersive interactions make brands **more memorable and engaging.**

4. **Future-Proofs Businesses for Web3:** Early adopters **gain a competitive edge** as digital ecosystems grow.

5. **Drives Innovation & Experimentation:** The metaverse enables brands to **test new digital products, services, and marketing techniques.**

How It Works

1. **Establish a Virtual Presence:** Companies create **virtual stores, branded worlds, or social spaces** in metaverse platforms.

2. **Integrate Blockchain & Digital Assets:** NFTs and cryptocurrency allow **users to buy, trade, and own virtual goods.**

3. **Develop Immersive Experiences:** Brands offer **gamified interactions, exclusive events, and digital collectibles** to engage users.

4. **Enable Social & Community Engagement:** Users interact with **brand ambassadors, influencers, and other customers** in real-time.

5. **Monetize Through Digital Commerce:** Businesses sell **virtual merchandise, event tickets, and brand collaborations.**

Application

- **Retail & Fashion: Nike, Gucci, and Balenciaga** sell digital fashion and virtual collectibles.
- **Entertainment & Events: Travis Scott's virtual concert in Fortnite** attracted millions of viewers.

- **Real Estate & Virtual Offices: Decentraland and The Sandbox** enable businesses to **own virtual land and conduct virtual meetings.**

- **Education & Training: Meta and Microsoft** use metaverse spaces for **virtual learning, simulations, and corporate training.**

- **Finance & Banking: JPMorgan's metaverse lounge** in Decentraland provides **financial services in virtual environments.**

Key Insights

1. **The Metaverse is Still Evolving:** While opportunities are vast, businesses must **adapt to technological advancements and user behaviours.**

2. **Blockchain Integration Enhances Security & Ownership:** Decentralized assets **increase trust and authenticity.**

3. **Virtual Goods & Experiences Drive Engagement:** Digital fashion, NFT art, and in-game purchases create **new business models.**

4. **Community Building is Essential:** The most successful metaverse brands foster **active, engaged user communities.**

5. **Scalability & Adoption Will Take Time:** Businesses must **experiment, iterate, and refine their strategies** as the metaverse matures.

Conclusion

The **Metaverse Strategy** represents the next frontier of digital business, enabling brands to create **immersive experiences, digital economies, and interactive communities.** Companies like **Nike, Gucci, and JPMorgan** are already investing in **virtual storefronts, blockchain integration, and digital engagement.** As the metaverse continues to evolve, businesses that **adopt innovative strategies, focus on user experience, and build digital-first communities** will gain a competitive advantage in this new digital era.

84. Web3 Strategy

Web3 Strategy: A Comprehensive Breakdown

Theory

The **Web3 Strategy** is a business approach that leverages decentralized technologies, blockchain, and token-based economies to create more transparent, user-controlled, and community-driven digital ecosystems. Unlike Web2, where centralized platforms (e.g., Google, Facebook, Amazon) control user data, Web3 empowers individuals through decentralization, smart contracts, and cryptographic security.

Key pillars of Web3 strategy include:

1. Decentralization: Instead of being controlled by corporations, Web3 applications run on blockchain networks like Ethereum, Solana, and Polkadot.

2. Tokenization & Digital Ownership: Users can own NFTs (non-fungible tokens), cryptocurrencies, and other digital assets that represent real-world or virtual value.

3. Smart Contracts & Automation: Self-executing contracts reduce the need for intermediaries in financial transactions, governance, and supply chains.

4. User Sovereignty & Privacy: Web3 prioritizes data ownership, self-sovereign identities (SSI), and peer-to-peer interactions.

5. Decentralized Finance (DeFi) & Monetization: Financial services, lending, and payments occur through DeFi platforms without traditional banks.

By integrating Web3 principles, businesses enhance transparency, increase user engagement, and open new revenue streams through token economies.

Example

A major example of Web3 in action is Axie Infinity, a play-to-earn (P2E) game where players earn cryptocurrency and NFTs that hold real-world value. This model transforms gaming into an economy, where players are financially incentivized to participate and contribute to the ecosystem.

Another example is Uniswap, a decentralized exchange (DEX) that allows users to trade cryptocurrencies without a central authority. By eliminating middlemen, Uniswap provides lower fees, more transparency, and better user control over digital assets.

Why It Works

1. Empowers Users & Reduces Centralized Control: Web3 removes reliance on large corporations and shifts power to individuals.

2. Increases Transparency & Security: Blockchain records transactions immutably, reducing fraud and ensuring trustless interactions.

3. Creates New Business & Revenue Models: Token economies, NFT marketplaces, and DeFi offer alternative monetization strategies.

4. Encourages Community Ownership & Governance: DAOs (Decentralized Autonomous Organizations) allow users to collectively manage projects and make decisions.

5. Future-Proofs Digital Businesses: As Web3 adoption grows, early adopters will gain a competitive advantage in the decentralized internet economy.

How It Works

1. **Adopt Blockchain & Smart Contracts:** Businesses integrate Ethereum, Solana, or Polygon to enable decentralized transactions and automation.

2. **Tokenize Assets & Create Incentives:** Companies issue utility tokens, governance tokens, or NFTs to incentivize participation.

3. **Enable Peer-to-Peer Transactions:** Web3 removes intermediaries, allowing direct user-to-user payments, content sharing, and commerce.

4. **Implement Decentralized Governance:** DAOs let users vote on protocol upgrades, product decisions, and revenue distribution.

5. **Focus on Data Privacy & Security:** Self-sovereign identities and decentralized storage protect user data and eliminate third-party tracking.

Application

- **Finance & DeFi:** Uniswap, Aave, and MakerDAO offer decentralized lending, staking, and crypto exchanges.

- **Gaming & Metaverse:** Axie Infinity and Decentraland use Web3 to enable play-to-earn economies and virtual ownership.

- **Content & Social Media:** Lens Protocol and Audius allow creators to monetize content without platform interference.

- **Retail & E-commerce:** Luxury brands like Gucci and Nike issue NFTs for exclusive digital fashion and collectibles.

- **Healthcare & Data Security:** Web3 identity solutions protect patient records and enable secure, user-controlled data sharing.

Key Insights

1. **Decentralization Reshapes Business Models:** Companies must rethink how they interact with customers, shifting from ownership to shared participation.

2. **Tokenization Unlocks New Value Streams:** Brands can monetize NFTs, staking models, and decentralized economies to drive revenue.

3. **Web3 is Still Evolving:** While opportunities are vast, scalability, regulation, and adoption remain key challenges.

4. **Community is the Foundation:** Success in Web3 depends on engaged, incentivized communities rather than centralized decision-making.

5. **Security & Trust are Critical:** Businesses must ensure blockchain security, smart contract integrity, and compliance with emerging regulations.

Conclusion

The **Web3 Strategy is revolutionizing digital business by introducing decentralized ownership, token economies, and user-driven governance. Companies like Axie Infinity, Uniswap, and Decentraland showcase how Web3 can transform gaming, finance, and digital commerce. Businesses that adopt blockchain, NFTs, and decentralized finance (DeFi) will position themselves at the forefront of the next internet era, offering more transparency, ownership, and community-driven innovation.**

85. Sustainability-Driven Strategy

Sustainability-Driven Strategy: A Comprehensive Breakdown

Theory

The **Sustainability-Driven Strategy** is a business approach that integrates **environmental, social, and governance (ESG) principles** into company operations, decision-making, and long-term planning. The goal is to **balance profitability with environmental responsibility and social impact**, ensuring that business success contributes positively to the planet and society.

Key pillars of this strategy include:

1. **Environmental Responsibility:** Reducing carbon footprint, waste, and resource consumption through **eco-friendly**

processes, renewable energy, and sustainable supply chains.

2. **Social Responsibility:** Ensuring ethical labour practices, diversity and inclusion, and investing in **community development**.

3. **Corporate Governance & Transparency:** Upholding responsible leadership, regulatory compliance, and **accountability in sustainability initiatives**.

4. **Sustainable Innovation:** Developing products and services that **reduce environmental impact while delivering value to consumers**.

5. **Circular Economy Principles:** Transitioning from a linear "take-make-dispose" model to **a circular system focused on recycling, reusing, and repurposing** materials.

Companies adopting sustainability strategies **enhance brand reputation, reduce risks, and improve long-term profitability** while addressing global challenges like climate change, pollution, and social inequality.

Example

A prime example of a sustainability-driven business is **Patagonia**, the outdoor clothing brand that integrates sustainability into every aspect of its operations. Patagonia uses **recycled materials, fair trade practices, and eco-friendly production methods** while advocating for **climate activism and responsible consumerism**. The company even launched the "Worn Wear" program, encouraging customers to **repair and recycle** clothing rather than buying new products.

Another example is **Tesla**, which revolutionized the automotive industry by promoting **electric vehicles (EVs) as a sustainable alternative to fossil fuel-powered cars**. By investing in **renewable energy, battery technology, and carbon reduction**, Tesla has driven widespread adoption of **clean energy solutions**.

Why It Works

1. **Aligns with Consumer & Investor Expectations:** Modern consumers and investors prefer brands committed to **sustainability, ethical sourcing, and social impact**.

2. **Reduces Costs & Increases Efficiency:** Sustainable practices like **energy efficiency, waste reduction, and water conservation** lower operating expenses.

3. **Strengthens Brand Loyalty & Competitive Advantage:** Companies that demonstrate **genuine sustainability efforts** build **trust, credibility, and long-term customer relationships**.

4. **Ensures Regulatory Compliance & Risk Mitigation:** Adhering to ESG regulations and sustainability standards **reduces legal and reputational risks**.

5. **Encourages Innovation & Market Differentiation:** Sustainability-driven companies create **eco-friendly products, ethical supply chains, and green technologies**, setting themselves apart.

How It Works

1. **Assess Environmental & Social Impact:** Conduct a sustainability audit to identify **areas for improvement in energy use, waste management, and ethical sourcing.**

2. **Set Clear & Measurable Sustainability Goals:** Commit to targets like **carbon neutrality, zero waste production, or ethical labour standards.**

3. **Integrate Sustainability into Supply Chains:** Work with **eco-conscious suppliers, use sustainable materials, and optimize logistics** for minimal environmental impact.

4. **Engage Stakeholders & Consumers:** Educate customers on sustainability efforts, implement **transparent reporting**, and involve communities in **corporate social responsibility (CSR) initiatives.**

5. **Leverage Technology for Sustainability:** Use **AI, IoT, and blockchain** to track emissions, monitor resource use, and ensure **supply chain transparency.**

Application

- **Retail & Fashion: Patagonia and H&M's Conscious Collection** promote **recycled materials and sustainable clothing.**

- **Automotive & Transportation: Tesla and Toyota's hybrid models** support **low-carbon mobility solutions.**

- **Food & Agriculture: Beyond Meat and Impossible Foods** reduce **environmental impact by offering plant-based alternatives.**

- **Energy & Manufacturing: IKEA and Unilever** invest in **renewable energy, zero-waste production, and circular economy principles.**

- **Finance & Investment: BlackRock and ESG-focused funds** allocate capital toward **sustainable businesses and green bonds.**

Key Insights

1. **Sustainability is a Long-Term Commitment:** Businesses must **continuously adapt, innovate, and refine sustainability initiatives** to remain relevant.

2. **Transparency & Accountability Build Trust:** Companies should report sustainability progress through **ESG disclosures and impact assessments.**

3. **Greenwashing is a Risk:** Brands must avoid **false sustainability claims** and ensure that initiatives are **genuine and measurable.**

4. **Collaboration Amplifies Impact:** Partnering with **NGOs, governments, and other businesses** accelerates sustainability goals.

5. **Sustainable Innovation Drives Growth:** Companies that embrace **eco-friendly technologies, carbon reduction, and ethical practices** will lead in the future economy.

Conclusion

The **Sustainability-Driven Strategy** is no longer optional—it is essential for businesses seeking **long-term success, consumer trust, and regulatory compliance.** Companies like **Patagonia, Tesla, and Unilever** have shown that **profitability and sustainability can coexist.** Businesses that prioritize **eco-conscious innovation, ethical practices, and responsible governance** will not only reduce environmental impact but also gain a **competitive advantage in a rapidly changing global market.**

86. Crisis Management Strategy

Crisis Management Strategy: A Comprehensive Breakdown

Theory

The **Crisis Management Strategy** is a structured approach businesses use to **prepare for, respond to, and recover from unexpected events** that could disrupt operations, damage reputation, or harm stakeholders. These crises can include **natural disasters, financial downturns, cybersecurity breaches, PR scandals, or supply chain disruptions.**

A well-developed crisis management strategy is based on **proactive planning, rapid response, and transparent communication.** The key components include:

1. **Risk Assessment & Preparedness:** Identifying potential crises, assessing vulnerabilities, and developing **contingency plans.**

2. **Crisis Response Team & Leadership:** Designating **decision-makers and spokespeople** to handle crises effectively.

3. **Crisis Communication Plan:** Crafting **clear, transparent, and timely messaging** to internal and external stakeholders.

4. **Operational Continuity & Recovery:** Ensuring that essential business functions **continue running or are quickly restored.**

5. **Post-Crisis Evaluation & Improvement:** Analyzing **lessons learned** and updating strategies for future resilience.

A strong **Crisis Management Strategy** helps businesses **mitigate damage, maintain trust, and recover quickly** while safeguarding long-term stability.

Example

A well-known example of effective crisis management is **Johnson & Johnson's response to the 1982 Tylenol poisoning crisis**. When several consumers died due to **tampered Tylenol capsules**, Johnson & Johnson **immediately recalled 31 million bottles, issued public warnings, and introduced tamper-proof packaging**. Their **swift action, transparency, and commitment to safety** helped restore public trust and solidify the company's reputation.

In contrast, **BP's response to the Deepwater Horizon oil spill in 2010** was widely criticized for **slow reactions, lack of**

accountability, and poor communication, leading to lasting damage to its brand and financial losses.

Why It Works

1. **Minimizes Financial & Reputational Damage:** Quick action reduces **losses, legal risks, and long-term brand erosion.**

2. **Enhances Public Trust & Stakeholder Confidence:** Transparent communication reassures **customers, employees, and investors.**

3. **Ensures Business Continuity:** Effective crisis planning prevents **operational shutdowns and minimizes disruption.**

4. **Strengthens Organizational Resilience:** Learning from crises helps **businesses become stronger and better prepared for future risks.**

5. **Improves Decision-Making Under Pressure:** A pre-established plan allows leaders to **act decisively and efficiently.**

How It Works

1. **Identify & Assess Risks:** Conduct risk assessments to **anticipate potential crises and develop response plans.**

2. **Establish a Crisis Management Team:** Designate key executives, PR specialists, legal advisors, and operational leaders.

3. **Develop a Crisis Communication Plan:** Create **pre-approved messaging templates** for public statements, social media, and press releases.

4. **Simulate & Train for Crisis Scenarios:** Conduct **crisis drills and scenario planning** to test preparedness.

5. **Implement & Adapt During a Crisis:** Activate response plans, communicate effectively, and **adjust strategies as the situation evolves**.

6. **Analyse & Improve Post-Crisis:** Evaluate the response, document lessons learned, and update **crisis management frameworks**.

Application

- **Retail & Consumer Goods: Johnson & Johnson and Nestlé** have handled **product recalls and safety crises** effectively.
- **Technology & Cybersecurity: Facebook and Equifax** faced data breaches, highlighting the importance of **cyber crisis response plans**.
- **Energy & Manufacturing: BP's oil spill and Toyota's faulty accelerator recall** demonstrated crisis **communication strengths and failures**.

- **Financial Services: Goldman Sachs and Wells Fargo** have managed crises related to **financial fraud and regulatory breaches.**
- **Hospitality & Airlines: United Airlines' customer removal incident** shows the impact of **poor crisis communication on brand reputation.**

Key Insights

1. **Preparation is Crucial:** Companies that plan ahead recover faster and **minimize brand damage.**
2. **Transparency Builds Trust: Honest, timely communication** is essential for maintaining **public confidence.**
3. **Speed Matters:** A delayed response often worsens **the impact of a crisis and fuels public backlash.**
4. **Post-Crisis Learning is Essential:** Every crisis should lead to **process improvements and stronger policies.**
5. **Crisis Management is an Ongoing Process:** Businesses must continuously **update risk assessments and train employees** for different crisis scenarios.

Conclusion

The **Crisis Management Strategy** is essential for businesses to **navigate unexpected disruptions, protect their reputation, and ensure long-term stability.** Companies like **Johnson & Johnson and Toyota** have demonstrated the power of **proactive planning, quick decision-making, and transparent communication.** Businesses that invest in **crisis preparedness, clear communication, and post-crisis learning** will be better equipped to handle challenges, minimize damage, and emerge stronger in the face of adversity.

87. Business Model Innovation Strategy

Business Model Innovation Strategy: A Comprehensive Breakdown

Theory

The **Business Model Innovation Strategy** is a strategic approach where companies **reinvent or modify their core business model** to create new value propositions, reach untapped markets, and gain a competitive edge. Instead of just innovating products or services, this strategy focuses on **rethinking how a company delivers, captures, and monetizes value.**

Key components of business model innovation include:

1. **Value Proposition Innovation:** Redefining what makes a product or service **unique and appealing** to customers.

2. **Revenue Model Innovation:** Changing **pricing strategies, monetization methods, or subscription-based models** to maximize profitability.

3. **Customer Experience Transformation:** Introducing **new ways of engaging with customers**, such as digital-first interactions or self-service models.

4. **Operational & Cost Structure Changes:** Optimizing **supply chains, partnerships, and production methods** for efficiency and scalability.

5. **Market Disruption & Expansion:** Entering new markets or disrupting existing industries by **offering a radically different value proposition.**

By **rethinking traditional business models**, companies can **unlock new revenue streams, improve efficiency, and create a sustainable competitive advantage.**

Example

A famous example of business model innovation is **Netflix**. Initially a DVD rental company, Netflix disrupted the entertainment industry by shifting to a **subscription-based streaming model.** This transition allowed it to **scale globally, leverage AI-driven content recommendations, and produce original content**, redefining how audiences consume media.

Another example is **Apple's iTunes and App Store**, which transformed **music and software distribution** by offering digital downloads and a revenue-sharing model for developers. This shift created **a multi-billion-dollar ecosystem** and changed how consumers access content.

Why It Works

1. **Creates Sustainable Competitive Advantage:** A **unique and evolving business model** is harder for competitors to replicate than a product innovation.

2. **Responds to Changing Market Conditions:** Companies can adapt **to new technologies, customer demands, and economic shifts.**

3. **Opens New Revenue Streams:** By **introducing subscriptions, licensing, or platform-based models**, businesses expand monetization opportunities.

4. **Improves Customer Loyalty & Retention:** Customer-centric models **enhance engagement, personalization, and long-term relationships.**

5. **Drives Scalability & Growth:** Digital and **platform-based models** allow businesses to **scale efficiently without increasing operational costs proportionally.**

How It Works

1. **Analyse Market Gaps & Customer Needs:** Identify **pain points, inefficiencies, or underserved segments** in the market.

2. **Reimagine the Core Business Model:** Explore subscription, platform, direct-to-consumer (DTC), or **decentralized models** based on market trends.

3. **Test & Validate New Models:** Use **pilot programs, A/B testing, and customer feedback** to refine the strategy before full implementation.

4. **Optimize Revenue & Cost Structures:** Adjust **pricing models, partnerships, and automation** to improve profitability.

5. **Scale & Continuously Innovate:** Monitor performance metrics and **adapt the business model** as market dynamics evolve.

Application

- **Technology & Media: Netflix and Spotify** shifted from ownership models to **subscription-based streaming.**

- **Retail & E-Commerce: Amazon and Shopify** revolutionized **online commerce through marketplace and logistics innovation.**

- **Transportation & Mobility: Uber and Airbnb** introduced **peer-to-peer platform models, disrupting traditional industries.**

- **Finance & Payments: PayPal and Square** changed the way businesses and consumers **transact digitally.**

- **Healthcare & Wellness: Telehealth providers and digital pharmacies** redefined **how medical services are delivered.**

Key Insights

1. **Business Model Innovation is More Powerful Than Product Innovation:** A new business model **can disrupt entire industries**, whereas a product innovation may only offer **short-term differentiation.**

2. **Customer-Centricity is Key:** Successful innovations focus on **enhancing customer experiences, convenience, and accessibility.**

3. **Technology Enables Scalability: AI, blockchain, and digital platforms** accelerate business model transformation and **unlock new efficiencies.**

4. **Experimentation & Agility Drive Success:** Businesses should **test and iterate rapidly**, rather than committing to rigid models.

5. **First Movers Gain Long-Term Advantage:** Companies that **pioneer new models** (e.g., Uber, Tesla, Airbnb) establish market dominance before competitors catch up.

Conclusion

The **Business Model Innovation Strategy** is a transformative approach that allows companies to **redefine industries, optimize** revenue streams, and future-proof their businesses. Companies like **Netflix, Apple, and Uber** have leveraged business model innovation to **disrupt traditional markets and create long-term competitive advantages.** Businesses that continuously **analyse market trends, embrace digital transformation, and prioritize customer needs** will thrive in an era of rapid change and evolving consumer expectations.

88. Hyperlocal Strategy

Hyperlocal Strategy: A Comprehensive Breakdown

Theory

The **Hyperlocal Strategy** is a business approach that focuses on **targeting customers within a specific geographic area** by tailoring marketing, services, and operations to meet local preferences and behaviours. It is especially effective for businesses that rely on **physical locations, localized supply chains, or community-driven engagement**.

This strategy is built on **personalization, proximity, and localized insights**, ensuring businesses align their offerings with **cultural, economic, and social dynamics of a specific region**. Key components include:

1. **Geolocation Targeting:** Using **GPS, mobile data, and AI-driven analytics** to engage nearby customers.

2. **Localized Marketing & Promotions:** Offering region-specific **advertising, discounts, and culturally relevant messaging.**

3. **Community Engagement & Partnerships:** Collaborating with **local influencers, businesses, and organizations** to strengthen brand presence.

4. **Tailored Product & Service Offerings:** Adjusting **inventory, menus, or services** to fit local demand and preferences.

5. **Real-Time Customer Interaction:** Leveraging tools like **Google My Business, social media, and hyperlocal apps** to interact with nearby customers instantly.

By prioritizing hyperlocal engagement, businesses create **stronger customer loyalty, better brand recognition, and higher conversion rates within a defined geographic market.**

Example

A standout example of a hyperlocal strategy is **Starbucks' location-based marketing approach**. Starbucks uses **mobile app geolocation data** to send personalized promotions when customers are near a store. Additionally, they **adjust menu items based on local preferences**, such as offering **matcha-based drinks in Japan and dulce de leche in Latin America**.

Another example is **Zomato**, a food delivery platform that personalizes app experiences based on **local cuisines, restaurant partnerships, and user behaviour in different cities**. By using real-time location data, targeted promotions, and hyperlocal restaurant recommendations**, Zomato significantly increases customer engagement and repeat orders.

Why It Works

1. **Enhances Relevance & Customer Connection:** Businesses that **align with local culture, language, and preferences** build deeper relationships.

2. **Increases Foot Traffic & Sales:** Targeting customers **at the right place and time** drives higher conversion rates.

3. **Improves Competitive Advantage:** Small and local businesses can **compete effectively with larger brands** by offering personalized, community-focused services.

4. **Boosts Brand Loyalty & Community Trust:** Customers feel more **connected to brands that engage with their local environment.**

5. **Optimizes Marketing Spend:** Hyperlocal advertising **reduces waste by targeting only high-intent local consumers.**

How It Works

1. **Analyse Local Consumer Behaviour:** Use **location data, surveys, and purchasing patterns** to understand regional needs.

2. **Develop Location-Based Offers & Content:** Craft **customized marketing messages, promotions, and experiences** tailored to local audiences.

3. **Leverage Geolocation & Mobile Technology:** Use **Google Ads, Facebook location targeting, and push notifications** to reach customers in specific areas.

4. **Partner with Local Influencers & Businesses:** Collaborate with **community leaders, micro-influencers, and local businesses** to enhance credibility.

5. **Monitor & Adapt Using Real-Time Data:** Continuously refine the strategy using **customer feedback, seasonal trends, and market shifts.**

Application

- **Retail & Restaurants: McDonald's and Starbucks** adjust **menus, pricing, and promotions** based on local market trends.

- **E-commerce & Delivery Services: Amazon and Zomato** use **hyperlocal logistics and geofencing** to optimize delivery times.

- **Healthcare & Wellness:** Local clinics and pharmacies offer **personalized healthcare solutions** based on regional health data.

- **Real Estate & Hospitality: Airbnb and real estate agencies** use **location-based recommendations** to match customers with ideal properties.

- **Finance & Banking: Regional banks and fintech startups** provide **localized financial services, loan offers, and credit solutions.**

Key Insights

1. **Hyperlocal Strategies Work Best with Digital Integration: AI, mobile apps, and geofencing** enable precise targeting and real-time engagement.

2. **Customer Insights Drive Success:** Businesses must continuously **analyse local trends, cultural influences, and seasonal demands** to remain relevant.

3. **Community Engagement Strengthens Brand Loyalty:** Active participation in **local events, sponsorships, and partnerships** enhances customer trust.

4. **Scalability Requires Adaptability:** Successful hyperlocal businesses **expand by replicating strategies while adapting to each new location.**

5. **Hyperlocal Marketing is Cost-Effective:** Targeting **smaller, high-intent audiences** ensures a higher return on investment (ROI).

Conclusion

The **Hyperlocal Strategy** is a powerful tool for businesses looking to **increase local engagement, optimize marketing efforts, and improve customer loyalty.** Companies like **Starbucks, Zomato, and McDonald's** successfully implement this approach by using **location-based marketing, community involvement, and personalized offerings.** Businesses that embrace **data-driven geolocation tools, cultural adaptability, and real-time customer interaction** will thrive in an increasingly localized and personalized marketplace.

89. Reverse Innovation Strategy

Reverse Innovation Strategy: A Comprehensive Breakdown

Theory

The **Reverse Innovation Strategy** is a business approach where companies develop innovations in **emerging markets first** and later introduce them to **developed markets.** Unlike the traditional **"trickle-down" innovation** model, where new products are created for wealthy nations and later adapted for lower-income countries, **reverse innovation flips this approach**, leveraging cost-effective, high-impact solutions from developing markets and scaling them globally.

Key principles of this strategy include:

1. **Cost Efficiency & Resource Optimization:** Innovations developed for **price-sensitive markets** often lead to **affordable, scalable, and efficient solutions.**

2. **Local Adaptation & Problem-Solving:** Reverse innovation focuses on **solving unique challenges in emerging markets**, such as **limited infrastructure, affordability constraints, and accessibility issues.**

3. **Scalability & Global Market Potential:** Once tested and refined in **developing economies**, successful innovations can **be adapted for mature markets** with additional features or premium pricing.

4. **Disrupting Traditional Business Models:** Reverse innovation encourages companies to **rethink conventional R&D processes, manufacturing, and distribution models.**

5. **Competitive Advantage & Market Differentiation:** Companies that master **reverse innovation gain a first-mover advantage** in global product adaptation.

By **developing cost-effective, high-value innovations in emerging markets**, businesses can **expand their global footprint, improve affordability, and introduce disruptive solutions** in wealthier economies.

Example

A well-known example of **reverse innovation** is **GE Healthcare's portable ultrasound device.** Initially developed for **rural India**

and China, where traditional ultrasound machines were too expensive and inaccessible, GE created a **compact, battery-powered, and affordable ultrasound machine**. The success of this innovation later led to **its adoption in the U.S. for emergency rooms, ambulances, and rural clinics**, proving its value beyond emerging markets.

Another example is **Tata Motors' Nano**, initially launched as the world's cheapest car in India. While the Nano did not achieve long-term success, it inspired **low-cost car manufacturing innovations** that were later adopted in European compact car markets.

Why It Works

1. **Drives Cost-Efficient Innovation:** Resource constraints in emerging markets **force companies to develop simpler, smarter, and more affordable solutions.**

2. **Unlocks Untapped Market Potential:** Innovations designed for **billions of underserved consumers** create **massive scaling opportunities**.

3. **Enhances Flexibility & Adaptability:** Reverse innovation promotes **modular design, frugal engineering, and lean business models** that work in multiple markets.

4. **Strengthens Competitive Edge:** Companies that innovate in **price-sensitive environments** develop **cost leadership and disruptive capabilities.**

5. **Expands Global Reach & Revenue Streams:** Successful innovations can **bridge gaps between emerging and developed markets,** creating **diverse revenue sources.**

How It Works

1. **Identify Unmet Needs in Emerging Markets:** Analyse **economic conditions, infrastructure gaps, and consumer behaviour** in **developing regions.**

2. **Develop Affordable & Scalable Solutions:** Focus on **low-cost, high-impact innovations** using **frugal engineering and simplified design.**

3. **Test & Validate Locally:** Pilot the product or service in the target market, gathering **real-time feedback and iterating improvements.**

4. **Adapt & Upgrade for Developed Markets:** Modify the successful innovation for **wealthier consumers by adding features, improving aesthetics, or integrating advanced technology.**

5. **Scale Globally & Optimize Distribution:** Expand the innovation into **Western markets, positioning it as a disruptive, cost-effective alternative.**

Application

- **Healthcare & Medical Devices: GE's portable ultrasound machines** were first designed for **rural India before being adopted in the U.S.**

- **Automotive & Transportation: Tata's low-cost vehicle designs** influenced **affordable car engineering worldwide.**

- **Consumer Electronics: Xiaomi's budget-friendly smartphones**, initially launched in China, expanded globally with **cost-effective, high-quality alternatives to premium brands.**

- **Financial Services & Fintech: M-Pesa's mobile banking**, developed in Kenya, inspired **cashless payment systems worldwide.**

- **Retail & E-commerce: Alibaba and Pinduoduo's mobile-first e-commerce models** influenced **U.S. and European e-commerce trends.**

Key Insights

1. **Emerging Markets Are Innovation Hubs:** Developing countries provide **unique challenges that drive creative, cost-effective problem-solving.**

2. **Frugal Engineering Is a Competitive Advantage:** Reverse innovation **prioritizes affordability, simplicity, and efficiency**, creating solutions with **broad global appeal.**

3. **Western Markets Can Benefit from Emerging Market Innovations:** Many products originally designed for **resource-limited environments** offer **efficiency and cost savings in developed economies**.

4. **Cultural Adaptation is Essential:** Innovations need **localized branding, pricing, and marketing strategies** when scaling to different regions.

5. **Reverse Innovation Can Disrupt Entire Industries:** Companies that successfully **export emerging market innovations to the West** create **game-changing market shifts**.

Conclusion

The **Reverse Innovation Strategy** is a powerful approach that enables businesses to **develop cost-effective, high-impact innovations in emerging markets** and later **scale them into developed economies.** Companies like **GE, Tata Motors, and M-Pesa** demonstrate how reverse innovation **disrupts industries, enhances affordability, and creates global competitive advantages.** Businesses that **embrace frugal engineering, customer-driven design, and cross-market adaptability** will be well-positioned to **succeed in a rapidly evolving global economy.**

90. Subscription-Based Business Model

Subscription-Based Business Model: A Comprehensive Breakdown

Theory

The **Subscription-Based Business Model** is a strategy where customers pay a **recurring fee (monthly, quarterly, or annually) to access products or services** instead of making one-time purchases. This model shifts revenue generation from **one-time transactions to long-term customer relationships, ensuring predictable income and higher lifetime value (LTV).**

Key elements of this model include:

1. **Recurring Revenue Stream:** Businesses generate consistent cash flow, reducing financial volatility.

2. **Customer Retention Focus:** The model emphasizes **long-term customer relationships and continuous engagement.**

3. **Tiered Pricing & Personalization:** Companies offer **multiple subscription levels** (basic, premium, enterprise) to accommodate different customer needs.

4. **Value-Driven Service Model:** Businesses provide **ongoing value through exclusive content, personalized offerings, or premium support.**

5. **Automated Billing & Convenience:** Subscriptions simplify payments, making it **easier for customers to stay engaged.**

By prioritizing **engagement, loyalty, and ease of access**, subscription models have become **widely adopted in software (SaaS), media, e-commerce, and consumer services.**

Example

A leading example of the subscription model is **Netflix**. Instead of selling individual movies or shows, Netflix offers **unlimited streaming for a fixed monthly fee.** This approach enhances **customer retention, allows for global scalability, and creates a**

recurring revenue stream. Netflix also uses **AI-driven personalization** to keep subscribers engaged.

Another example is **Amazon Prime**, which bundles multiple services (free shipping, streaming, and exclusive discounts) under a single subscription. This model increases **customer loyalty and cross-platform engagement**, encouraging users to stay within the Amazon ecosystem.

Why It Works

1. **Ensures Stable & Predictable Revenue:** Businesses **forecast earnings more accurately** and reduce reliance on one-time sales.

2. **Enhances Customer Lifetime Value (CLV):** Instead of a single purchase, companies earn **sustained revenue over time**.

3. **Encourages Customer Loyalty & Retention:** Subscribers are **less likely to switch brands** if they receive continuous value.

4. **Enables Scalability & Market Expansion:** Digital subscription services (e.g., SaaS, streaming) can scale **without significant operational costs.**

5. **Improves Business Valuation & Investment Appeal:** Investors favour subscription models due to **recurring revenue stability and growth potential.**

How It Works

1. **Define Value Proposition & Subscription Tiers:** Offer **basic, standard, and premium** plans to target diverse customer segments.

2. **Implement a Seamless Billing System:** Automate **recurring payments** to ensure uninterrupted service.

3. **Focus on Customer Onboarding & Retention:** Provide **free trials, onboarding support, and personalized experiences** to minimize churn.

4. **Monitor & Optimize Engagement Metrics:** Track **churn rate, average revenue per user (ARPU), and user activity** to refine offerings.

5. **Introduce Loyalty Perks & Exclusive Benefits:** Reward long-term subscribers with **discounts, early access, or special content.**

Application

- **SaaS & Cloud Computing: Adobe Creative Cloud, Microsoft 365** replaced one-time licenses with **monthly software access.**

- **Streaming & Media: Netflix, Spotify, and Disney+** deliver on-demand entertainment through paid subscriptions.

- **E-commerce & Retail: Amazon Prime and Dollar Shave Club** offer **membership perks and curated product deliveries.**

- **Health & Fitness: Peloton and Fitbit Premium** provide subscription-based workouts and personalized coaching.

- **Finance & Education: MasterClass, Coursera, and fintech apps** monetize **learning and financial services via subscriptions.**

Key Insights

1. **Retention is More Important Than Acquisition:** Subscription businesses must **minimize churn by delivering ongoing value.**

2. **Personalization Enhances Customer Engagement:** AI-driven recommendations **increase user satisfaction and retention.**

3. **Flexibility & Transparency Reduce Cancellations:** Offering **pause, downgrade, or easy cancellation options** improves trust.

4. **Bundling Increases Value Perception:** Adding complementary services **boosts subscription appeal** (e.g., Amazon Prime's multi-service bundle).

5. **Freemium Models & Trials Drive Conversions:** Offering **free trials or limited free access** encourages users to upgrade to paid plans.

Conclusion

The **Subscription-Based Business Model** is transforming industries by **shifting focus from one-time transactions to customer lifetime value.** Companies like **Netflix, Amazon Prime, and Adobe Creative Cloud** have successfully built **recurring revenue streams through personalization, automation, and continuous value delivery.** Businesses that **prioritize retention, optimize pricing strategies, and create engaging subscription experiences** will **sustain long-term profitability and market dominance.**

Industry-Specific Business Strategies

91. Direct-to-Consumer (DTC) Strategy

Direct-to-Consumer (DTC) Strategy: A Comprehensive Breakdown

Theory

The **Direct-to-Consumer (DTC) Strategy** is a business model where brands **sell directly to customers** without relying on third-party retailers, wholesalers, or intermediaries. By **owning the entire sales process**, companies can **control pricing, branding,**

customer experience, and data collection while maximizing profit margins.

Key principles of the DTC strategy include:

1. **Eliminating Middlemen:** Selling directly to consumers **increases profitability and pricing control** by avoiding retailer markups.

2. **First-Party Data Collection:** Businesses gather **customer insights, shopping behaviours, and preferences** for personalized marketing.

3. **Brand-Owned Distribution Channels:** Companies use **e-commerce platforms, branded stores, and social media** to engage customers directly.

4. **Stronger Customer Relationships:** A DTC model **improves engagement and loyalty** through direct interaction and personalized experiences.

5. **Faster Product Innovation & Testing:** Businesses can **launch, test, and iterate new products quickly** based on real-time customer feedback.

By bypassing **traditional retail models**, the DTC approach **enhances control, improves customer experience, and accelerates brand growth.**

Example

A standout example of a DTC success story is **Warby Parker**. The eyewear brand disrupted the optical industry by **selling stylish,** affordable glasses directly to consumers online. By offering a home try-on program, eliminating middlemen, and maintaining a strong online presence, Warby Parker **lowered costs and created a superior customer experience** compared to traditional optical retailers.

Another example is **Tesla**, which sells its electric vehicles **directly through its website and brand-owned showrooms**, bypassing car dealerships. This allows Tesla to **control pricing, customer interactions, and brand messaging** while collecting valuable user data for ongoing improvements.

Why It Works

1. **Maximizes Profit Margins:** Removing intermediaries **reduces distribution costs** and allows for **competitive pricing.**

2. **Strengthens Customer Loyalty & Brand Identity:** DTC brands build **direct relationships with consumers**, increasing retention.

3. **Gains Complete Control Over Marketing & Messaging:** Companies maintain **full creative control** over branding and storytelling.

4. **Leverages Data for Personalization:** First-party data enables **AI-driven recommendations, targeted ads, and customized shopping experiences.**

5. **Speeds Up Market Adaptation:** Businesses can **quickly test new products, gather feedback, and refine offerings** based on direct consumer interactions.

How It Works

1. **Develop an Online-First Sales Channel:** Use **e-commerce websites, mobile apps, and social media storefronts** for direct sales.

2. **Implement Personalized Marketing:** Utilize **AI-driven recommendations, email campaigns, and retargeting ads** based on consumer behaviour.

3. **Leverage Social Commerce & Influencer Marketing:** Partner with **influencers, user-generated content (UGC), and digital campaigns** to drive engagement.

4. **Optimize Fulfilment & Logistics:** Ensure **fast shipping, seamless returns, and subscription options** to enhance customer convenience.

5. **Create Exclusive Brand Experiences:** Offer **limited drops, VIP memberships, or customization options** to differentiate from competitors.

Application

- **Fashion & Apparel: Nike and Gymshark** use DTC e-commerce to **reduce reliance on retailers and build stronger brand communities.**

- **Beauty & Skincare: Glossier and The Ordinary** leverage social media and direct sales to **personalize customer interactions.**

- **Consumer Electronics: Tesla and Apple** sell directly to customers, **avoiding dealership markups and maintaining premium brand experiences.**

- **Food & Beverage: HelloFresh and Blue Apron** use **DTC subscription models for meal kits**, cutting out grocery store distribution.

- **Health & Wellness: Peloton and Hims** provide **direct-to-consumer fitness and telemedicine solutions** without relying on intermediaries.

Key Insights

1. **DTC Brands Must Master Digital Marketing:** Since there are no retailers promoting products, **brands must invest in paid ads, SEO, and influencer partnerships.**

2. **Customer Experience Drives Retention:** Fast shipping, **seamless checkout, and personalized engagement** are essential for long-term success.

3. **Data is the Biggest Asset:** Direct access to **consumer behaviour insights fuels better product development and targeted marketing.**

4. **Scaling DTC Requires Operational Efficiency:** Companies must ensure **cost-effective logistics, warehousing, and fulfilment** to maintain profitability.

5. **Hybrid DTC & Retail Models Are Emerging:** Some DTC brands **eventually open physical stores or partner with select retailers** for omnichannel growth.

Conclusion

The **Direct-to-Consumer (DTC) Strategy** empowers brands to **own their customer relationships, maximize profits, and build stronger brand loyalty.** Companies like **Warby Parker, Tesla, and Glossier** have disrupted traditional industries by **leveraging digital channels, personalized experiences, and first-party data.** Businesses that invest in **e-commerce, social media engagement, and customer-driven innovation** will thrive in the evolving **DTC landscape.**

92. Dropshipping Strategy

Dropshipping Strategy: A Comprehensive Breakdown

Theory

The **Dropshipping Strategy** is an **inventory-free e-commerce model** where businesses sell products **without stocking them physically.** Instead, when a customer places an order, the retailer **purchases the item from a third-party supplier**, who then **ships it directly to the customer.** This means the seller **never handles the product**, reducing inventory and operational costs.

Key principles of the Dropshipping model include:

1. **Low Startup Costs:** Since there is **no need to buy inventory upfront**, entrepreneurs can **launch with minimal capital.**

2. **No Need for Warehousing:** Sellers avoid **storage costs and inventory management challenges.**

3. **Flexibility & Scalability:** Drop shippers can sell **a wide range of products without production constraints.**

4. **Supplier Reliance:** The business depends on **third-party suppliers for stock availability, fulfilment, and shipping.**

5. **E-commerce & Digital Marketing Focus:** Since drop shippers **don't manufacture products, success relies on branding, advertising, and customer experience.**

Dropshipping is ideal for **new entrepreneurs, online retailers, and niche markets** due to its **low-risk, high-opportunity structure.**

Example

One of the most famous examples of Dropshipping success is **Gymshark**. Initially, the fitness apparel brand started as a **Dropshipping business**, sourcing products from third-party manufacturers while focusing on **branding, influencer marketing, and e-commerce sales**. As it scaled, Gymshark **transitioned to owning production** while maintaining a strong DTC strategy.

Another example is **AliExpress-based Shopify stores**, where entrepreneurs **resell trending products** by importing them from **Chinese suppliers** and marketing them via Facebook ads. These stores scale rapidly by identifying **viral product trends** and leveraging **targeted digital advertising**.

Why It Works

1. **Eliminates Inventory Risks:** Businesses don't need to **forecast demand or deal with unsold stock.**

2. **Enables Fast Market Entry:** Entrepreneurs can **launch online stores quickly** without manufacturing delays.

3. **Reduces Financial Barriers:** No need to **invest in production, warehousing, or logistics** before making sales.

4. **Scalability Without Overhead Costs:** Businesses can **add or remove products easily** without major financial risks.

5. **Leverages E-commerce & Digital Advertising:** Success comes from **SEO, Facebook ads, TikTok marketing, and influencer collaborations** rather than physical operations.

How It Works

1. **Select a Niche & Find Suppliers:** Identify **high-demand, low-competition products** and partner with **reliable Dropshipping suppliers** (e.g., AliExpress, CJ Dropshipping, Spocket).

2. **Set Up an E-commerce Store:** Use **Shopify, WooCommerce, or Wix** to create a **professional online store** with a strong brand identity.

3. **Import Products & Optimize Listings:** Add **product descriptions, images, and pricing** that differentiate the store from competitors.

4. **Run Targeted Digital Ads & Social Media Marketing:** Utilize **Facebook Ads, Google Ads, TikTok, and influencer partnerships** to drive traffic.

5. **Manage Orders & Customer Service:** When a sale is made, the supplier **handles fulfilment, while the drop shipper focuses on marketing and customer support.**

Application

- **Fashion & Accessories:** Many Shopify stores sell **jewellery, watches, and streetwear** through AliExpress suppliers.

- **Tech Gadgets & Electronics:** Dropshipping is common for **smartphone accessories, headphones, and LED lighting.**

- **Home & Kitchen Products:** Niche stores focus on **eco-friendly kitchenware, home decor, and unique gadgets.**

- **Fitness & Wellness:** Dropshipping **yoga mats, resistance bands, and supplements** is a popular e-commerce strategy.

- **Pet Products:** Online retailers sell **custom pet accessories, toys, and grooming products** without inventory costs.

Key Insights

1. **Branding is Essential for Long-Term Success:** Since anyone can sell the same products, **strong branding, storytelling, and design** are crucial.

2. **Quality Control & Supplier Reliability Matter:** A **bad supplier can lead to slow shipping times, refunds, and negative reviews.**

3. **Customer Experience Defines Success: Fast communication, strong policies, and engaging content** help businesses stand out.

4. **Product Trends Drive Profitability:** Winning products come from **market research, trend analysis, and viral marketing strategies.**

5. **Dropshipping is Competitive But Lucrative:** Success requires **testing ads, optimizing offers, and continuously refining the sales funnel.**

Conclusion

The **Dropshipping Strategy** enables **low-risk, cost-efficient e-commerce businesses** by eliminating **inventory management and upfront capital investments**. Companies like **Gymshark and Shopify-based entrepreneurs** have proven its potential when combined with **smart branding, digital marketing, and supplier reliability.** Businesses that focus on **niche selection, customer experience, and viral marketing** will have the highest chance of **long-term success in the Dropshipping industry.**

93. On-Demand Economy Strategy

On-Demand Economy Strategy: A Comprehensive Breakdown

Theory

The **On-Demand Economy Strategy** is a business approach that provides **instant access to goods and services** through digital platforms, allowing consumers to **order what they need in real time, whenever and wherever they want.** This model leverages **technology, mobile apps, and gig workers** to offer **speed, convenience, and flexibility.**

Key components of the on-demand economy include:

1. **Instant Access & Convenience:** Customers can **request products or services immediately**, reducing wait times.

2. **Technology-Driven Operations:** Businesses rely on **mobile apps, AI-driven logistics, and digital payments** to facilitate fast transactions.

3. **Gig & Freelance Workforce:** Companies use **independent contractors** instead of full-time employees to provide services efficiently.

4. **Scalable, Asset-Light Models:** Businesses **do not own physical inventory or large infrastructures**, making scaling **easier and cost-effective.**

5. **Personalization & AI Integration:** Platforms use **AI and data analytics** to offer **personalized recommendations, dynamic pricing, and demand forecasting.**

This strategy **revolutionizes traditional industries** such as transportation, food delivery, home services, and entertainment, offering **greater flexibility for consumers and service providers alike.**

Example

A major success story in the on-demand economy is **Uber**, which transformed the **traditional taxi industry** by offering **ride-hailing through a mobile app.** Instead of waiting for taxis, users can **book a ride instantly, track the driver in real time, and pay digitally.** Uber's **scalable, asset-light model** (not owning cars) and **gig-based workforce** made it a **dominant force in transportation.**

Another example is **DoorDash**, which disrupted **food delivery services** by connecting consumers with local restaurants. Unlike traditional food chains, DoorDash **partners with independent drivers** who fulfil orders **without requiring restaurants to hire their own delivery staff**, creating an **efficient, scalable model.**

Why It Works

1. **Solves Consumer Pain Points:** Offers **instant gratification, eliminating long wait times and traditional service inefficiencies.**

2. **Low Operational Costs & High Scalability:** Companies **avoid heavy infrastructure investments**, focusing on **platform development and workforce management.**

3. **Expands Workforce Flexibility:** The gig economy allows workers to **choose their hours, increasing supply availability.**

4. **AI & Data Optimization Enhance Efficiency:** AI-driven **route optimization, surge pricing, and demand prediction** improve service quality.

5. **Encourages High Customer Retention:** Fast service and **personalized experiences** create **repeat usage and brand loyalty.**

How It Works

1. **Develop a Digital Platform:** Build an **app or web-based marketplace** where customers can request services instantly.

2. **Recruit & Onboard Service Providers:** Use **freelancers, gig workers, or third-party vendors** to fulfil demand without hiring full-time staff.

3. **Implement AI & Automation:** Use **real-time tracking, dynamic pricing, and demand forecasting** to optimize delivery or service efficiency.

4. **Focus on Speed & Convenience:** Ensure **fast response times, streamlined payments, and user-friendly interfaces** for a seamless experience.

5. **Scale Regionally & Then Globally:** Expand into **multiple cities or industries**, leveraging **network effects and brand trust.**

Application

- **Transportation & Mobility: Uber, Lyft, and Bolt** disrupted traditional taxi services with app-based ride-hailing.

- **Food & Grocery Delivery: DoorDash, Instacart, and Uber Eats** provide **on-demand meal and grocery deliveries.**

- **Home Services: TaskRabbit and Handy** allow users to **hire freelancers for home repairs, cleaning, and assembly.**

- **Healthcare & Wellness: Zocdoc and Heal** enable **on-demand doctor appointments and telemedicine.**

- **Retail & E-commerce: Amazon Prime Now** offers **same-day deliveries**, catering to the **instant gratification economy**.

Key Insights

1. **Consumer Expectations Are Shifting Toward Instant Access:** Companies must prioritize **speed, reliability, and frictionless digital interactions**.

2. **Scalability Requires a Strong Digital Infrastructure:** A **robust app, AI-driven logistics, and automated payments** are critical.

3. **The Gig Economy is Both an Opportunity & a Challenge:** While flexible labour pools enhance scalability, **regulatory issues around worker rights remain a concern**.

4. **Trust & Safety Measures Are Crucial:** Businesses must **verify service providers, protect customer data, and implement fair pricing models** to maintain credibility.

5. **Future Growth Lies in Industry Expansion:** The **on-demand model** is evolving beyond **transportation and food** into **healthcare, education, and professional services**.

Conclusion

The **On-Demand Economy Strategy** is reshaping industries by **prioritizing speed, convenience, and digital-first interactions.**

Companies like **Uber, DoorDash, and Instacart** have proven that **technology-driven, asset-light business models** can disrupt traditional markets. Businesses that **embrace AI, optimize gig workforce management, and enhance user experiences** will continue to **lead in the on-demand economy revolution.**

94. Frugal Innovation Strategy

Frugal Innovation Strategy: A Comprehensive Breakdown

Theory

The **Frugal Innovation Strategy** is a business approach that focuses on **creating high-value solutions with minimal resources** by simplifying products, reducing costs, and maximizing efficiency. This strategy is particularly relevant in **emerging markets and resource-constrained environments**, where affordability and accessibility are critical. Instead of using expensive R&D and cutting-edge technologies, frugal innovation relies on **clever problem-solving, repurposing existing technologies, and cost-effective design.**

Key principles of frugal innovation include:

1. **Minimalism & Essentialism:** Developing **simpler, affordable solutions** that meet basic needs without unnecessary complexity.

2. **Cost-Effective Production:** Using **local materials, lean manufacturing, and optimized supply chains** to reduce expenses.

3. **Scalability & Accessibility:** Ensuring solutions are **widely available and affordable** to a broad audience.

4. **Sustainability & Resource Efficiency:** Designing **eco-friendly, low-energy, and waste-reducing** innovations.

5. **User-Centric Design:** Prioritizing **functionality and usability over premium features** to serve mass markets effectively.

Frugal innovation is widely used in **healthcare, consumer goods, financial services, and technology**, making products **affordable without sacrificing quality.**

Example

A standout example of frugal innovation is **GE Healthcare's portable ECG device**. Traditional ECG machines cost thousands of dollars and require trained professionals, making them inaccessible in rural India. GE **developed a battery-powered, lightweight ECG machine for just $500**, making heart monitoring affordable and widely available.

Another example is the **Tata Nano**, initially designed as the world's cheapest car at $2,500. Tata Motors **eliminated non-essential features** and redesigned production processes to **create an ultra-low-cost vehicle**, making car ownership possible for low-income families in India.

Why It Works

1. **Addresses Real Market Needs:** Frugal innovation **solves essential problems for price-sensitive consumers**, creating strong demand.

2. **Reduces Production & R&D Costs:** By focusing on **lean development, cost-effective design, and local sourcing**, companies **lower overhead expenses**.

3. **Encourages Rapid Market Adoption:** Affordable, functional products **reach mass audiences quickly**, driving sales volume.

4. **Enhances Business Resilience:** Companies using frugal innovation **adapt to economic downturns and resource constraints more effectively**.

5. **Drives Social & Environmental Impact:** Sustainable and affordable solutions **improve lives in underserved regions while minimizing waste**.

How It Works

1. **Identify Market Gaps & Constraints:** Focus on **high-impact problems** in **low-income, resource-limited markets**.

2. **Develop Simplified, Low-Cost Solutions:** Remove unnecessary features while maintaining **core functionality and reliability**.

3. **Leverage Local Resources & Partnerships:** Use **local suppliers, affordable materials, and grassroots distribution networks**.

4. **Test, Iterate & Scale Efficiently:** Launch **low-cost prototypes**, gather feedback, and **refine based on real-world usage**.

5. **Ensure Sustainable Production & Distribution:** Implement **eco-friendly materials, energy efficiency, and low-cost logistics** for long-term scalability.

Application

- **Healthcare & Medical Devices: GE's low-cost ECG and Aravind Eye Care's affordable cataract surgeries** bring healthcare to underserved populations.

- **Automotive & Transportation: Tata Nano and Mahindra's budget-friendly vehicles** offer cost-effective mobility solutions.

- **Consumer Electronics: Xiaomi's budget smartphones** provide high-quality tech at a fraction of premium brand costs.

- **Financial Services: Airtel and M-Pesa's mobile banking solutions** enable affordable financial access in emerging markets.

- **Sustainable Energy: Solar-powered LED lamps and off-grid electricity solutions** provide **low-cost, renewable energy alternatives.**

Key Insights

1. **Frugal Innovation is Not About Low Quality:** It focuses on **efficiency, necessity, and affordability** without compromising essential functionality.

2. **Emerging Markets are a Goldmine for Frugal Innovation:** Developing nations provide **massive demand for cost-effective solutions.**

3. **Technology Can Be Simplified & Repurposed:** Businesses can **redesign existing technologies for affordability and accessibility.**

4. **Sustainability & Frugality Go Hand-in-Hand:** Eco-friendly materials and low-cost production **reduce waste and carbon footprints.**

5. **Frugal Innovation Can Disrupt Premium Markets:** Cost-effective products **can challenge traditional brands** in high-income markets as well.

Conclusion

The **Frugal Innovation Strategy** is a powerful approach that allows companies to **deliver high-value, affordable solutions with minimal resources**. Businesses like **GE Healthcare, Tata Motors, and Xiaomi** have successfully leveraged this strategy to **expand into new markets, drive social impact, and increase profitability**. Companies that embrace **simplicity, resource efficiency, and user-centric design** will not only thrive in **emerging economies** but also **create innovative solutions for global markets**.

95. Hyperautomation Strategy

Hyperautomation Strategy: A Comprehensive Breakdown

Theory

The **Hyperautomation Strategy** is a business approach that leverages **advanced automation technologies**, such as **Artificial Intelligence (AI), Machine Learning (ML), Robotic Process Automation (RPA), and Low-Code/No-Code Platforms**, to **streamline operations, increase efficiency, and reduce human intervention**. Unlike traditional automation, which focuses on individual tasks, **Hyperautomation integrates multiple automation tools** to create **end-to-end intelligent workflows**.

Key principles of Hyperautomation include:

1. **End-to-End Process Automation:** Automating entire workflows rather than isolated tasks, leading to **seamless operational efficiency.**

2. **AI-Driven Decision-Making:** Using **AI and ML** to analyse data, detect patterns, and automate **complex decision-making.**

3. **Scalability & Adaptability:** Hyperautomation evolves **with business needs**, improving over time with **self-learning capabilities.**

4. **Human & Machine Collaboration:** Employees **focus on high-value tasks**, while automation handles **repetitive, time-consuming work.**

5. **Enterprise-Wide Digital Transformation:** Hyperautomation is implemented across multiple departments, from **customer service to finance and HR.**

By combining multiple automation technologies, Hyperautomation helps businesses **increase speed, reduce costs, and enhance accuracy** while fostering **innovation and agility.**

Example

A prime example of Hyperautomation is **Amazon's fulfilment centres**. Amazon uses **robotic process automation (RPA), AI-driven forecasting, and smart logistics systems** to automate order processing, warehouse management, and customer support. These technologies **work together to reduce manual labour, accelerate deliveries, and improve inventory

management, giving Amazon a **massive competitive advantage in e-commerce.**

Another example is **JP Morgan's COIN (Contract Intelligence) platform,** which uses **AI and Natural Language Processing (NLP)** to automate legal contract reviews. What previously took **thousands of human hours** is now completed **in seconds with near-zero errors,** significantly increasing efficiency.

Why It Works

1. **Boosts Productivity & Efficiency:** Hyperautomation eliminates **manual bottlenecks, speeding up processes and reducing errors.**

2. **Reduces Costs & Labor Dependency:** Automating **repetitive and rule-based tasks** lowers **operational expenses and workforce dependency.**

3. **Enhances Decision-Making with AI:** AI-driven insights improve **accuracy, forecasting, and strategic planning.**

4. **Improves Customer Experience:** Automated workflows ensure **faster responses, reduced errors, and personalized interactions.**

5. **Ensures Business Continuity & Scalability:** Businesses can **scale operations efficiently** without additional human labour.

How It Works

1. **Identify & Prioritize Automation Opportunities:** Analyse workflows to find **high-impact, repetitive, and time-consuming tasks.**

2. **Integrate Multiple Automation Technologies:** Combine **RPA, AI, chatbots, and analytics** to create intelligent end-to-end automation.

3. **Implement Low-Code/No-Code Platforms:** Enable business users to **automate processes without extensive coding knowledge.**

4. **Use AI & ML for Continuous Optimization:** Implement self-learning models that **improve automation accuracy over time.**

5. **Monitor, Optimize, and Scale:** Continuously analyse **performance metrics, refine algorithms, and expand automation capabilities** across departments.

Application

- **Retail & E-Commerce: Amazon and Walmart** automate **inventory management, order fulfilment, and customer support.**

- **Finance & Banking: JP Morgan and Wells Fargo** use AI-driven automation for **fraud detection, risk assessment, and customer service.**

- **Healthcare & Pharmaceuticals: IBM Watson and Medtronic** automate **patient diagnostics, medical record management, and drug research.**

- **Manufacturing & Supply Chain: Tesla and Siemens** leverage **AI-powered robotics and predictive maintenance** for optimized production.

- **HR & Administrative Functions: Workday and SAP** use Hyperautomation for **recruitment, payroll processing, and compliance tracking.**

Key Insights

1. **Hyperautomation is the Future of Digital Transformation:** Businesses must **continuously integrate AI, RPA, and analytics** to stay competitive.

2. **AI & Machine Learning Enhance Automation's Intelligence:** Automation is no longer limited to repetitive tasks—it can **predict, analyse, and optimize workflows.**

3. **Scalability & Flexibility Are Critical for Success:** Hyperautomation must be **adaptable and scalable** across different business functions.

4. **Security & Compliance Must Be Prioritized:** As automation expands, **cybersecurity, data privacy, and regulatory compliance** become crucial.

5. **Human Expertise Remains Essential:** While machines handle repetitive work, **human oversight is necessary for creativity, strategy, and ethical considerations.**

Conclusion

The **Hyperautomation Strategy** is reshaping industries by integrating AI, RPA, and analytics to create fully automated, intelligent workflows. Companies like **Amazon, JP Morgan, and Tesla** have successfully leveraged Hyperautomation to **increase efficiency, reduce costs, and enhance decision-making.** Businesses that **invest in Hyperautomation, prioritize AI-driven optimizations, and ensure seamless human-machine collaboration** will **achieve long-term growth, agility, and market leadership.**

96. Decentralized Business Strategy

Decentralized Business Strategy: A Comprehensive Breakdown

Theory

The **Decentralized Business Strategy** is a model in which decision-making, operations, and resource allocation are **distributed across multiple units, teams, or even independent contributors, rather than being controlled by a central authority.** This strategy promotes **autonomy, flexibility, and**

innovation by allowing different parts of an organization—or an ecosystem of independent players—to operate with greater independence.

Key principles of a decentralized strategy include:

1. **Distributed Decision-Making:** Authority is spread across multiple departments, regional offices, or autonomous teams, allowing for **faster, localized decision-making**.

2. **Agility & Flexibility:** Decentralized businesses **adapt quickly to market changes, customer needs, and emerging trends** without waiting for corporate approval.

3. **Empowerment & Innovation:** Employees, stakeholders, or even users have **greater autonomy**, leading to **higher creativity, engagement, and accountability**.

4. **Blockchain & Web3 Integration:** Some decentralized businesses use **blockchain-based governance models, smart contracts, and DAOs (Decentralized Autonomous Organizations)** to enable **peer-to-peer transactions without intermediaries**.

5. **Scalability Through Network Effects:** By decentralizing operations, businesses can **scale without excessive overhead costs, leveraging distributed teams, independent franchises, or a community-driven model**.

This strategy is particularly effective in **tech-driven industries, blockchain ecosystems, multinational corporations, and remote-first organizations** that benefit from **distributed leadership and decision-making power**.

Example

A leading example of decentralized business strategy is **Bitcoin**, the world's first decentralized cryptocurrency. Unlike traditional financial institutions that rely on central banks, **Bitcoin operates on a peer-to-peer network** where transactions are validated by a distributed network of miners rather than a single authority. This model ensures **trust, transparency, and resilience** without relying on a central institution.

Another example is **Spotify**, which employs a **decentralized "Squad Model"** for product development. Instead of a rigid hierarchy, Spotify organizes employees into **small, autonomous teams (Squads)**, each responsible for a specific feature or innovation. This approach allows for **rapid iteration, cross-functional collaboration, and high levels of ownership.**

Why It Works

1. **Enhances Speed & Responsiveness:** Localized or independent teams **make quicker decisions** without waiting for corporate approval.

2. **Promotes Innovation & Creativity:** Decentralized teams **experiment more freely**, leading to faster innovation cycles.

3. **Boosts Employee & Community Engagement:** When teams and users have **greater autonomy**, they feel more invested in the business's success.

4. **Reduces Bureaucracy & Overhead Costs:** Decentralization eliminates unnecessary layers of management, **streamlining operations.**

5. **Increases Transparency & Trust:** Blockchain-enabled decentralized businesses **reduce fraud, ensure data security, and empower users** through transparent governance models.

How It Works

1. **Distribute Authority & Decision-Making:** Instead of a rigid top-down approach, empower **regional teams, product squads, or blockchain-based governance systems** to operate independently.

2. **Implement Technology-Driven Decentralization:** Leverage **AI, blockchain, and automation** to enable decentralized operations, smart contracts, and digital governance.

3. **Foster a Culture of Autonomy & Responsibility:** Encourage **self-management, cross-functional teams, and decentralized leadership** to enhance agility.

4. **Use Network Effects for Scalability:** Businesses can expand through **independent contributors, decentralized marketplaces, or open-source communities** rather than centralized expansion.

5. **Monitor & Optimize Decentralized Systems:** Implement **real-time data analytics, transparent reporting, and**

adaptive strategies to ensure decentralized operations remain efficient and aligned.

Application

- **Cryptocurrency & Blockchain: Bitcoin and Ethereum** operate on decentralized networks, enabling **peer-to-peer financial transactions without central oversight**.

- **Tech & Software Development: Spotify's squad model and GitHub's open-source platform** enable **distributed innovation and agile development**.

- **E-commerce & Marketplaces: Shopify and Etsy** empower **independent sellers and merchants** rather than controlling all inventory.

- **Media & Content Creation: DAOs and decentralized platforms like Mirror.xyz** allow creators to **monetize content without intermediaries**.

- **Remote & Distributed Workforces: Automattic (WordPress) and GitLab** operate fully remotely, using decentralized teams across different time zones.

Key Insights

1. **Decentralization Boosts Agility & Innovation:** Organizations that decentralize decision-making **respond faster to market shifts and customer needs**.

2. **Technology Enables Decentralized Models:** AI, blockchain, and automation allow businesses to **scale without relying on traditional management structures**.

3. **Trust & Transparency Are Critical:** Decentralized businesses must establish **clear governance models and accountability frameworks** to maintain integrity.

4. **Not All Businesses Should Be Fully Decentralized:** Some industries still require **central oversight for compliance, security, or legal reasons**.

5. **Hybrid Models Are Emerging:** Many businesses use a **semi-decentralized approach**, where **some decisions are centralized while others are delegated** to autonomous teams.

Conclusion

The **Decentralized Business Strategy** is transforming industries by **removing traditional hierarchies, leveraging peer-to-peer networks, and empowering teams or communities**. Companies like **Bitcoin, Spotify, and GitHub** have successfully demonstrated how decentralization fosters **innovation, agility, and efficiency**. As blockchain technology and digital collaboration tools evolve, businesses that **embrace decentralization strategically** will gain a **competitive edge in the digital economy**.

97. Co-Branding Strategy

Co-Branding Strategy: A Comprehensive Breakdown

Theory

The **Co-Branding Strategy** is a business approach where two or more brands collaborate to create a **joint product, service, or marketing campaign**, leveraging each other's strengths, customer bases, and brand equity. The goal is to **enhance brand perception, increase market reach, and create a unique value proposition** that benefits both companies.

Key types of co-branding include:

1. **Ingredient Co-Branding:** One brand integrates another's product into its offering (e.g., **Intel processors in Dell laptops**).

2. **Same-Industry Co-Branding:** Two brands within the same industry collaborate to enhance product appeal (e.g., **Nike and Apple's fitness tracker integration**).

3. **Cross-Industry Co-Branding:** Brands from different industries partner to tap into new markets (e.g., **Red Bull and GoPro's extreme sports campaigns**).

4. **Retail Co-Branding:** A retailer partners with a brand for exclusive collections (e.g., **H&M x Balmain fashion line**).

5. **Cause-Related Co-Branding:** Brands align with a **social cause** to strengthen brand trust (e.g., **IKEA and UNICEF's charity partnerships**).

By **combining resources, audiences, and brand authority**, co-branding helps companies **increase market share, drive sales, and create innovative offerings**.

Example

A standout example of successful co-branding is **Nike and Apple's partnership**. Nike, a leader in athletic wear, teamed up with Apple to create **Nike+**, integrating Apple's wearable technology with Nike's fitness ecosystem. This collaboration:

- **Expanded Apple's reach into fitness enthusiasts.**

- **Boosted Nike's brand positioning as a tech-savvy sports brand.**
- **Provided a unique, value-added experience for customers.**

Another example is **Doritos and Taco Bell's "Doritos Locos Tacos"**, where Doritos provided the taco shell, and Taco Bell handled the rest. This led to **over $1 billion in sales**, proving how co-branding can drive massive success when two strong brands align.

Why It Works

1. **Combines Brand Strengths:** Each brand **leverages the other's expertise, credibility, and market presence** to enhance product appeal.

2. **Increases Market Reach & Customer Base:** Brands tap into each other's **existing customer bases**, reaching **new audiences effortlessly.**

3. **Reduces Marketing & Development Costs:** Sharing **resources, R&D, and marketing budgets** makes co-branding a **cost-effective growth strategy.**

4. **Enhances Product Differentiation & Perceived Value:** Customers view co-branded products as **exclusive, premium, and innovative**, increasing demand.

5. **Boosts Brand Loyalty & Awareness:** Co-branding strengthens brand affinity, **deepening consumer engagement and trust**.

How It Works

1. **Identify a Strategic Partner:** Choose a brand with **aligned values, complementary strengths, and a shared target audience**.

2. **Define a Clear Value Proposition:** Ensure the collaboration **offers unique value to consumers**, whether through product enhancement, exclusivity, or experience.

3. **Create a Joint Marketing Strategy:** Leverage **social media, influencer partnerships, and co-branded content** to maximize visibility.

4. **Execute & Monitor Performance:** Track **sales, customer engagement, and brand sentiment** to measure success.

5. **Iterate & Expand If Successful:** If the partnership proves successful, brands can **expand their collaboration into new products or markets**.

Application

- **Technology & Sportswear: Nike x Apple** (fitness technology integration).

- **Food & Beverage: Starbucks x Spotify** (in-store curated playlists).

- **Luxury & Retail: Louis Vuitton x Supreme** (exclusive streetwear collection).

- **Entertainment & Consumer Products: Marvel x Fortnite** (crossover in gaming and entertainment).

- **Automotive & Electronics: BMW x Louis Vuitton** (luxury travel accessories for BMW vehicles).

Key Insights

1. **Brand Alignment is Critical:** A mismatch in brand values or audience expectations can lead to **co-branding failures**.

2. **Exclusivity Drives Demand:** Limited-edition or exclusive co-branded products **create urgency and increase perceived value**.

3. **Marketing & Storytelling Matter:** Effective co-branding requires **compelling campaigns that highlight the synergy between brands**.

4. **Legal & Financial Terms Must Be Defined Clearly:** Contracts should outline **profit-sharing, intellectual property rights, and exit strategies**.

5. **Co-Branding Can Be a Long-Term Growth Strategy:** If successful, partnerships can evolve into **multi-product collaborations and ongoing alliances**.

Conclusion

The **Co-Branding Strategy** is a powerful method for brands to **expand market reach, enhance product offerings, and create unique consumer experiences**. Companies like **Nike & Apple, Taco Bell & Doritos, and Starbucks & Spotify** have shown that **when two strong brands align strategically, they can drive massive growth, innovation, and customer loyalty**. Businesses that execute **thoughtful, well-aligned co-branding initiatives** will benefit from **increased revenue, enhanced brand equity, and market differentiation** in an increasingly competitive landscape.

98. Ecosystem Strategy

Ecosystem Strategy: A Comprehensive Breakdown

Theory

The **Ecosystem Strategy** is a business approach where companies **collaborate with multiple partners, industries, and stakeholders** to create **a connected, interdependent value network**. Unlike traditional linear business models, ecosystems leverage **shared resources, data, and innovation** to enhance customer experiences, increase market reach, and drive sustainable growth.

Key principles of an ecosystem strategy include:

1. **Interconnected Value Creation:** Companies within an ecosystem **offer complementary products or services** to create a **seamless customer experience**.

2. **Network Effects & Scalability:** As more participants join, the ecosystem **grows stronger, offering greater value to users**.

3. **Platform-Based Integration:** Many ecosystem businesses rely on **digital platforms that connect users, service providers, and third-party developers**.

4. **Data & AI-Driven Optimization:** Shared **customer insights and analytics** enable businesses to **personalize offerings and improve efficiency**.

5. **Flexibility & Co-Innovation:** Businesses within an ecosystem can **adapt, collaborate, and innovate faster** compared to traditional models.

Ecosystem strategies allow businesses to **expand their influence, build strong partnerships, and create long-term competitive advantages.**

Example

A prime example of an ecosystem strategy is **Apple's iOS ecosystem**. Apple **integrates hardware (iPhones, iPads, Macs),** software (iOS, macOS), and services (App Store, iCloud, Apple Pay, Apple Music) into a **seamless digital ecosystem**.

- **Developers contribute apps to the App Store**, expanding Apple's ecosystem.
- **Third-party businesses integrate with Apple Pay, HomeKit, and CarPlay**, enhancing user experience.
- **Customers stay within the Apple ecosystem**, as products and services work better together, leading to **higher brand loyalty and lifetime value**.

Another example is **Amazon**, which connects **e-commerce, cloud computing (AWS), smart home devices (Alexa), and digital content (Prime Video, Kindle)** into a **holistic ecosystem** that serves multiple customer needs.

Why It Works

1. **Enhances Customer Loyalty & Retention:** Customers benefit from **integrated, frictionless experiences**, making them **less likely to switch brands**.
2. **Increases Revenue Streams & Monetization Opportunities:** Businesses **earn from core products, partner contributions, and platform commissions**.

3. **Encourages Innovation & Collaboration:** Open ecosystems **allow third-party developers, businesses, and entrepreneurs** to create new value.

4. **Drives Competitive Advantage Through Network Effects:** The more users and partners an ecosystem has, the **more valuable it becomes**.

5. **Optimizes Cost Efficiency & Resource Sharing:** Companies **reduce costs by leveraging shared infrastructure, technology, and data analytics**.

How It Works

1. **Define the Core Value Proposition:** Establish **the core product, service, or platform** that will **anchor the ecosystem**.

2. **Attract Key Partners & Developers:** Build a **network of businesses, suppliers, developers, and third-party providers** to expand offerings.

3. **Integrate Seamless Technology & Data Sharing:** Create an infrastructure where **different services work together, enhancing user experience**.

4. **Monetize Through Multiple Channels:** Generate revenue via **subscriptions, partnerships, commissions, and premium services**.

5. **Continuously Expand & Optimize:** Leverage **AI, analytics, and customer feedback** to refine and grow the ecosystem over time.

Application

- **Technology & Platforms:** Google (Android, Search, YouTube, Ads), Apple (iOS, App Store, Apple Pay)
- **E-commerce & Retail:** Amazon (Marketplace, AWS, Prime, Alexa), Alibaba (E-commerce, Finance, Logistics)
- **Finance & Payments:** PayPal & Visa (partner networks for digital payments)
- **Automotive & Mobility:** Tesla (Electric Cars, Charging Stations, Autopilot AI)
- **Healthcare & Wellness:** Fitbit (Wearable Devices, Fitness Apps, Third-Party Integrations)

Key Insights

1. **Ecosystem Strategies Require Long-Term Vision:** Businesses must **build relationships, integrate technologies, and continuously innovate** over time.

2. **User Experience is the Core of a Successful Ecosystem:** Seamless, **integrated services keep customers engaged and loyal**.

3. **Third-Party Collaboration Drives Ecosystem Growth:** Encouraging **partners, developers, and suppliers** to contribute enhances value.

4. **Data & AI are Key to Optimization:** Shared data insights allow **personalization, predictive analytics, and continuous improvement**.

5. **Ecosystem Failure Can Lead to Customer Abandonment:** If businesses **restrict flexibility or fail to innovate**, users may leave for **more open, dynamic ecosystems**.

Conclusion

The **Ecosystem Strategy** is a powerful way to **connect businesses, customers, and partners into an interdependent value network**. Companies like **Apple, Amazon, and Google** have demonstrated that **strong ecosystems lead to higher customer retention, revenue growth, and competitive differentiation**. Businesses that **leverage partnerships, technology, and seamless user experiences** will **thrive in an increasingly interconnected economy**.

99. User-Generated Content (UGC) Strategy

User-Generated Content (UGC) Strategy: A Comprehensive Breakdown

Theory

The **User-Generated Content (UGC) Strategy** is a business approach that encourages customers, fans, and community members to **create and share content** related to a brand, product, or service. This content can be in the form of **social media posts, reviews, testimonials, blogs, videos, and images**, which are then leveraged by the brand to enhance credibility, engagement, and brand awareness.

Key principles of the UGC strategy include:

1. **Authenticity & Trust:** Consumers trust **peer recommendations** more than traditional advertising, making UGC a powerful marketing tool.

2. **Community Engagement & Loyalty:** Encouraging user contributions builds a **sense of belonging and advocacy** among customers.

3. **Cost-Effective Marketing:** UGC reduces **content creation costs**, as brands can repurpose customer-generated content instead of producing everything in-house.

4. **Social Proof & Influence:** Seeing real people using and endorsing a product **influences purchasing decisions and increases conversion rates.**

5. **Scalability & Virality:** UGC spreads **organically across social media**, reaching wider audiences without excessive advertising spend.

This strategy works particularly well in industries where **visual storytelling, brand experience, and social engagement** play a crucial role.

Example

One of the best examples of a successful UGC strategy is **GoPro**. The company encourages users to **capture and share adventure videos** using their GoPro cameras. By featuring these videos on **YouTube, Instagram, and its website,** GoPro:

- **Showcases real-life product performance**, increasing brand credibility.
- **Encourages community engagement**, making users feel part of the brand's lifestyle.
- **Reduces marketing costs**, as customers generate most of the brand's content.

Another great example is **Starbucks' "#RedCupContest"**, where Starbucks invites customers to share creative photos of their holiday-themed red cups. The campaign generates **massive engagement, free brand exposure, and a viral effect on social media**.

Why It Works

1. **Builds Brand Trust & Credibility:** Seeing real customers using a product **validates its quality and reliability**.

2. **Enhances Engagement & Community Building:** UGC fosters **deeper emotional connections** between brands and customers.

3. **Increases Content Volume Without High Costs:** Brands get a **steady stream of authentic, shareable content** at minimal expense.

4. **Boosts SEO & Organic Reach:** UGC generates **higher engagement and shares**, improving search engine rankings and social media visibility.

5. **Encourages Word-of-Mouth Marketing:** Satisfied customers **naturally become brand ambassadors**, driving **organic growth**.

How It Works

1. **Create a UGC-Friendly Campaign:** Launch contests, hashtags, or community challenges that **encourage users to create and share content**.

2. **Feature User Content on Brand Channels:** Showcase UGC on **social media, websites, emails, and advertisements** to amplify reach.

3. **Engage & Reward Participants:** Respond to user content with **likes, comments, shares, and incentives** to keep engagement high.

4. **Leverage Influencers & Micro-Creators:** Partner with **loyal customers, niche influencers, and brand advocates** to encourage more UGC.

5. **Monitor & Moderate Content Quality:** Use **AI tools or manual curation** to ensure brand-safe, high-quality content is being shared.

Application

- **Fashion & Beauty: Nike and Glossier** use UGC from customers showcasing **outfits and makeup looks** on social media.

- **Travel & Hospitality: Airbnb and Expedia** feature **guest travel photos and experiences** to attract more bookings.

- **Food & Beverage: Coca-Cola and Starbucks** run **hashtag challenges** to encourage photo-sharing.

- **Technology & Gadgets: GoPro and Apple's "Shot on iPhone" campaign** promote **real-life product use through customer photography.**

- **Retail & E-commerce: Amazon and Sephora** leverage **customer reviews, video testimonials, and social proof** to drive conversions.

Key Insights

1. **UGC Strengthens Brand-Consumer Relationships:** Encouraging participation fosters a sense of **community and loyalty**.

2. **Authenticity is More Valuable Than Perfection:** Consumers prefer **real, relatable content over highly polished brand advertisements**.

3. **Hashtags & Challenges Drive Virality:** Creative campaigns like **TikTok trends or Instagram challenges** fuel massive engagement.

4. **Incentives Increase Participation:** Contests, giveaways, or simple recognition **motivate users to create content**.

5. **Quality Control is Essential:** Brands should **monitor and curate UGC** to maintain a consistent, positive brand image.

Conclusion

The **User-Generated Content (UGC) Strategy** is a powerful tool for brands looking to **increase engagement, build trust, and reduce marketing costs**. Companies like **GoPro, Starbucks, and Apple** have successfully used UGC to **leverage social proof, boost brand credibility, and create viral marketing campaigns**. Businesses that effectively **encourage, showcase, and reward user-generated content** will experience **higher customer engagement, organic reach, and long-term brand loyalty**.

100. Reverse Logistics Strategy

Reverse Logistics Strategy: A Comprehensive Breakdown

Theory

The **Reverse Logistics Strategy** is a business approach that focuses on **managing the return, reuse, recycling, and disposal of products** after they reach the customer. Unlike traditional supply chains, which move goods **from manufacturer to consumer**, reverse logistics **moves goods from the consumer back to the company** for purposes such as **returns, repairs, refurbishing, or recycling**.

Key principles of reverse logistics include:

1. **Product Returns & Exchanges:** Managing customer returns **efficiently and cost-effectively** to maintain customer satisfaction.

2. **Refurbishing & Reselling:** Repairing or reconditioning returned items for **resale at a lower price or as refurbished goods.**

3. **Recycling & Sustainability:** Breaking down products into **raw materials for reuse**, reducing waste and promoting **eco-friendly practices.**

4. **Warranty & Repairs Management:** Handling **defective or damaged products** under warranty to enhance **customer trust and brand loyalty.**

5. **Disposal & Compliance:** Ensuring **safe and legal disposal** of non-recyclable or hazardous items **in accordance with environmental regulations.**

Reverse logistics helps businesses **reduce waste, recover value from returned products, and enhance sustainability efforts**, making it an **essential part of modern supply chain management.**

Example

A well-known example of an effective reverse logistics strategy is **Amazon's returns system**. Amazon allows customers to return products **easily through drop-off locations, pickup services, or self-shipping options**. The returned items are then:

- **Refurbished and resold through Amazon Warehouse Deals** (if in good condition).
- **Recycled or disposed of sustainably** if beyond repair.
- **Returned to manufacturers** for warranty claims or resale.

Another strong example is **Apple's Trade-In Program**, where customers return old devices in exchange for discounts on new ones. Apple then **refurbishes and resells these devices or recycles components**, reducing e-waste while recovering valuable materials.

Why It Works

1. **Enhances Customer Satisfaction & Loyalty:** Easy returns and exchanges improve **brand reputation and consumer confidence.**

2. **Reduces Environmental Impact:** Recycling and refurbishing **minimize waste and lower carbon footprints.**

3. **Improves Cost Efficiency:** Businesses recover **value from returned goods**, reducing losses.

4. **Ensures Regulatory Compliance:** Proper disposal and recycling prevent **legal issues and fines related to waste management.**

5. **Creates Additional Revenue Streams:** Refurbished goods and resale programs **generate extra income** while keeping products in circulation.

How It Works

1. **Develop a Clear Returns & Reverse Logistics Policy:** Define how **returns, repairs, and recycling** will be handled.

2. **Implement Efficient Return Processing:** Use **automated tracking, AI-based sorting, and customer-friendly return methods.**

3. **Establish Refurbishment & Resale Programs:** Repair and resell used products through **outlet stores, certified refurbishers, or discount platforms.**

4. **Integrate Recycling & Disposal Systems:** Partner with **recycling firms or set up in-house recycling** for responsible waste management.

5. **Monitor & Optimize the System Continuously:** Use **data analytics to track return rates, customer preferences, and process inefficiencies** for continuous improvement.

Application

- **E-commerce & Retail: Amazon, Walmart, and Best Buy** offer **hassle-free returns, refurbishment, and resale programs.**

- **Technology & Electronics: Apple and Dell** use trade-in and recycling programs to **recover valuable materials.**

- **Automotive Industry: Tesla and Toyota** implement **battery recycling and vehicle refurbishment programs.**

- **Fashion & Apparel: Nike's Move to Zero and Patagonia's Worn Wear** allow customers to return used clothing for resale or recycling.

- **Pharmaceuticals & Healthcare: Hospitals and medical companies** use reverse logistics to **dispose of expired or unused medications safely.**

Key Insights

1. **Reverse Logistics is a Competitive Advantage:** Businesses that offer **hassle-free returns and eco-friendly disposal** stand out in the market.

2. **Sustainability & Profitability Can Coexist:** Companies can **reduce waste while recovering costs through resale and recycling programs.**

3. **Technology Enhances Efficiency:** AI, IoT, and automation streamline **sorting, tracking, and managing returns.**

4. **Customer-Friendly Returns Drive Sales:** Offering **easy return policies increases consumer trust and purchase confidence.**

5. **Regulatory Compliance is Crucial:** Companies must **adhere to environmental and safety regulations** when disposing of products.

Conclusion

The **Reverse Logistics Strategy** is essential for businesses aiming to **improve efficiency, reduce waste, and enhance customer satisfaction**. Companies like **Amazon, Apple, and Nike** have demonstrated that **integrating refurbishing, recycling, and responsible disposal** into supply chains can **drive profitability while benefiting the environment**. Businesses that implement **smart, customer-friendly, and sustainable reverse logistics systems** will gain **a competitive edge in the circular economy.**

BEST OF LUCK APPLYING THESE BUSINESS STRATEGIES IN YOUR ORGANISATION

OTHER BOOKS IN THIS 100 SERIES – SCAN HERE

100 COGNITIVE AND MENTAL MODELS TO HELP YOUR CAREER: Mental Shortcuts for Smarter Choices, Sharper Thinking, and Success

-

ANOTHER 100 MENTAL MODELS TO HELP YOUR CAREER - VOLUME 2: Another 100 Powerful Mental Models for Clarity, Confidence, and Climbing the Career Ladder

-

100 HEURISTICS AND HEURISTIC MODELS: The Hidden Rules of Smart Thinking Used by Experts, Entrepreneurs, and Machines

-

100 GAME THEORIES AND DECISION MODELS FOR RATIONAL DECISION MAKING IN COMPETITIVE

SITUATIONS: 100 Winning Strategies for Rational Thinking in High-Stakes Scenarios

-

100 BUSINESS STRATEGIES PROVEN TACTICS FOR GROWTH, INNOVATION AND MARKET DOMINATION: Actionable Strategies to Scale, Disrupt and Lead in Any Industry

-

100 LEADERSHIP MODELS AND STRATEGIES FOR EFFECTIVE DECISION-MAKING FOR ORGANIZATIONAL SUCCESS: Empowering Your Leadership, 100 Proven Strategies and Models to Enhance Decision-Making & Drive Success

-

100 BUSINESS GROWTH HACKS AND STRATEGIES TO GROW PROFIT AND INCREASE YOUR COMPETITIVE ADVANTAGE: Proven Techniques to Scale Faster, Boost Revenue, and Dominate Your Market with Actionable Growth

-

100 ECONOMIC THEORIES DEMYSTIFIED : A Guide To The World's Most Influential Economic Ideas From Keynesian Economics To Debt-deflation Theory

-

100 PASSIVE INCOME STREAM SIDE HUSTLES, MASTERING SIDE HUSTLES AND SMART INVESTMENTS: How to Make Money While You Sleep and Secure Your Financial Future

-

WHILST YOU ARE HERE, WHY NOT SCAN THIS TO SEE IF THERE ARE ANY MORE BOOKS PUBLISHED YET

OR FOLLOW ME AT @DANDANMUSICMAN ON X AND @DANDANMUSICMANUK ON INSTAGRAM

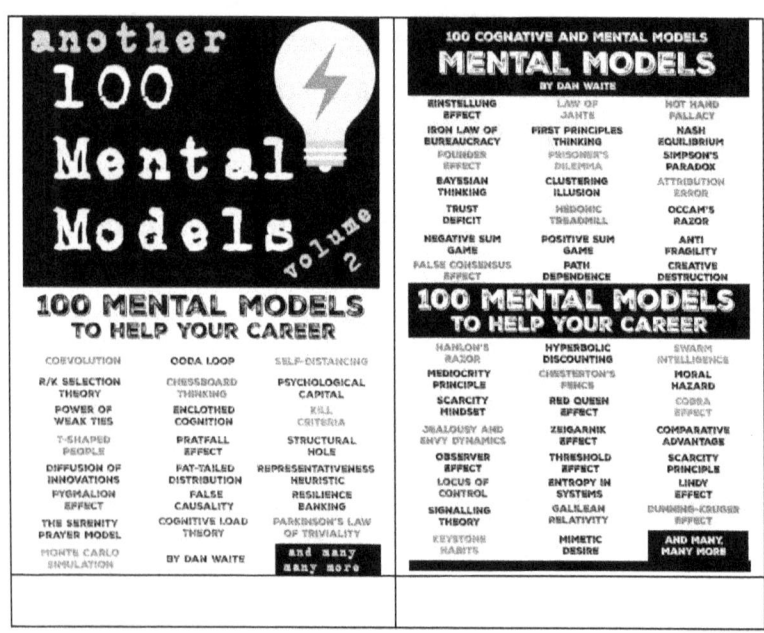

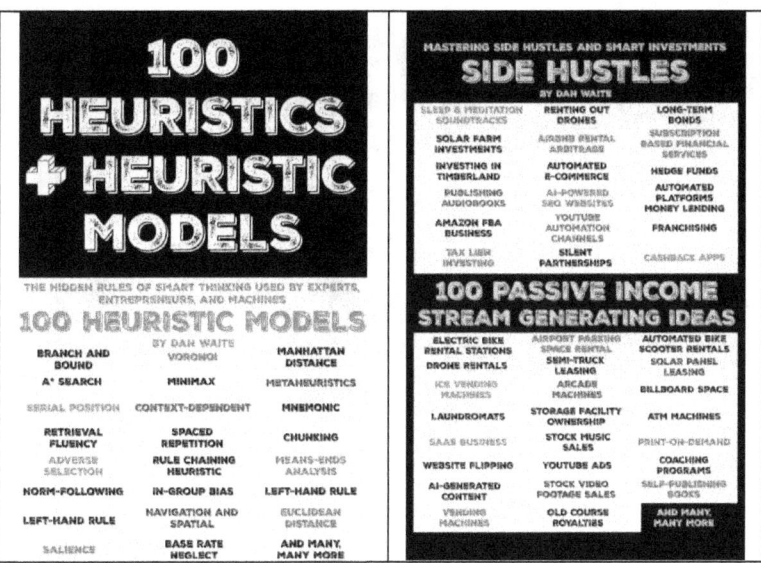

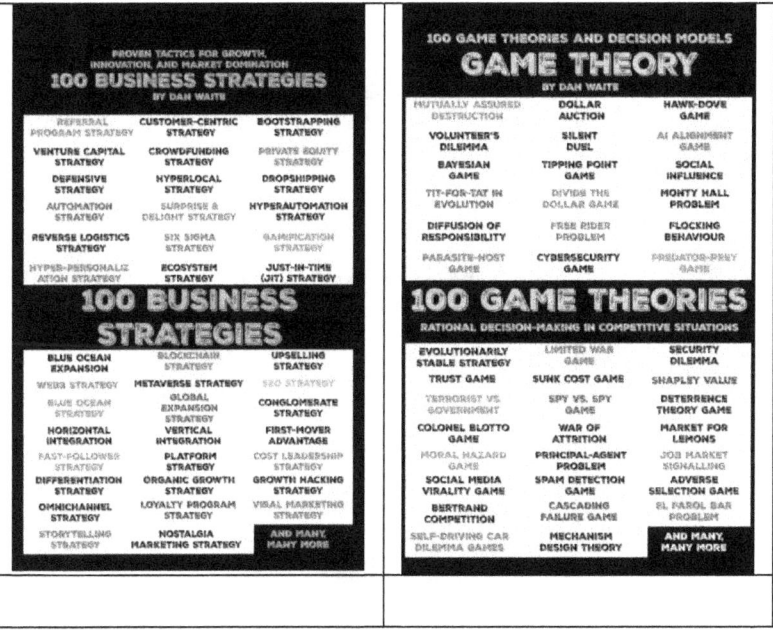

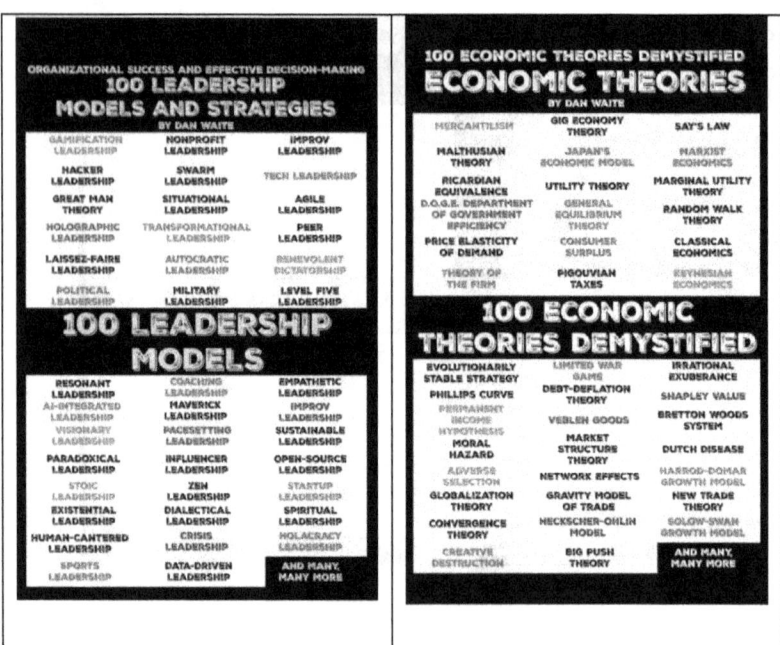

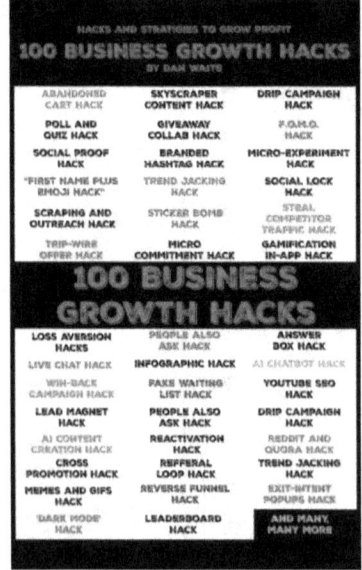

www.ingramcontent.com/pod-product-compliance
Lightning Source LLC
Chambersburg PA
CBHW071957150426
43194CB00008B/905